Home Ecology

Home Ecology

Simple and Practical Ways to Green Your Home

Karen Christensen

Illustrated by
Judy Strafford

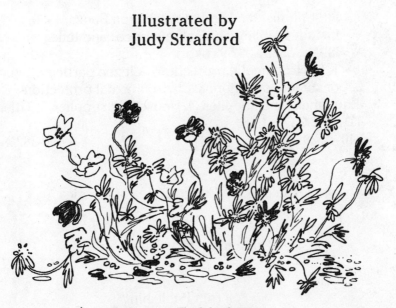

Fulcrum Publishing
Golden, Colorado

First published in 1989 by
Arlington Books (Publishers) Ltd.
London, England.

Cover Photograph by Bryan Dahlberg
Illustrations by Judy Strafford
Quilt courtesy of The Margaret Cavigga Quilt Collection

Library of Congress Cataloging-in-Publication Data

Christensen, Karen, 1957–
     Home ecology : simple and practical ways to green
your home / Karen Christensen : illustrated by Judy
Strafford.
          p.   cm.
     First published: London : Arlington Books, 1989.
     Includes bibliographical references and index.
     ISBN 1-55591-062-9 (pkb.)
     1. Environmental protection—Citizen participation.
2. Consumer education. 3. Environmental protection-
-Equipment and supplies. 4. Household supplies. I. Title.
TD171.7.C47   1990
640–dc20   90-38258
                                                                CIP

Printed in the United States of America

0   9   8   7   6   5   4   3   2   1

Printed on Recycled Paper

Fulcrum Publishing
350 Indiana Street, Suite 350
Golden, Colorado 80401

For Roxanne,
with thanks for planting the seed

CONTENTS

ACKNOWLEDGMENTS

When I started work on this book, I knew far more about "The Waste Land" than I did about the ozone layer or sustainable agriculture, so I must acknowledge the work of the many environmental writers and organizations who educated and guided me. Friends of the Earth UK was especially helpful, and the Worldwatch Institute in Washington provided both information and inspiration.

Bob Fromer deserves special mention for looking through a confused first draft and writing many pages of notes and suggestions. Patrick Green, Michel Odent, Walter Patterson, and Tony Webb commented on the drafts of certain chapters. Many people encouraged me, sent me clippings and books, and contributed ideas: Maggie Chudley, Adrian Howe, Cathy Keir, Cecilia Mueller, Melissa Moore, Lydia Umney, and Catrina Ure. The eagerness with which the Women's Environmental Network adopted *Home Ecology* gave me great pleasure, and I appreciate their support.

Roxanne Wolfe (then Teske) was majoring in environmental studies when I was engrossed in Anthony Trollope and Jane Austen. We used to have 6 A.M. picnics on the beach in Santa Cruz after wandering along the shore looking for shells. She planted the idea of *Home Ecology* in my mind by talking about small personal choices—using tampons with cardboard rather than plastic tubes, and not letting her father buy seashells for her collection because living animals were killed to obtain them. Those ideas lay dormant in me for over ten years, but they eventually brought forth this book.

My editor, Alan Stark, advised, teased, and cajoled me through the project, and kept me working on it when I longed to escape. His encouragement, and that of Linda Tiley Stark, helped me through a difficult time. I am also grateful to the rest of the staff at Fulcrum for their enthusiasm and for helping to educate me about the publishing process, and to Peter Danckwerts at Arlington Books in London.

Most of all, my love and thanks go to my parents (who were

bemused by my latest obsession but enthusiastic and supportive nonetheless), to my brothers and sister (David, Jim, Judy,
and Dan—who are, respectively, a chef, a computer programmer,
an administrator, and a soldier in the U.S. Army Special Forces),
to Andy Cotton (who was always happy to use cloth diapers), to
my five-year-old son Tom (who defines mommy's work as "fighting for the environment *peacefully*") and to Rachel (whose conception coincided with that of *Home Ecology*).

INTRODUCTION

Once our personal connection to what is wrong becomes clear, then we have to chose: we can go on as before, recognizing our dishonesty and living with it the best we can, or we can begin the effort to change the way we think and live.
—Wendell Berry, *The Unsettling of America,* 1977

When I was 13 my father started making "ecology runs" every Saturday afternoon. This meant mustering as many kids as possible and driving up into the foothills above California's Santa Clara Valley to gather cans, bottles, paper, and plastic which had been thrown along the roadside. The trash was sorted into boxes in the back of our big station wagon—aluminum cans went to the recycling center, soda bottles went back to the grocery store, and the rest was bagged for garbage collection. Dad arrived home glowing with accomplishment.

I grew to hate the word *ecology* and I never once went on one of Dad's ecology runs. This became a point of honor. Every week I had to devise some new scheme to avoid taking part. I resented the fact that Dad's "ecology" meant good citizenship instead of political activism. His quiet statement of civic responsibility was too tame for me. Trash was messy. It wasn't my problem. I was incapable of seeing a connection between the state of the roads and the state of my world.

Only after my son was born in 1985 did it dawn on me that my concern about his well-being and future was connected with the environmental problems I read about. Early lessons came to mind and I began to feel uncomfortable. I knew I should be recycling bottles and tin cans, and that detergents were a bad thing. I suddenly wanted to do my part, to make a contribution.

The idea of individual action—simple things we can do to help save the planet—seems obvious now after Earth Day 1990. What a change from 1987, when I first began work on *Home*

Ecology. I had difficulty convincing the environmentalists I talked to that individual action was of any importance, and my friends looked embarrassed when I said that I was writing a book about ecology. Nowadays, when I say that I'm an environmental writer people nod and smile and tell me about the recycling facilities in their neighborhood. My friends no longer see me as a crank. (You might like to know that E. F. Schumacher, the author of *Small Is Beautiful,* was happy to be called a crank. He explained that cranks are small, efficient tools that make revolutions.)

But many environmentalists still have reservations about the role the individual can play in saving the earth. "Green consumerism"—the notion that consumers can change industry simply by asking for environment-friendly products—is fraught with contradictions. It shifts the blame for environmental problems, and the quest for environmental solutions, to the individual and away from corporate polluters and government policy.

That's not to say, of course, that the individual doesn't matter. We have the ability, and a responsibility, to care for our home planet in small ways. We can improve our homes in the process, creating healthy, satisfying places to spend time with the people we love most.

I sympathize with dedicated campaigners who feel that only political action has any chance of changing the destructive course on which we have set ourselves. Institutional change, in governments and corporations, is essential. But so is home ecology. Both kinds of change, in institutions and in the way we live, are necessary. Like an army at war, there's no point throwing all our troops into a battle on one front if we are threatened on several sides.

Whenever I hear someone criticize the current emphasis on what the individual can do, I come back to three certainties. The first is that personal change is an essential part of changing people's attitudes, and it is public attitudes which will force the necessary changes in industry and technology, in the way we deal with our garbage, and in safety standards for dangerous products and processes.

Second, all of us need to become active participants in society. One of the most debilitating psychological consequences of the Cold War was a general feeling that we were standing on the sidelines, with no control over our own future. As I began to learn about the environmental problems which we face, I felt overwhelmed. But once I began to carry a string bag to the grocery store and draftproof my windows and stop buying things I didn't need, I found that I could cope with discouraging information because I no longer felt powerless.

Third, you and I are the ones who will figure out how to make our homes and communities sustainable, healthy, and satisfying places to live. I disagree with the authors of *The Green Consumer,* who believe that we are hooked on convenience and consumption, and that the best we can do is to lessen our destructive impact on the earth. I think that many of us want to make substantial changes and simply need to know where to start. While *Home Ecology* by no means provides all the answers, it is a realistic starting point.

Let's face it, not everyone can work for Friends of the Earth or Greenpeace. In an article entitled "Activism in Daily Life," in *Utne Reader* (March/April 1988) Marty Teitel wrote:

> For political and social action to become broad-based rather than just the territory of "professional activists," the price of admission should be low enough to include as many of us as possible. We should each be able to do small things in our daily lives that we know will work toward changing the world.... Those people who will dedicate their entire lives to making changes in society deserve our respect and our thanks. But we can also pay attention to those who care, but whose family responsibilities, economic conditions, or other factors make them unable to single-mindedly devote their lives to activism.

The word *ecology* means the study of homes and comes form the Greek *oikos.* It is a branch of biology which studies the interrelationships between organisms and the environment. *Home Ecology* looks at the home as an ecological system, part of the larger ecosystem of a neighborhood, town, and region. *Home Ecology* is not a green consumer guide. It is about living better, not buying better—about beginning the process of long-term change to a sustainable way of life.

A common complaint is that what one person does can't possibly make any difference. Why bother? True, your choosing a biodegradable dishwashing soap isn't going to stop our lakes from filling up with algae growing on an excess of nitrates (from fertilizers) and phosphates (from detergents). The amount of plastic which you throw out each day is only a miniscule fraction of what has to be dealt with around the world. And your can of hairspray will not make a very big hole in the ozone layer.

A more constructive approach is to recognize that although every choice you make may not change the world, at the very least it changes *you*. And a positive choice this time makes it far easier to make the right choice next time—passing up a fast food hamburger, say, or walking to the shops instead of driving.

The battle for the planet is one we can all fight. Every small contribution was welcome during the Second World War. Victory gardens, helping to create a more self-sufficient nation, can be just as relevant now. Small things—turning down your thermostat, reusing envelopes, growing your own organic tomatoes—do matter.

Some changes are much easier than others. Giving up the car entirely would be a difficult change for most people. But a reduction in the amount you use it, by carpooling, walking, or taking the bus, is easy.

The evening news often sounds like an environmental bulletin these days, and it seems that we need to be scientists in order to understand the issues. I hope that *Home Ecology* will enable you to assess what you are told on the basis of some simple principles of ecological earth-keeping. Knowledge will give you confidence in your ability to make decisions about the many choices which face us, in the supermarket and in the voting booth. Confidence in yourself as a discerning citizen will make you want to delve more deeply into particular areas.

Some people imagine that an ecologically sound way of life will be dreary, difficult, and expensive. There are politicians who would like us to think that the costs of cleaning up our act are just too high. Environmentalists are frequently accused of being against progress. Progress means "to advance or develop toward a better state." The ozone layer above the earth has a hole in it reaching three times the size of the United States. People in Third World countries are getting poorer and hungrier all the time. The world is heating up as the result of our intensive burning of coal, gas, and oil. Civilization, or at least our western version of it, has its own crippling plethora of diseases. Is this really progress?

I am not suggesting that we turn our backs on technology. Technological innovation, especially in the area of renewable energy, is an important part of environmental strategy. Sometimes the past looks infinitely safe and cosy by comparison with the ever-changing, insistent, demanding world we live in. But this is our world, our moment of history. *Home Ecology* is not mystical rhetoric, talking to plants and hugging trees. It means practical choices about everyday things, such as washing the dishes, feeding the dog, or choosing a vacation destination for next year. Making these choices will not solve the world's problems, but they are a vital part of the move to a sustainable way of life.

This book was first published in England, where I have spent a good deal of my time since graduating from college in 1981. I have been influence by the European green movement and the global perspective of British environmentalists—something I appreciate at a time when we need to take to heart the admonition to "think globally, act locally."

Home Ecology is full of practical suggestions. Most of the ideas won't cost much, and many will save you money. As you read, mark or highlight those you want to try. Make the book your own. Although I would be happy if you read *Home Ecology* through from cover to cover, it would please me even more to have it sitting within easy reach, beside your favorite cookbooks. I want it to provide you with friendly encouragement as well as information and practical tips.

When you get excited about cleaning up your home environment, that enthusiasm may be contagious and your partner or housemates or children may jump on the bandwagon. But they may cling ever more tightly to the remote control device and the microwave instruction booklet, flaunt their drycleaning, and throw away the box of used newspaper you were saving for the recycling center. Don't try to do too much, too soon. Change can be very threatening, and you cannot force real cooperation. With patience, it will come in time.

Whenever possible I have listed a mail order source for any

product I recommend. You may, however, find the same product in local stores, or something even better. Urban and suburban centers have a wide variety of shops and facilities, but if you live in the country, there may be a local farm which sells fresh honey and eggs or chemical-free meat. You may decide to keep your own hens, or be able to get ahold of bales of straw to mulch your garden. Wherever you live ask around, make contacts, and read the notice boards at your wholefood store. You may be surprised at what is available.

I hope that as you read your curiosity will be piqued and you will want to know more about the larger environmental, health, and social issues discussed here. There are plenty of contact addresses and book references for you to follow up. Rather than tackling everything at once, concentrate on one or two areas which really interest you and learn as much as you can about them.

If, after reading a few chapters, you find yourself hesitant about getting started, figure out what is holding you back. Are you afraid of ridicule? Work out how you will explain your new activities to friends and family. Perhaps you don't feel you have enough information or experience. Or maybe the problems sound so immense that you feel overwhelmed. The answer is to decide on a few small steps which you can take today. No matter how small the beginning, it is always better to do something than to do nothing. If something is worth doing well, it is also worth doing a little at a time.

Stephanie Winston, author of *Getting Organized,* has a few tips for dealing with procrastination:

- Don't be trapped by thinking you have to clear the boards (finish that mountain of ironing or get all the kids in school) before starting something new.
- If the big picture is overwhelming, make a list of 5-minute tasks. Then do a couple each day. Your list might include dropping those old cans of paint at the toxic waste facility, clearing a space under the kitchen sink for a couple of boxes to hold "recyclables," or writing to Seventh Generation for its catalog of products which are easy on the environment (for their address, see page 66).

Gradual change is far more likely to be permanent than a crash program, as anyone who has struggled to lose weight will know. Remember that new ways of doing things soon become old ways. Keep a sense of perspective and don't be hard on yourself when you slip from the straight environmental path. Relish the ironies of life, and don't fret when the children regale your mother-in-law with a body count of the wine bottles in the last load they put out for curbside collection. You won't convert anyone to the green cause by being grim and miserable.

We live in challenging times, and the next few decades will demand some hard choices. But there will be pleasures too—the pleasure of good work, of a new sense of community, and of a renewed appreciation for the natural world. After I've done the dirty work, rinsed out my daughter's cloth diapers and lugged a bucket of kitchen scraps to the compost bin, I settle down to read to my children with a sense of hope and optimism about their future.

I'd love to hear from readers who have further ideas and suggestions for Home Ecology. Please write to me c/o Fulcrum Publishing, 350 Indiana Street, Suite 350, Golden, CO 80401.

Karen Christensen
Washington, DC, May 1990

Home Ecology

1
TIME

If a man does not keep pace with his companions, perhaps it is because he hears a different drummer. Let him step to the music which he hears, however measured or far away.

—Henry David Thoreau, *Walden*

THE TIME OF YOUR LIFE
    Time and the Environment—Chronobiology—Living Well in Time—A Different Drummer—*For the Compulsively Busy—For the Apathetic*
GETTING ORGANIZED
    Finding Time—Planning—*Storage Checklist—Shopping Checklist*
SOURCES

The Time of Your Life

Are you frantically busy, harassed by incessant demands on your time and energy? When I suggest that you switch to cloth diapers or make soup from kitchen leftovers, your first reaction may be, "But I don't have the time for things like that!" When I mentioned that I was writing a book about what each of us could do to improve the environment, some friends reacted angrily. Their lives were so difficult, so full, that the idea of trying to do anything extra was devastating.

You may be dealing with the conflicting demands of children, home, and work. Surveys show that women, mothers in particular, are the group most concerned about the environment, but they are the people who have least time to spare.

Now you know why I decided to start *Home Ecology* with a

chapter about time—because your waking hours are what you start with. Before looking at particular environmental issues, we need to think about how we can find the time and energy to make changes in the way we live. First, let's look at the way time—or our perception of it—makes us tick.

Benjamin Franklin espoused an obsessive (and common) attitude toward time:

> Remember that TIME is Money. He that can earn Ten Shillings a Day by his labor, and goes abroad, or sits idle one half of that Day, tho' he spends but Sixpence during his Diversion or Idleness, ought not to reckon That the only Expence; he has really spent or rather thrown away Five Shillings besides.
> —*Advice to a Young Tradesman*, 1748

If every moment spent relaxing, playing with your children, or contemplating the ocean waves was a penny lost, every human activity could be quantified in terms of its monetary value. How much is your baby's smile worth, or a game of chess, or helping a 10-year-old with her math homework? How about a day spent decorating the house for Christmas, or an afternoon in bed with your beloved?

Our attitude toward time affects everything we do. We may want it to pass quickly. Think of the last week of school before summer vacation, waiting for news after an accident, or the long hours spent washing dishes at a summer camp when you were 18. On the other hand, many of us long for 36-hour days, when stretched to the limit by the conflicting demands of home and work.

Some people compulsively fill every second of each day with projects, while others proceed at a leisurely pace, always ready to sit down and talk over a cup of coffee. Who's right?

In economic terms it seems that we always have a role to play. If we aren't earning money we should be spending it. A good example of this, pointed out by Ivan Illich in *Limits to Medicine* (see Sources), is the way women have been encouraged to switch from breast to bottlefeeding: the change has provided industry with working mothers who are clients for a factory-made formula.

Money can sometimes buy time—for example, by making it

possible to hire someone to do a task you dislike or aren't good at—but the idea that time is money is misleading. People end up trapped by the need to finance a luxurious lifestyle and may in fact have far less free time than those who live more simply. E. F. Schumacher (*Small Is Beautiful*) summed this up with what he called the first law of economics: "The amount of real leisure a society enjoys tends to be in inverse proportion to the amount of labor-saving machinery it employs"—and, presumably, to the amount of money it has. In the same way, the more money a society has, the less real leisure time people enjoy.

Contrary to the notion that we have more free time than our ancestors (a notion fostered by a culture which needs our continual contribution as employees and as consumers), people in primitive agricultural or hunter-gatherer societies enjoyed far more leisure than we do. As a rule, they spent between 15 and 20 hours a week providing for themselves and their children—leaving the remainder of their time for socializing and relaxing ("Why tribal peoples and peasants of the Middle Ages had more free time than we do," Susan Hunt, *Utne Reader*, September/October 1987). Note that this is not the case for many Third World women today, however; the chores of obtaining scarce water and firewood take up an increasingly large proportion of their day.

Our need to do things faster has lead to a vast increase in convenience products—from frozen meals and fast-drying paint to permanent press clothes. We are also being sold the idea of convenience, because a sense of urgency and helplessness about everyday chores is one way of increasing consumer demand. The cost of this convenience is a loss of quality, along with a number of environmental price tags. "As far as food engineers are concerned, the microwave oven is one lousy cooking device ... but consumers are very forgiving when it comes to microwave foods. They readily swap quality for speed" ("Brave New Foods," Erik Larson, *Harper's*, May 1988).

The time-saving nature of convenience products is often illusory—natural rice needs to cook for longer than the instant variety, but it takes no more of your time to set it cooking. As we consider the *quality* of life we want, our priorities will change. Cooking and sharing a meal and doing the dishes afterwards takes more time than sticking individual frozen pizzas into the microwave, but eating together plays a vital role in any human group, and shared preparation is both creative and pleasurable.

An expenditure of time—the decision to stop for an impromptu picnic in a beautiful spot instead of hurrying home to get a load of washing hung out—can make an addition to what Christian writer Edith Schaeffer calls our "museum of memories." She stresses the importance of traditions and of taking opportunities to add to our precious stock of memories in her book *What Is a Family?* (see Sources). Think of the extent to which friendships are built up by years of shared experiences. Taking a child to a museum or building a dollhouse together is likely to mean far more in later years than any number of purchased toys.

The way we spend our time is a reflection of our values. Only you can decide about your own days and years, but taking time to consider how you want to spend the time of your life is the first step in home ecology.

Time and the Environment

In *Time Wars: The Primary Conflict in Human History,* activist and philosopher Jeremy Rifkin looks at the social, physiological, and political dimensions of the way we perceive time, and at how the computer is making "a revolutionary change in time orientation, just as clocks did several hundred years ago when they began the process of replacing nonautomated timepieces as society's key time-ordering mechanisms."

Computers measure time in nanoseconds. A nanosecond is a billionth of a second, which we can conceive of theoretically but which we cannot experience. "Never before," says Rifkin, "has time been organized at a speed beyond the realm of consciousness."

As more and more people use increasingly powerful computers, psychologists and sociologists are expressing concern about the effect this new perception of time will have on our relationships with each other and with the environment.

> The desire, especially of the Western world, to produce and consume at a frantic pace has led to a depletion of our natural endowment and the pollution of our biosphere. Nature's own production and recycling rhythms have been so utterly taxed by the twin dictates of economic efficiency and speed that the planetary ecosystems are no longer capable of renewing resources as fast as they are being depleted, or recycling waste as fast as we discard it.
>
> —*Time Wars*, p. 12

Just as E. F. Schumacher pointed out the holes in the notion that bigger is better with his *Small Is Beautiful,* Rifkin takes on the current assumption that faster is better. He claims that our obsession with speed has gone too far. If going faster means a loss of quality (artificial ripening of fruit), of human contacts (shopping by computer), and of human values (traditional village life, for example, and a responsible and responsive relationship with the place we live), we ought to think about slowing down, and we ought to slow down while we think.

Chronobiology

Plants, animals, and human beings have inbuilt "clocks." Seasonal growth cycles, mating patterns, and the way we wake up on New York time after a flight to London are examples of this.

Studies have found that the effects of a given drug can vary depending on the time of day it is administered. Long distance truck drivers are three times as likely to have an accident at five o'clock in the morning. The nuclear accident at Three Mile Island, Pennsylvania, occurred at around 4:00 A.M., because of errors made by workers who had been "rotating shifts around the clock every week for a month and a half" (Rifkin, p. 38).

Job satisfaction, general health, and productivity were dramatically improved at a plant in Montana when a new schedule allowed workers to stay on the same shift for three weeks instead of one, and when the rotation went forward rather than backward; this makes a difference because most people's biological clock runs on a 25-hour rather than 24-hour day. Shift work and jet lag can cause dramatic changes in mood and mental clarity, but trying to live by "social time" can pose problems for people whose natural biorhythm has unsocial peaks and troughs.

Organizing expert Stephanie Winston (*Getting Organized*) stresses the importance of finding your own prime time before you try to start a new task—this includes tackling the suggestions in the rest of *Home Ecology*. If you aren't sure about your own biorhythms, consider the following:

❏ Are you more likely to feel chilled in the morning or the evening? Body temperature tends to peak along with alertness.

❏ Try doing a crossword puzzle at different times of the day—when is it easiest?

❏ Exercise for five minutes in the morning and again in the late afternoon or evening. Does one session leave you feeling exhausted and the other energized?

Living Well in Time

Think of someone you know who is really healthy and vibrant, full of energy and enthusiasm. Isn't it surprising that more people don't fit that description, considering our affluence and our knowledge about good eating habits and exercise? Many of us barely manage to get through each day, and underneath superficial energy is weariness which we just can't seem to shake off.

There are a number of explanations for this—psychological, social, and economic. Fatigue and depression are common symptoms of environmental stresses, which range from poor diet or working in a modern "sick" office block to a sensitivity to household chemicals. In one way or another, the way we live is to blame.

Look at some of the bigger home issues. Why do you work and live where you do? How do you travel to work? What about your health—how do you feel most of the time? What about stress in your life? How happy are you?

All these things are interrelated, and need to be considered as you take on the ideas and suggestions in *Home Ecology*. It's possible that making changes in your home and the way you live will cure the blues by dealing with a problem you weren't conscious of, or by providing a new way to look at the pressures in your life.

A Different Drummer

Some suffer from compulsive busyness, every minute carefully preplanned in a datebook. Others are apathetic in the face of the many conflicts of modern life, becoming couch potatoes who retire each evening with a microwave meal and a stack of videotapes. Here are a few suggestions.

FOR THE COMPULSIVELY BUSY

❑ Take your watch off for a day or two. Does it really matter whether it is 2:36 or 2:39? Eat when you feel hungry; go to bed when you get tired.
❑ Spend a weekend doing nothing much, preferably in good company (no television).
❑ Get involved in a time-consuming craft: pottery or knitting or bookbinding.
❑ Plant some seeds or grow lentil sprouts in a jar.
❑ Spend half an hour or so walking, every day for a week, a different route each day. Use the time for quiet reflection, or concentrate on the trees, sky, houses, and people you see.

❏ Do something extraordinary for someone you care about without spending any money.

FOR THE APATHETIC

❏ Get involved in something: learning a language or finding a new apartment or volunteer work.
❏ Put the television away for a few days.
❏ Cook a special meal or refinish that old pine table. Make sure what you choose is something you actually enjoy but normally can't find the energy for.
❏ Start walking or riding a bike every day. Look around you, notice your environment. If you have literary inclinations, you may want to spend some time writing about your observations—your world is an interesting place. *Nature Notes*, an illustrated "blank book" might help you get started (see Sources).
❏ Surprise your lover, or your mother, with concert tickets or a new tablecloth.

Getting Organized

An ecologically sound life requires a little more organization than an unsound one. Separating your trash for recycling, for instance, is going to take more foresight than putting everything into one big plastic bag.

Living in an ecologically sound way is not a hobby, like needlework or tennis. It is a set of attitudes and habits that you will acquire gradually. The key is establishing a routine, and good storage arrangements. It will become natural to put glass bottles to one side, and you'll find that with familiarity a new method of washing clothes or feeding your pet will soon take half the time it did when you first tried it.

Time is not the only thing in short supply. You may worry that this is going to cost too much, but although you may spend more on some things, on balance the suggestions in *Home Ecology* will save you money, while improving the quality of your life.

Space is also at a premium, particularly in an apartment. You may have a tiny kitchen like mine, where we have to move the trash can to get to the oven and half the time I end up putting waste aluminum foil into the compost bucket, instead of into the jar where it belongs, because both recycling containers are squeezed onto the same narrow shelf.

Finding Time

Home Ecology is not like one of these beauty books which tells you that in 10 to 15 minutes a day you can significantly improve the state of your nails, and in the next chapter asks for 10 to 15 minutes for your eyebrows, half an hour for your face,

and 20 minutes for meditation—so that when you add it up you would be spending more time on the author's program than you spend at work.

To make any change takes a special degree of effort, and possibly (although not necessarily) extra time or money. But living more simply can bring dividends of extra leisure, because you decide that you're just not going to bother doing some things any more!

Think about ways you might eliminate clutter from your home, and about the worries or responsibilities that make for mental clutter. What can you get rid of, stop doing, do less often, or get someone else (partner, children, hired help) to do? What can you do more simply: food, makeup, clothes, decorating, vacations?

Try not to become overwhelmed by the prospect of filtering your water, changing cleaning products, and spending more time in natural light, all this week. Specialize—decide what matters to you or bothers you most. Concentrate on the things you like—finding good secondhand furniture for your new apartment or retuning your car engine for improved efficiency.

Planning

It's time to sit down with a pad of paper. In fact, why not start a household notebook where you can keep track of ideas which you want to try and questions which come to mind as you read, and where you can do a little problem solving too, perhaps about how to cut down on car use.

If you are an inexperienced cook, planning your grocery shopping and meals is a great help. This does not have to be complicated—even a sketchy plan will help, and it's reassuring to know that pasta with sauce and a salad is on the menu for Thursday.

Planning ahead saves both time and money, and you avoid last minute dashes to the store, once again cutting car use. A large wall calendar is useful for recording things like the bi-monthly newspaper collection in your area.

STORAGE CHECKLIST

❏ A good spring cleaning is the place to start. Try to get the whole household involved in this. Unwanted items can go to charity.

❏ Decide where to store reusable items and things for recycling, donations, mending, etc.

❏ You'll need room for any extra cooking equipment you acquire and bulk purchases of staple foods, as well as bicycles, gardening tools (out of the rain!), and walking gear.

Ecologically sound living is undoubtedly easier in a sprawling house in the country. If you live in crowded quarters, think about storage before you start saving bottles or paper for recycling.

SHOPPING CHECKLIST

Shopping may take a bit longer at first, as you buy less at the supermarket and more from other stores, but you will probably find yourself spending less time in the long run. Organization makes an enormous difference and your shopping time should be much more enjoyable. Here are some tips:

❏ Stock up as much as your budget and cupboard space allow. Whole grains and legumes, toilet paper and cleaning products can be bought in bulk and last virtually forever. This not only saves money and the hassle of running out in the middle of the holidays, but eliminates a considerable amount of packaging.

❏ Keep track of things you are running low on by ensuring that there is a pad of paper and a pencil in the kitchen and the bathroom. Everyone in the household should learn to add to these lists. There's nothing worse than cutting up mounds of vegetables for a Chinese stir-fry only to discover that you've run out of something basic like rice.

❏ Make out a shopping checklist of everything you normally keep on hand, arranged into categories to speed things up when you get to the store. The list can be photocopied, or you can put it in a plastic folder and use a grease pencil to mark the items you plan to buy, ticking them off as you put them into your basket.

❏ Try to find stores which you like and can visit regularly— knowing the layout and staff speeds shopping considerably.

❏ Don't forget to check local stores. People who commute may not realize that an excellent meat market or produce stand is just down the road—there's always Saturday morning.

❏ Save the car for long distance and/or bulk shopping.

❏ Make shopping enjoyable by combining it with outings, to the local park or crafts shop, for instance. The personal contact of buying from small producers is a delightful change from impersonal department stores.

Mail order is a good way to save time while helping small producers of specialist food, clothes, and household articles.

Sources

Books

Getting Organized: The Easy Way to Put Your Life in Order, Stephanie Winston (New York, Norton, 1978).

Limits to Medicine, Ivan Illich (Marion Boyars Publishers, 24 Lacy Road, London SW15 1NL, 1976).

Nature Notes, Margaret O'Brien and Ursula Shepherd (Golden, CO, Fulcrum Publishing, 1990).

Small Is Beautiful: Economics as if People Mattered, E. F. Schumacher (New York, Harper & Row, 1975).

Time Wars: The Primary Conflict in Human History, Jeremy Rifkin (New York, Henry Holt & Company, 1987).

What Is a Family? Edith Schaeffer (Old Tappan, NJ, Fleming F. Revel Co., 1982).

2
FOOD

A change of diet is not an answer . . . [but it is] a way of saying simply: I have a choice. That is the first step. For how can we take responsibility for the future unless we can make choices now that take us, personally, off the destructive path that has been set for us?
—Frances Moore Lappé, *Diet for a Small Planet*

Introduction

The food we eat affects our health, of course, but our shopping choices have wider consequences too. The store we shop in, the way food has been processed and packaged, and where it comes from are all important. First, let's just think about what we are buying and eating right now.

It's entertaining and educational to look into other people's shopping carts and guess what sort of people they are, or who's coming to dinner. I look at my own purchases guiltily sometimes, and argue with my son about what he's going to have for lunch. What do your groceries say about you?

Processing

How much of your weekly shopping is basic, unprocessed food? Processing is not, in itself, a bad thing: when you prepare a meal at home you are processing the food—peeling the onions and making gravy.

But commercial food processing has a number of nasty side effects. It removes nutrients and fiber, and adds considerable quantities of salt, sugar, and cheap fats, along with a huge range of chemical additives. It is the high percentage of processed food we eat, going hand in hand with our excessive consumption of fats, sugars, and salt, that concerns nutritionists.

Don't think that you avoid waste by buying processed food. The waste just goes somewhere else, and the expense and energy cost of processing and packaging are substantial.

Packaging

It isn't only what's in the food that matters, but what the food is in. Plastics do not biodegrade and should therefore be avoided whenever possible; they are also undesirable from the point of view of human health. Think of how new plastic smells, or how coffee tastes when you drink it out of a plastic cup. These are both signs that chemicals are being released into the air and into your food.

Plastic film wrapping may not smell but it is recognized that the plasticizers it contains, which are known to be carcinogenic, leak into food wrapped in it, particularly into fatty foods like cheese or bacon. You can now buy wrapping labeled "non-PVC" or "contains no plasticizers," but it's better to avoid it altogether. Even plastic bags can contaminate food. Natural (and biodegradable) cellophane is preferable.

One of my cookbooks advises against covering a pasta dish containing (acid) tomatoes with aluminum foil because the foil will "shed" into the sauce. Not a pleasant prospect when you consider recent findings about the relationship between aluminum and Alzheimer's disease.

Cans, too, should be avoided as much as possible, both because it is seldom possible to recycle them and they require a great deal of energy and raw material to produce, and because generally they are soldered with a compound containing lead.

A new concern is over dioxin in bleached paper products. Traces of the highly toxic chemical have been found in milk cartons and in the long-life cartons in which fruit juices and other foods are packed.

What this adds up to is choosing foods with little or no packaging. You can do this by buying fresh foods and by purchasing in bulk.

Green Shopping

Wouldn't you like to know about the social and environmental record of the companies which make the foods you buy? It's easy now. The Council for Economic Priorities publishes a pocket-sized guide called *Shopping for a Better World* which will certainly change your buying habits, as will *The Green Consumer* by John Elkington, Julia Hailes, and Joel Makowa (see Sources).

Ecologically Sound Food

Organic Produce

For years I didn't bother to look for organic vegetables—I didn't shop anywhere that had them, and the articles I saw in the paper invariably reported that scientists were not convinced that organic food was any more nutritious than conventional produce.

When my son was six months old and I started to think about what solid food to start him on, I suddenly realized that I

didn't want him to have anything which could possibly be contaminated with dangerous chemicals. His first food was scrapings of organically grown pears, and our switch to organic food has progressed from there.

The International Federation of Organic Agriculture Movements sets out the following points in its document on organic standards: organic agriculture should (1) maintain the long-term fertility of soils, (2) avoid all forms of pollution, (3) reduce the use of fossil energy in agriculture, and (4) treat livestock humanely.

Current agricultural policy and practice are in confusion. Famine in the Third World stands in lamentable contrast to costly overproduction in the First World. There is a worldwide problem with soil degradation and the loss of topsoil, and the battle against insect damage to crops is proving far more costly, financially and environmentally, than anyone could have imagined when chemical pesticides first appeared. Since the 1940s pesticide use has increased tenfold and crop losses to insects have doubled, according to Lawrie Mott and Karen Snyder, authors of *Pesticide Alert*. Even conventional growers are cutting back on chemical use with a method called Integrated Pest Management (IPM), simply because it is a more effective way of dealing with insect pests. As pointed out in *Joy of Cooking*, "guarding against losing helpful insects is as important as destroying insect enemies—a fact stressed less often than is the need to solve the equally knotty problem of pesticide poisons in the food chain. We can no longer afford to ignore the interrelationships on which global food supplies depend."

Another serious problem is nitrate fertilizer. It is used in vast quantities, much of it being washed off into lakes and streams and eventually turning up in our drinking water. Nitrates are also absorbed into plant tissue in higher concentrations from artificial sources than from natural nitrogen-rich fertilizers like manure, and we ingest them in the food we eat.

In addition, farmers are now threatened with the uncertain effects of the hole in the ozone layer (with a resultant increase in ultraviolet rays) and the greenhouse effect—rising CO_2 levels and global temperature, resulting from the burning of fossil fuels.

Consumer worries about pesticide residues in food have been placated for many years. At last, however, there is some official recognition that we have a serious problem. Baby food manufacturers are refusing to buy produce which has been sprayed with certain chemicals, and even the larger retailers are deciding to get tough with their suppliers in the face of inadequate legal controls.

Government safety levels are seriously flawed. Pesticides, herbicides, and fungicides are, by their nature, poisons and it is probably wrong to suggest that there is such a thing as safe levels. Organic agriculture is the obvious alternative.

Fungicides are thought to be particularly dangerous—be cautious of fruit and vegetables from warm, humid climates. Apples, peppers, cucumbers, citrus fruits, and eggplants are often coated with a wax, made of petroleum products and animal fat, to improve their appearance and increase shelf life. The wax may contain fungicides and cannot be washed off.

Here's a horror story, quoted by Jane Grigson in her *Fruit Book*: "Commercial dates are customarily dusted with Malathion or a similar toxic insecticide to keep down the date beetle [and] when picked are customarily washed with detergent. Because they are then wet, [they] must customarily be treated with a mould inhibitor [and then] coated with glycerine or something similar to make them look sticky again." Did you think dates were a health food?

PESTICIDES CHECKLIST

❑ Whenever you can, buy organically grown food. Bulk purchases of rice, potatoes, onions, and other staples will keep costs down. Try your local health food store and farmer's market—many small growers use organic methods.

❑ Grow your own food. You could start with herbs and a tub of tomatoes on the patio (see Chapter 13 for more information).

❑ More than half the pesticides we consume come from meat and dairy products—a good reason to cut back on these items. Chemical-free, humanely reared meat is delicious. Local organic farmers may have small amounts of meat to sell.

❑ Wash all chemically grown produce. A mild solution of biodegradable dish soap and water will remove some, but not all, surface pesticide residues.

❑ Peel chemically grown fruit and vegetables. This means extra work and losing some of the valuable nutrients contained in fresh food, but will completely remove surface residues.

❑ Buy U.S.-grown foodstuffs, and fruits and vegetables in season. These contain fewer pesticide residues.

❑ Beware of perfect-looking produce. A few superficial flaws do not affect the quality or flavor of what you buy. Some 60 percent of total pesticide use merely enhances the appearance of the food, and retailers insist that this is what the public demands. Nowadays I welcome a few worm holes!

❑ Press for comprehensive labeling of the pesticides used on food by writing to the general manager of the supermarket you shop at, and ask for organic products.

❑ Write to your representative to support comprehensive testing of pesticides, as well as regenerative agriculture.

❑ Learn more about pesticides—(see Sources for pesticide newsletters).

Local Supplies

Because most of us grew up on packaged and processed food and insipid modern vegetables, we don't know what really fresh food tastes like. Food that has been shipped thousands of miles, and which is bred or formulated for its ability to stand being stored for many weeks, is not going to be really tasty. We are usually satisfied if a banana isn't bruised, without reflecting much on whether it has any flavor.

While we may not be self-sufficient individually, we can aim for considerable regional and national self-sufficiency. The Cornucopia Project began when a few people at Rodale Press (famous for its magazines *Organic Gardening* and *Prevention*) realized that New Yorkers were eating broccoli which had been shipped 2,700 miles from California, when broccoli would grow better in New York's cool climate. After a look at the statistics, it seemed that the only people who were gaining were the trucking and oil companies and agribusiness—the huge firms which control most of American agriculture. The consumer was getting food that was less fresh, less nutritious, and more expensive than it might have been, and which did not encourage local employment.

One serious danger with food from the Third World is that agricultural chemicals which are banned in the West are exported to Third World countries, so we may be consuming trace chemicals which have been proved cancer-causing or mutagenic. Recent trials have found that pesticide residues on imported fruits and vegetables were higher than on domestic produce, and the types of pesticides were often more hazardous.

Try to find local sources for some of your food. A neighbor may be willing to sell excess from a flourishing garden; there may be farms nearby where you can buy eggs or milk or honey; and there are city farms in some urban areas.

Thinking about using local produce has changed the way I shop. While it is exciting to buy French cider, Italian cheese, and Greek olives, this may lead us to undervalue and ignore New Mexico salsa, Wisconsin cheese, and numerous other regional specialties. Growing your own food—even a tiny proportion of it—will improve your health, and give you increased independence and genuine contact with your environment. Add to your yard's productive capacity by planting fruit and nut trees.

Seasonal Items

When I first went to England I was astounded to find that fruits and vegetables had such definite seasons: there were peas and new potatoes in the spring, and in June the strawberries arrived. To my delight I also found that fresh food was best when it was cheapest, so that I could save money and eat well by concentrating on whatever was in season. Many cookbooks have charts to guide you in shopping for produce in season.

"Fresh" fruits and vegetables are not necessarily fresh. They may have been shipped thousands of miles and kept in cold storage for months. These lengthy delays lead to deterioration in food value, especially as regards volatile vitamins like vitamins A and C. One food scientist tested supermarket brussels sprouts and cabbage and found no detectable vitamin C! Fruits stored for long periods need extra doses of pesticides and fungicides to preserve them.

Shopping

Keeping Costs Down

You may be alarmed that many of the foods I am recommending cost more than similar items from a supermarket. This is largely compensated for by a reduction in meat consumption and by cutting out many convenience and snack foods, but it is still important to think about how to obtain good quality food at reasonable prices. People on a low income have far poorer diets and spend a larger proportion of their income on food than do people who have more money. Only by making a truly adequate diet accessible to everyone (this includes food free from dangerous additives and pesticides) can we expect real improvements in health.

If you are concerned about how much you spend on food, try to figure out why the bill always seems to be higher than you have budgeted for. Advertising on boxes, special displays, bullying from the children, and the fact that you skipped breakfast may all contribute to unnecessary purchases.

As the organic food market grows, prices will come down—your purchases act as an investment in organic agriculture. Neighborhood food co-ops are an excellent idea but require quite a bit of time and commitment, especially in the beginning. Organizing a cooperative scheme among a few friends is easy. Get together to order chemical-free meat, buy from your nearest wholefood warehouse (grains, legumes, and dried fruits keep for long periods, so you can stock up) or buy directly from organic farms and dairies in your area.

Emphasize seasonal foods, and let inexpensive grains, legumes, vegetables such as potatoes and carrots form the mainstays of your diet. Good vegetarian cookbooks are essential; borrow some from the library so you can find out whose cooking style suits you. There's no need to eat brown rice and baked potatoes day in and day out. Cookbooks provide the ideas and inspiration to turn inexpensive staples into delicious meals.

Where to Shop

Frances Moore Lappé, author of *Diet for a Small Planet*, points out that the question may not be which supermarket to shop at but whether we wouldn't be better off shopping somewhere else. Many of us assume that we save time by using supermarkets and shopping centers, but a smaller wholefood store, which you get to know and which doesn't offer an overwhelming range of unhealthy and overpackaged goods, may well be faster.

Of course you are not going to give up your weekly supermarket shopping trip immediately. Make changes gradually, as you get to know the alternatives in your area. Over the past couple of years I have found my supermarket shopping lists grow shorter as I've found other sources for our food.

Try to buy from small farms and local businesses. In Britain, demand for real ale has put small brewers back in business. T. S. Eliot, who was a great cheese fan, mourned the demise of English cheesemaking some 40 years ago. He would be delighted to see the present revival of traditional double Glouchester and white Cheshire.

While buying from farms isn't as quick as piling everything into a cart at the supermarket, you can combine weekend outings with a little shopping—we keep shopping guides in the car so that we don't find ourselves in new surroundings with no idea of what treasure might lie just a mile or two off our course.

Boycotts

Avoiding certain types of food or the products of particular countries or companies is a powerful consumer tool. I cannot give a complete list of things to boycott, but current campaigns ask that shoppers avoid buying tuna since tuna fishing is causing the death of thousands of dolphins because of the types of nets used; and pass up Icelandic fish as Iceland is one of the few countries that allow commercial whaling. Avoiding South African goods is a common ethical choice.

Susan George, researcher on international food issues, has suggested a boycott of products from "corporate junk food mongers"—makers of soft drinks, sugary children's cereals, and artificial baby milk—because these companies aggravate malnutrition in the Third World by promoting their nutritionally marginal products as alternatives to indigenous staple foods. While we're at it, why not a similar boycott on junk food promoters here at home? Boycotting is more effective if you write to the manufacturers to explain why you are no longer buying their product.

Co-op America publishes a quarterly newsletter, *Building Economic Alternatives* (see Sources), which includes a summary of major boycott activities, and many environmental groups list products or companies to boycott in their membership magazines.

What About Meat?

I saw an advertisement recently for a firm of "environment-friendly" builders. When I asked one of the partners what they did differently from other builders, he said that he and his partner had been vegetarians for 10 years. Some environmentalists feel that eating meat—any meat—is unacceptable. Butchers feel beleaguered these days, with all the publicity about the evils of animal fats and intensive farming practices, while public awareness about dietary fiber has made many of us shift to eating more whole grains and less meat.

Cutting down on the amount of meat we eat will contribute to a more equitable and balanced agriculture and economy throughout the world. Frances Moore Lappé's *Diet for a Small Planet*, first published in 1972, set out a startling discovery. If the grain (corn, wheat, soybeans, etc.) we in the West use to feed our animals were instead used directly as food for people, there would be plenty for everyone on the planet.

The waste involved in commercial meat production is taking food out of the mouths of the starving, especially when the grain comes from the Third World. More than half the world's grain harvest goes to feed livestock, an enormous and incredible waste of food. The conversion ratio of pounds of grain or soybean protein needed to produce one pound of animal protein ranges from 3:1 for eggs and broiler chickens to 6:1 for pigs, and 16:1 for cows.

Hunger activists and environmentalists join ranks in saying that we should move away from a meat-centered diet. Don't think, however, that you have to become a 100 percent vegetarian. Reducing the amount of meat you eat, and cutting back drastically on beef (especially luxurious grain-fed beef) will be good for the environment, other people, and for your health, too.

Responsible Meat Eating

Is there any place for meat in the diet of the ecologically concerned? I think there is. Traditional farming methods depend on animal manures, and mixed farming creates a neat ecological cycle: animals graze fallow land and eat scraps which would otherwise be wasted (free-range chickens do even more: they eat large numbers of pests), and provide manure to fertilize the next crop.

On the other hand, factory or intensive methods of raising animals for slaughter are appalling. We hear a great deal about battery chickens, but other animals are kept under similarly barbaric conditions. The emphasis for environmentalists should be on eliminating these practices, via the marketplace and political pressure.

Look for meat from animals which have been humanely treated and raised without routine antibiotics, growth promoters and hormones, and for meat without chemical additives. Some specialist food stores sell "naturally reared meat." Ask what this means, where the meat comes from, and whether the animals are fed an organic diet. Another thing to look out for is meat from rare old breeds. They have a more robust flavor than modern meats, and by supporting the small breeders who specialize in these animals you are promoting genetic diversity.

If you are buying from a supermarket, try to stick to non-chemically fed chicken, game, and fish. While offal is nutritious—and delicious—these organs, especially the liver, tend to store poisons. Avoid them if you do not have a source of organic meat.

Vegetarianism

A common misconception is that a vegetarian diet is unhealthy, whereas the opposite is true. Although in the Third World many people don't get enough protein, we get more than enough. Premature aging and degenerative diseases have even been associated with eating too much protein. Vegetarians have lower rates of heart disease and tend to be slimmer than meat eaters.

Old-fashioned vegetarianism —substituting an omelet for a steak—might be boring, but the modern meatless diet certainly is not. Many ethnic cuisines are vegetarian, and there are dozens of inspiring cookbooks available (see Sources).

Veganism means eating no animal products whatsoever, with the possible exception of honey, and using synthetic materials to replace leather and wool. This seems unnecessarily severe to me, but I've experimented with vegan cooking and been delighted by the results. Soy products like tofu and miso feature heavily, and make for low-fat meals which are easy on the environment.

Healthy Food

Perhaps you feel pulled this way and that by dietary advice: Eat a hearty breakfast to start the day right; don't eat breakfast; have plenty of bran fiber; wheat bran is bad for you, but oat bran will cure cancer. Who's right? How should we eat, to avoid illness and to achieve good health? Some of my favorite cookbooks are the ones which show blithe disregard for fussy modern fads. "Plenty of salty farmhouse butter," says a recipe, and I feel inclined to obey.

Most of us know the basics for healthy eating: less fat and sugar, more fresh fruits and vegetables, less meat and more roughage. The most important list to make, if you want to improve your eating habits, is "Good food I like.". This is a lot more constructive than concentrating on the bad things you eat and feel guilty about.

Supplements

Concentrate on good food before considering nutritional supplements. There are a number of nutritious foods which you can emphasize in your diet—seaweeds, yogurt, garlic—which are whole foods, not health foods. How do you rate a natural foods store? What I want to see is a large selection of simply packaged whole grains, legumes, nuts and dried fruits; a reasonable range of organically grown produce (which should be in good condition); and cool cabinets with untreated milk, yogurt and cheese, tofu and tempeh products. I do not want to see endless shelves of "healthy," overpackaged potato chips, cookies, and soft drinks across from shelves of tablets and powders with pictures of muscular men and women on the labels.

For some suggestions about supplements, please see the Supplements Checklist in Chapter 9.

The Fat Fallacy

There is considerable disagreement among scientists about the role of cholesterol in heart disease, although the public has now been thoroughly indoctrinated with the idea that polyunsaturates are desirable and saturated fats are bad.

Margarine is one of the most highly refined foods in the modern diet, yet health conscious people continue to eat it because of worries about cholesterol. These worries allow unscrupulous manufacturers to market low-quality products with a health label—for example, a no-cholesterol coffee cake made from refined flour, white sugar, chemically refined fat, and half a dozen artificial additives.

According to Thomas J. Moore, author of the well-documented and persuasive *Heart Failure,* there is no conclusive evidence that lowering blood cholesterol will save lives. In addition, a clear relationship between diet and cholesterol levels has never been established. Moore points out that the real beneficiaries of the cholesterol craze are doctors and drug companies.

Nonetheless, many people continue to eat chemically extracted vegetable fats because they think this will safeguard them from heart attacks. The vegetarian cookbook *Laurel's Kitchen* points out that margarine is the most highly processed food many of us eat.

For an alarming look at the links between national health policy, the medical profession, and the pharmaceutical industry, read *Heart Failure*, and subscribe to Nikki and David Goldbeck's excellent and entertaining *True Food Newsletter* to keep up-to-date on the cholesterol debate (see Sources). A well-balanced, unfaddy diet and plenty of exercise is an unexceptionable prescription for good heaelth.

Too much unsaturated fat seems to have the deleterious effect of suppressing the immune system and promoting tumor growth. According to Michael Weiner, author of *Maximum Immunity*, some scientists suspect that the increased use of polyunsaturated fats in our diet is responsible for the high incidence of cancer in western civilization, and that the more unsaturated a fat is, the more it can harm your immunity.

Unsaturated fats—containing essential fatty acids—are indeed needed for good health, but only in small amounts. They should come from a natural, untreated source such as fresh raw seeds, unrefined oils or fish and fish oils. Cookies and cakes in which vegetable fats are listed as an ingredient are likely to contain highly saturated palm or coconut oils, or hydrogenated vegetable oils.

Monosaturated olive oil seems particularly desirable although researchers are not entirely clear about the reasons for the relatively low incidence of heart disease in Mediterranean countries where it is the main source of fat.

Commercial vegetable oils are extracted with a solvent, which may be benzene, ethyl ether, or methylene chloride (known carcinogens which leave minute traces in the final product), and are then bleached and deodorized. In *Fruit Book,* Jane Grigson gives a description of the processing of vegetable oils:

> First, the oils have to be degummed and neutralized [after, of course, being chemically extracted]. Phosphoric acid is injected into the oil and mixed under pressure to precipitate the gums. Then it is mixed with caustic soda which forms a soap containing gums and color which can be separated easily from the oil. Next stage is to wash the oil, dry it, bleach it with fuller's earth and filter it. At this point it's a fully refined oil but the original taste and smell still remain, making it unacceptable for consumption. The final stage, therefore, is deodorization to ensure a bland, odorless oil that won't tinge the flavor of what's cooked in it.

Grigson adds that this is why she prefers to stick to butter, lard, and olive oil. I'm with her—I cannot believe that a highly refined product that contains traces of hazardous chemicals is better for me than natural, unrefined foods. The traditional diet of Eskimos is high in animal fats but they don't suffer from heart disease. Another point to consider is that pesticides and other chemicals concentrate in fats, both animal and vegetable.

FATS CHECKLIST

❑ Reduce fats from all sources. The "good" fats recommended below are more expensive than those you've probably been using, an excellent deterrent to overconsumption.

❑ Use unrefined, mechanically pressed (sometimes called first pressing or extra virgin) oils, and heat them as little as possible. They should be stored in a cool place.

❑ If you deep fry, use fresh oil each time.

❏ Use butter (in small amounts) in preference to highly processed margarine.

❏ Choose organic dairy products whenever you can, and buy meat which has been raised without antibiotics, growth promoters, and hormones.

❏ Cut the fat off your meat and choose lean cuts, especially if you are buying meat at a meat market or supermarket meat counter. Fatty meat will contain higher levels of pesticide residues than lean meat.

❏ Lard is a useful cooking fat, but commercial varieties contain traces of pesticides and growth promoters and also have added antioxidants as preservatives. To get traditional lard you will almost certainly have to make your own (it's not difficult, if you enjoy leisurely kitchen tasks).

❏ Cold-pressed oils have distinctive flavors, unlike bland commercial oils. You'll need to experiment to find ones you like. I find sunflower and safflower oils too strong and prefer to use corn oil. Sesame oil (not the dark, toasted kind used as a flavoring) is also bland. On salads, use olive oil or—even more expensive, and delicious—walnut or hazelnut oil.

Cooking

Organization

A common mistake among the health conscious is to make huge bowls of salad each mealtime, because we ought to eat more salad, and throw half of it away afterwards. This bad planning is based on unrealistic ideas. Many soups, and most stews, and chili con carne taste much better after standing overnight, and even better on the third day.

Knowing your audience is crucial, as is having the right equipment and a good stock of basic ingredients and seasonings. Favorite recipes should be somewhere accessible, and it's a good idea to keep cookbooks in or near the kitchen, rather than on the bookshelves in the bedroom, so that they are at hand to provide inspiration and information.

Planning meals and shopping—with anyone who is going to share in them—can also be great help, even if you aren't terribly precise about it. Keeping tabs on what you have on hand in the

fridge helps to avoid shriveled carrots and moldy cheese, and prevents a build-up of unidentifiable containers lingering on the back shelf.

Conserve energy by letting dishes cook in their own heat. Nutritionist Adelle Davis recommends bringing a soup or spaghetti sauce to a boil and then turning off the heat and allowing the pot to stand for a couple of hours, instead of simmering.

You can save yourself a great deal of work by doubling or even tripling recipes, assuming you have the right size pans and bowls (be careful if you're an inexperienced cook). It's not much more trouble to make a huge batch of lasagna than a tiny one. Eat half now, and save the other half for another meal. Double cooking is easiest if you have a freezer, because you can have the second dish a week or two later. If possible, freeze food in the dish in which it is to be cooked. A collection of inexpensive glass baking dishes make this possible.

Pots and Pans

Even stainless steel cookware needs to be looked after with care: there are suggestions that if it is once scoured with abrasive powder or steel wool, tiny amounts of toxic metals such as chromium and nickel will leach into whatever you cook in it.

A far greater concern is aluminum, which has been associated with a number of brain disorders. Have you noticed that you can clean an aluminum pan by cooking something acid (tomato soup or rhubarb, for instance) in it? Guess where the surface of the pan has gone. Try to get rid of your aluminum cookware—and, most important, throw out any aluminum teapots.

Enameled pots and pans are probably safest of all, and uncoated cast-iron pans can add small but beneficial amounts of iron to your diet. Glass is safe, and so is terra cotta, as long as the glaze does not contain lead.

Teflon is a fluorine-based plastic that should be avoided. If Teflon-coated pans are put over a high flame, they release toxic fumes. Nonstick coatings are made from plastics and will gradually release their constituents. The surface eventually gets worn so that small particles chip off into your food.

The best stainless steel and enameled iron pans are expensive. Accumulate them gradually, and in the meantime try to stop using aluminum, particularly for acid foods and long-cooking soups and stews.

In the Kitchen

As we lead more hectic lives, convenience foods become an increasingly and excessively important part of our diet. Many people, especially those who work outside the home, feel that these foods are the only way to escape the tyranny of hours spent over a hot stove. One of the most important changes needed to help us to eat soundly is more cooperation from our partners.

A recent survey found that the maximum amount of time Americans wanted to spend preparing a meal was 30 minutes. Many people would be happy to come home and eat a piece of cheese and some cherry tomatoes, or a bowl of soup, but sometimes their partners are miserable if there isn't a plateful of something serious in the offing.

As partners in a relationship, we should think hard about our actual, manual contribution to preparing meals. Many people simply feel awkward in the kitchen, and hate cooking under someone else's supervision. Learning to cook takes time, practice, and making a few mistakes along the way—but you should be able to count on a sympathetic reception if you decide to master the art.

Ensure, jointly, that you always have a supply of things that do not need to be cooked: fruit, vegetable sticks, yogurt, cheese, and good bread. Even small children can make an adequate supper on these.

Inexperienced Cooks

If you are inexperienced in the kitchen, enlist the help of a couple of user-friendly cookbooks or, preferably, a skilled friend. Be prepared to scrub vegetables and whip egg whites while you watch and learn.

Start by making a list of "Things I want to be able to make myself," and work up to them gradually. It's fun to specialize a little: Indian food, Japanese, old-fashioned country cooking, soups, salads and vegetables, or whatever else you fancy.

My own choice is soups, and I can recommend them as the ideal unprocessed fast food, especially during cold months. A couple of years ago we replaced our aluminum soup kettle with an enormous stainless steel pot. It has a thick bottom which heats evenly and prevents sticking, and in the winter it is kept pretty constantly full of things like corn chowder and spinach-kasha soup.

Quick Meals

Frankly, most of what we eat falls into this category. When it gets to the table to may not look as though it came out of "Fast and Furious" (the cookbook I keep meaning to write), but when it comes to making a meal after a long day at the office or coping with a pair of toddlers, or with teenagers whining that they are hungry, plans for a leisurely casserole go out of the window.

I once saw a newspaper column called "The 60-Minute Gourmet." What I'd like to read is "The 60-Second Gourmet." Well, up to about 10 minutes would be okay. What I have in mind are meals that take minimal effort and don't dirty more than one pan.

In fact, a good rule for deciding whether a recipe is easy or not is to count the number of bowls and pans it requires. Another clue is the number of ingredients, though this can be misleading because some cookbook writers list ten herbs and spices for a single sauce, which really doesn't complicate things much.

Make out a list of your own Rock Bottom Six easy meals, just to prove that you can get through a week of eating at home. Baked potatoes, omelets or scrambled eggs, pasta, grilled fish, cheese and salad, stir-fried vegetables, for example. These will take you through six evenings, and the seventh night you eat at your mother's, cadge a meal from a friend who loves to cook, or go to a restaurant. Or don't eat at all!

Microwave Cooking

Microwave ovens are good at cooking dishes which have been engineered to suit their peculiar requirements, but they are a flop when it comes to real, fresh food. Have you ever read a microwave cookbook? Prawn curry, an "easy" dish which takes 20 minutes according to one recipe, has six separate stages of microwave cooking. Minted lamb chops, less easy, require ten separate stages. Although you might be able to produce a dish in slightly less time with a microwave (and the cookbook times do not take account of chopping and measuring, exactly the same for conventional and microwave cooking), you are almost certain to spend just as much time working at it.

My heart sinks when I hear the ding of a microwave from the direction of a restaurant kitchen, moments after I've ordered a bowl of homemade soup. When the soup arrives, it is searingly hot and there is a dried ring around the edge of the bowl, a dead giveaway.

In the United States, far in "advance" of the rest of the world with at least one microwave oven in 70 percent of homes, there is an enormous market for foods designed specifically for microwaving. In "Brave New Foods" (*Harper's*, May 1988), Erik Larson points out that these are the costliest, most intensively engineered foods in history, and describes a popular microwave cake: "It did not smell like cake. It did not look like cake. It had the feel of sweaty human flesh. . . . If you saw it on the kitchen counter, you would try to wipe the sink with it."

Along with many other people, I have serious reservations about the effect microwaves have on food. In Indian yogic tradition foods have varying amounts of "life force." This idea correlates with the system of biogenics, a term coined in the 1920s by Edmond Szbhely, who ran a health center in California where the diet consisted of organically grown and mostly uncooked fruits and vegetables. In Europe, a similar food cure was promoted by Ralph Bircher, inventor of Bircher muesli. These theories, which have been successfully tested on thousands of people, may tie in with modern physics and its discovery of subtle energy patterns in matter. Certain successful cancer therapies use fresh, raw foods to fortify the immune system.

Cooking for One

The main problem here is inspiration. It just isn't as much fun to cook for yourself as for or with other people. Why not eat with other single friends, perhaps on a regular basis by forming a supper club?

A freezer makes it possible to cook in quantity: make a batch of soup or a casserole which will serve six, divide it into portions (size depending on your figure and appetite), keep one out to eat tonight, and freeze the rest. Don't be careless about labeling—you'll end up thawing a tomato sauce when you wanted black currant mousse.

Mollie Katzen, in *The Enchanted Broccoli Forest*, includes a section called "Light Meals for Nibblers," and starts with a pep-talk for solitary eaters:

> Do you regularly miss out on the pleasure of Dining, because it doesn't seem worth the trouble to make things Nice if they're only for you (and the 6 o'clock news announcer, who is your steady dinner companion)? Perhaps you can be convinced that you, yes you, are indeed deserving of good food and a little extra attention. Try these suggestions, and dinner with your Self can become something you eagerly anticipate, . . . a Pleasurable Experience.

She suggests setting aside time each week to prepare one soup and one main dish, which you divide into single portions and freeze. With a steady supply of fresh fruits and vegetables and good bread, you are set. Soup with raw vegetables and a simple dip from the Nibblers chapter one night, and a portion of the main dish with a spectacular salad the following night. Vary with omelets, which can be made quickly and easily in single servings.

Eating Your Greens

The trick to eating fresh vegetables, something we all need to do more of, is preparation. If the salad greens are washed and the green onions trimmed, you can pull out a bowl, spend a minute or two dicing and tearing, and be ready to eat. A little dressing mixed up in advance or some good oil and vinegar make it a cinch.

Katzen believes that a major deterrent to the use of fresh, as opposed to frozen or canned, vegetables is an aversion to chopping. While a food processor makes this much easier, it does not have the skill of a good chef handling a good knife. Learning to prepare fresh vegetables yourself is an essential culinary skill, and *The Enchanted Broccoli Forest* has five pages of tips on cutting, with illustrations.

If you can't stand plain steamed vegetables, switch things around and make a vegetable dish the main course. Ethnic cookbooks are full of ideas.

Avoiding Waste

American society is the most affluent in the world, and the most wasteful. There is a lot you can do in your kitchen to break the pattern of over-indulgence and waste, from basic energy conservation to backyard composting.

Even though clearing our plates is not going to save a child in the Sudan from starvation, some changes in the way we use food can change our attitudes (and where else does any real change start?), as well as save money—money which might actually help the starving child.

Ensuring that children take no more food than they need is a healthier step than forcing them to eat more than they want. Many adults find it difficult to break the clear-your-plate syndrome and have weight problems as a result. Why not skip the occasional meal—or fast for a whole day? Make a guess at how much money you have saved and donate it to Save the Children.

Some people like to do without meat or desserts. If you are trying to lose weight and want to do something for the world at large too, put a quarter in a piggy bank each time you pass up a packet of potato chips or a chocolate truffle.

An important and rare culinary skill these days is making full use of every bit of food. Of course most of us don't have farmhouse kitchens or time to make our own sausages, but we could make far better use of the food we buy.

Leftovers are something of a joke, but if you establish one area of the fridge for things to be used up, the family will know to look there for that piece of lasagna to warm for lunch, and you'll notice the juice left from a tin of tomatoes in time to add it to a sauce.

It was estimated some years ago that the average family throws away in its potato peelings the amount of Vitamin C in 95 glasses of orange juice, the iron in 500 eggs, and the protein in 60 steaks. I have a simpler reason for not peeling potatoes—lack of time. Scrub them with a vegetable brush and cut out any spots. Some organic potatoes have more skin blemishes than chemically grown potatoes, but the more I learn about chemically grown produce, the happier I feel about signs of insect attention.

Unpeeled potatoes roast and mash perfectly well—though if you are accustomed to creamy white mashed potatoes they'll take a little getting used to. If you love baked potato skins, that's a good start.

Another point of view, vehemently espoused by a friend, is that mashed potatoes should be white and that they taste different with the skin left in. I don't mind, as long as he peels them. Anna Thomas, author of *The Vegetarian Epicure*, makes soup stock from potato peelings and says that she is sometimes hard pressed to use up the peeled potatoes!

Two other important ways of avoiding waste are to conserve energy (see the Kitchen Energy Use Checklist in Chapter 5) and to compost kitchen scraps (see Chapter 13).

Eating Out

Restaurants

An environmental activist was all in favor of restaurant eating because, he said, it meant fresh, bulk purchase food (saving packaging) prepared in large quantities (saving energy). But there are a few special hazards:

❑ Many restaurants, even expensive ones, serve prepackaged and processed foods. Good ethnic restaurants may be the best choice, and you can always ask if the vegetables are fresh or frozen when you order, and whether the soup is homemade.

❑ Many restaurants cook in aluminum because it is cheap and light. It also pits easily and is therefore not as hygienic as stainless steel or enamel pans.

❑ Restaurant food can contain hefty amounts of monosodium glutamate and salt, as well as cheap fats (why should they care about your heart or waistline?).

❑ Even wholefood restaurants microwave food these days. Although some waiters look terribly offended, the only thing to do is ask in advance.

Fast Food

There are plenty of reasons for feeling guilty about grabbing a hamburger grease-fix, but the habit won't be broken until we understand the attractions of fast food and find realistic alternatives. Why do people eat at fast food joints? They want something *now*, are in a hurry, and don't want to spend much.

Yet fast food restaurants have contributed to the destruction of tropical rainforests (destroyed forever in order to raise beef for a couple of seasons), add huge amounts of plastic and paper waste to the disposal stream, and give us thoroughly unhealthy food to boot. International hamburger chains also tend to homogenize cultures. Why on earth do people want to eat the same hamburger and French fries in Tokyo and Peking and Paris?

If you find yourself going out for a hamburger because it's 10 at night, you are starving, and there is nothing in your refrigerator except a couple of moldy tomatoes, get a piece of paper right now and make a list of ways you can avoid that situation in the first place. This is a lot more constructive than feeling guilty.

Laying in a supply of some kind of wholesome, nonperishable, and almost instantaneous food at home is a helpful step— eggs, dried pasta, tortillas in the freezer, and a copy of Martha Schulman's *Fast Vegetarian Feasts*. Don't forget simple foods. Bread, wine, and cheese make a good supper, especially if you have the right companion.

Alternatives

The food you get at service stations or fast food restaurants is usually processed and overpackaged, and it's pretty awful to eat. You can enjoy better food and save money by ensuring that you always have basic picnic equipment in the glove compartment or in your overnight case.

This sort of eating will remind you of picnics in France. While you may not be able to buy garlic sausage and baguettes, it is still possible to assemble a pleasant and satisfying meal if you have the following supplies with you: a sharp knife for cheese, fruit, and bread—a Swiss Army knife is good if you are traveling on foot or by train or bicycle; a corkscrew; a few pieces of cutlery; small hand towels for napkins and wiping up; salt, pepper, and mustard.

For long journeys it helps to lay in plentiful supplies of drinks and snack foods. A big thermos of iced water is good in warm weather, and in the winter there is nothing more welcome

than a hot drink—apple juice spiked with cinnamon is delicious. Cartons of juice, crackers, fresh fruit, cut up raw vegetables in a plastic bag, dried fruit, and nuts travel well and are easy to eat.

You might think about carrying real mugs along to avoid getting coffee or tea in a plastic cup (saves waste and tastes much better). With an old-fashioned wicker picnic basket you can transport wine glasses, and a tiny camping stove makes it possible to brew a fresh cup of tea or coffee.

When you travel by air, you can phone ahead and order vegetarian meals, which are often better than ordinary plane fare. But it is fun to plan a survival pack, with fresh fruit and some special cheese or whatever you fancy. Some health writers say that jet lag can be reduced by not eating anything but fruit during the flight—bring a bag of apples to munch on. Drink plenty of water and avoid alcohol, too.

Eating Together

Psychologists have begun to point out that sitting down for a meal is an important part of family life, another obvious fact confirmed by academic research. Eating together is fundamental to human groups. Sadly, mealtime is one of the casualties of our way of life and restoring it sometimes requires quite a lot of effort.

In *The Hidden Art of Homemaking*, Edith Schaeffer writes about restoring shared meals to their proper place in our lives:

> The art of living together, of being a family, is being lost, just as the wealth of the earth is being lost by man's carelessness in his ignoring the need for conservation of forests, lakes and seas. The "conservation" of family life does not consist of sticking a rose in the middle of the table, it is a deeper thing than that. However, whether one is sketching a face, building a house, designing a dress or planting a forest, one has to start somewhere. And in this need to get back to "gracious living," to real communication among people living together, it seems to me one place to start could be the meal-time moments, and the careful preparation of the background for conversations at that time.

Food is an absorbing and nearly endless subject because it is a continual part of our daily lives. The purchase, preparation, and consumption of food has important ecological consequences—and even more importantly, it is central to the fabric and substance of our families, work groups, and society. I hope that an ecological approach to the home and to food will encourage people to see shared meals as an essential part of good living.

Don't let worries about health or the environment stop food from being a source of pleasure. Food is the simplest, most socially acceptable sensual experience we can have. Breaking bread together promotes harmony. Regular, happy meals with people you love will do more for your health than the most carefully selected food eaten with no joy. As Proverbs 15:17 reminds us, "Better is a dinner of herbs where love is, than a stalled ox and hatred therewith." Bon appetit!

Sources

Books

The Catalog of Healthy Food, John Tepper-Marlin with Domenick Bertelli (New York, Bantam, 1990). A good guide to sources for healthy, delicious, whole food.

Diet for a New America, John Robbins (Walpole, NH, Stillpoint Publishing, 1987). Lots of reasons to stop eating meat.

Diet for a Small Planet, 10th Anniversary Edition, Frances Moore Lappé (New York, Ballantine 1982). Good recipes, but even more important for ideas and inspiration.

The Enchanted Broccoli Forest, Mollie Katzen (Berkeley, Ten Speed Press, 1982). Not everyday recipes, but excellent for the novice vegetarian cook with some time to spare.

Fast Vegetarian Feasts, Martha Schulman (New York, Doubleday, 1986). One of my favorite everyday cookbooks.

Food First, Frances Moore Lappé and Joseph Collins (New York, Ballantine, 1979). The authors went on to found the Institute for Food and Development Policy, 1885 Mission Street, San Francisco, CA 94103-3584. Become a member and receive *Food First News*.

Heart Failure, Thomas J. Moore (New York, Random House, 1990).

The Hidden Art of Homemaking, Edith Schaeffer (Wheaton, IL,

Tyndale House Publishers, 1985).

Jane Grigson's Fruit Book, Jane Grigson (New York, Atheneum, 1982). If you are a vegetarian or eat little meat, Grigson's books will provide a whole new repertoire (though some recipes do include meat).

Joy of Cooking, Irma S. Rombauer and Marion Rombauer Becker (New York, Macmillan, 1986).

Maximum Immunity, Michael Weiner (New York, Pocket Books, 1987). A fascinating review of ways to help your body to help itself.

The Moosewood Cookbook, Mollie Katzen (Berkeley, Ten Speed Press, 1977).

The New Laurel's Kitchen, Laurel Robertson et al. (Berkeley, Ten Speed Press, 1986).

Nicki & David Goldbeck's American Wholefood Cuisine, Nikki and David Goldbeck (New York, New American Library, 1983). This is an excellent basic cookbook.

Pesticide Alert: A Guide to Pesticides in Fruits & Vegetables, Lawrie Mott and Karen Snyder (San Francisco, Sierra Club Books, 1988). Distributed by Random House, New York.

Recipes for a Small Planet, Ellen Ewald (New York, Ballantine, 1973). Good sections on vegetarian camping, food co-ops, and composting. Recipes too!

Shopping for a Better World (Council for Economic Priorities, 1989, 30 Irving Place, New York, NY 10003; (800) U-CAN HELP). A pocket-sized guide that will transform your weekly shopping trip.

The Smart Kitchen, David Goldbeck (Woodstock, NY, Ceres Press, 1989). Get this book if you are interested in building a new kitchen or want to alter your present one—full of fascinating information and practical tips.

The Ten Day Pure Body Plan, Leslie Kenton (New York, Pocket Books, 1987).

The Vegetable Book, Jane Grigson (Michael Joseph Ltd., 27 Wright's Lane, London W8 5TZ, 1978).

The Vegetarian Epicure, Anna Thomas (New York, Random House, 1972). An emphasis on Polish and French dishes.

The Vegetarian Feast, Martha Rose Shulman (New York, Harper & Row, 1986). Elaborate, delicious recipes with lots of information about preparing for parties.

Newsletters

Building Economic Alternatives, Co-op America, 2100 M St. NW, Washington, DC 20063. (202) 872-5307. Their quarterly newsletter includes a summary of major boycott activities.

Food First News, Institute for Food and Development Policy, San Francisco, CA 94103. The institute was founded by Frances Moore Lappé and Joseph Collins.

The National Boycott Newsletter, 6506 28th Avenue NE, Seattle, WA 98115, (206) 523-0421. A comprehensive but irregularly published guide to boycotts.

Nutrition Action Healthletter, Center for Science in the Public Interest, 1501 16th Street NW, Washington, DC 20036. (202) 322-9110. A national consumer organization which focuses on health and nutrition issues.

True Food Newsletter, Nikki and David Goldbeck, P.O. Box 87, Woodstock, NY 12498. A quarterly newsletter which will keep you up to date on food additives, pesticides, biotechnology and agriculture—with fascinating facts, recipes and guest interviews.

Organizations

Center for Science in the Public Interest, 1501 16th Street NW, Washington, DC 20036. (202) 332-9110. A national consumer organization which focuses on health and nutrition issues. Send for their free catalog of publications, or become a member and receive the *Nutrition Action Healthletter*.

Farm Animal Reform Movement, Inc., Box 30654, Bethesda, MD 20824. (301) 530-1737.

Project for Public Spaces Inc., 153 Waverly Place, New York, NY 10014. (212) 620-5660. Send SASE for a list of local farmers' markets.

International Federation of Organic Agriculture Movements, Oekozentrun Imfbach, D6695 Tholey-Theley, West Germany. A group of some 80 organic monitoring organizations in 30 countries. They hold conferences and are trying to establish international organic standards.

Mothers and Others for Pesticide Limits, 40 West 20th Street, New York, NY 10011. Write for details about their newsletter, *tlc*, and their book *For Our Kids' Sake*.

National Coalition Against the Misuse of Pesticides, 530 7th Street SE, Washington, DC 20003. Newsletter and other publications.

The National Cooperative Business Institute, 1401 New York Avenue NW, Suite 1100, Washington, DC 20005. (202) 638-6222. They will help you find, or start, a co-op.

Organic Food Mail Order Supplies, list free with SASE from Americans for Safe Food, 1501 16th Street NW, Washington, DC 20036. (202) 332-9110.

3
SHOPPING

Good workmanship—that is, careful, considerate, and loving work—requires us to think considerately of the whole process, natural and cultural, . . . because the good worker does not share the industrial contempt for "raw material." . . . The good worker understands that a badly made artifact is both an insult to its user and a danger to its source. We could say, then, that good forestry begins with the respectful husbanding of the forest that we call stewardship and ends with well-made tables and chairs and houses, just as good agriculture begins with stewardship of the fields and ends with good meals.

—Wendell Berry, *Home Economics*

Introduction

When I wrote the first draft of this book, in early 1988, I was worried that readers would think that an ecology book should concentrate on recycling instead of discussing our purchasing habits. Today, attitudes have changed and green consumerism is trendy. This raises a whole new set of questions. Is any product 100 percent environment-friendly? Isn't consumerism the antithesis of caring for the environment? Can we buy our way to a better world?

Consumer Society

All the things we throw away—and should try to recycle— are things we have bought. This includes packaging: the cost of a sturdy cardboard box and styrofoam casing is included in the price you pay for your new home computer. Packaging accounts for approximately 5 percent of all consumer spending. Of course the computer needs to be protected by some sort of packaging, but the styrofoam was probably expanded with CFCs and it is not biodegradable.

When the cheap beach shoes you bought at the end of last summer go into the wastebasket, there is still a price to be paid for disposing of them. Some of it is burned, creating air pollution, and the remainder goes into landfill sites. Estimates reckon that approximately 75 percent of our trash could be reused or recycled, plastics and toxic products being the main exceptions. Recycling is infinitely better than disposal, but we need to consider how we create so much waste in the first place.

Do you have a bathroom cabinet full of makeup and different brands of cough syrups, or half a dozen different bottles of shampoo by your bathtub? The packages were tempting, you were in a hurry, or a friend recommended that new shampoo. Perhaps the salesperson insisted that Druff Away really worked and you were in a mood to believe anything. In the same way, your closet may be groaning with clothes or the workshop with gadgets.

Economic growth is supposed to be a good thing. Increasing productivity and efficiency is supposed to be a good thing, no matter what the human and social cost. The more people buy, the better this is for the country.

Think this through. An ever-rising standard of living, for everyone? Or a rising standard of living for some, with corresponding deterioration for others? Charts and numbers are not good at measuring quality of life. As long as we continue to measure standard of living in terms of cars and washing machines and other things we *own*, instead of giving some thought to the quality of the life we *live*, we will stay on the road to ecological and social disaster.

The common notion of growth doesn't make sense. See Sources for The Other Economic Summit (TOES). All production depends on the input of raw materials which come from the earth, and which are in limited supply or replace themselves relatively slowly. What happens when they run out? Is it appropriate to use things up (whether the process takes 10 years or 300) without ensuring that they will be replaced? There are costs involved in this kind of development which are not taken into account in annual business reports. Economic growth has the capacity to destroy our world, and each of us is part of the process. Increasing output depends on our willingness to buy ever increasing quantities of things. More cars, more clothes, more toys (for children and adults), more kinds of writing paper, fancier diaries and kitchen equipment.

Advertising

The typical American consumer receives 1,000 advertising messages every day according to a recent study, so many that even the marketing people are worried about overloading the public with advertising clutter; perhaps we could call this advertising pollution.

Some advertising is informative and necessary. We put up with a lot that is neither because it pays for our newspapers and magazines and television programs. Most advertising, however, is designed to make you unhappy with what you've got.

Your hair needs a lift and your bed hasn't got the latest support system. Good grief, if you settle in with that nice tweed jacket and neat little pigskin planning diary you bought in 1989 (both of which will easily last till the end of the century), business will take a nosedive. You need a denim jacket, they tell you, and some new organizer will be essential this autumn. Our insecurities grease the wheels of commerce.

Value Judgments

Although recent moves toward a green consumer ethic are welcome, we need to think primarily of reducing the volume of consumption and questioning the prevailing ethic of consumerism.

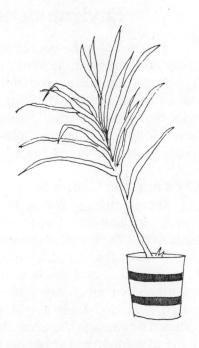

Do we want to be consumers? Consumers consume—that is, use things up—not a particularly satisfying function for most human beings. Most of us would prefer to think that we produce, that we are acting in the world, affecting other people, creating something of value.

The first step toward ecologically sound consumption is to think carefully about what you really need and want. This is not as simple as it might appear. Take time right now to jot down a list of your goals and aspirations. Do you think more about what you want to buy than about what you want to do or be? Are your choices about the future determined by what you own?

Many people have made a conscious decision to simplify the way they live, putting money aside for causes which matter to them. We could all resolve to live a little more lightly on the earth.

Maybe if you stop buying so much you'll end up with too much money. But you can give some away or invest it (ethically, of course). Or you could cut back on the time you spend working, to have more time for your family, or gardening, or travel—for campaigning on environmental issues or writing the novel you've always talked about.

Environmental Price Tags

A friend of mine was bemused as she looked around her crowded apartment, "How can one person buy this much stuff?" If you are a compulsive consumer, perhaps considering some of the following points will help you slow down. Environmental price tags are not written in dollars and cents—though they do have a long-term financial cost—but they can make even cheap items far too expensive for a concerned consumer.

CFCs and the Ozone Layer

Manufacturers are at last responding to scientific and public concern about the deterioration of the ozone layer—or at least to the likelihood of boycotts—although they have continued to insist that a link between the use of CFCs (chlorinated fluorocarbons) and the hole in the ozone layer has not been scientifically proven. Some manufacturers are adopting a label which says that their product does not contain propellants "alleged to damage the ozone layer."

But aside from the ozone problem, aerosols are a wasteful and expensive form of packaging. The very fine particles into which they disperse their contents can be a health threat. Aerosols can explode if left next to a source of heat or even in sunlight, and are a hazard to disposal workers. Choose an alternative product whenever possible—for example, shaving soap and a brush instead of a can of foam.

Styrofoam also contains CFC gases, which are used to expand it. As it breaks up the CFCs are released into the atmosphere. Fast food restaurants have been much criticized for using CFC-blown foam packaging and many have stopped using it. Even without CFCs, styrofoam packaging, especially for food, is wasteful and contributes to disposal problems.

Energy and Transport

The price of everything we buy includes a percentage for the energy needed to produce and transport it. Chemically based agriculture is extremely energy-intensive, both in the fertilizers and pesticides required and in the mechanical equipment used. Cotton, for example, requires the equivalent of its own weight in oil to produce it. Taking this cost into ac-

count—including the impact of energy generation—is a change
we should look forward to.

Pernicious Plastic

Plastics can be water-resistant, light, and almost unbreakable. They are also cheap. The trouble is that they last forever, for all practical purposes, and although recycling is possible in theory, it is a long way off in practice. Much packaging is made from layers of different plastics, which cannot be reprocessed in combination. There are also toxicity problems associated with plastics, and dangerous dioxins are given off when they are incinerated.

Plastics pose a grave danger to marine life—a simple thing to do is to snip six-pack rings before discarding them; avoid them altogether if possible. Plastic fishing nets are often discarded and left to drift in the sea until the weight of dead fish causes them to sink to the bottom.

Litter

Do you have to kick your way through a sea of broken fast food cartons, potato chip wrappers, and styrofoam cups when you go jogging?

Very little of this trash could be recycled, even if someone collected it. Concern about the social impact of litter and the difficulty and expense of disposing of the mountains of nonbiodegradable packaging we generate has led to important and innovative legislation in Suffolk County, Long Island. Almost all nonbiodegradable packaging at retail establishments throughout the county has been banned with particular emphasis on styrofoam and polyvinyl chloride (common plastic packing materials).

The environmental question includes the esthetics of walking through drifts of trash every time we go outside. The problem isn't restricted to urban areas: walks in the countryside are marred by inescapable and unmistakable signs of the people who have been there before you and who couldn't be bothered to pick up after themselves. Bright purple candy bar wrappers and "disposable" diapers catch the eye, instead of black-eyed susans and goldenrod.

It is all too easy to throw a wrapper down, especially when

there's no garbage can available and your scrap is only a drop in the oceans of plastic. Each of us needs to think about this, and discuss it with our children. There is no excuse, ever, for adding to the mess. The ecologically sound alternative snack is an apple, best of all from a tree in your backyard. Keep an apple in your purse or briefcase at all times. You'll never be embarrassed by it the way you are by a candy bar, and it isn't messy like a peach or fussy like grapes. Eat the core (for roughage) and toss the stem into the nearest potted plant.

NIMBY: Not in My Backyard

Just as we think of what comes into the ecosystem that is our home, we also need to consider what goes out again. Have you ever thought about what happens to the contents of the garbage can—or two, or even three—that you leave out on Friday morning? The garbage collectors heave the bags into the huge metal jaws of their truck. That's it, as far as we're concerned.

But landfill sites throughout the developed world are filling up. Many are already closed and it's harder to open new ones. Trash has to be transported further and further for burial, adding to costs. Landfills pose special problems: primarily the dangerous leakage of methane gas (which could, however, be used as fuel) and toxic leachate which enters groundwater supplies. Even domestic trash contains its share of toxic waste.

Incineration is a potentially useful source of heat and energy, but has special hazards. When some materials are burned they emit dangerous gases.

None of us wants this trash in our backyard, but everywhere is someone's backyard. There are ethical questions raised by the prospect of American trash being buried in Cornish tin mines or West German industrial waste in northern Cyprus. It should be obvious that our waste is our problem, while the waste of other nations is theirs. Responsible waste management is essential domestic housekeeping for everyone.

Ethical Issues

Many of the things offered in our stores come from countries with oppressive regimes or where production is causing ecological degradation or economic hardship. Countries which could easily produce enough food to feed their own population instead grow crops for sale to richer nations in order to pay off high interest bank loans, which were often taken out in the first place to finance expensive and inappropriate western technology. This problem cannot be separated from land rights issues in the producer countries, or from the economic hold which multinational companies have on Third World economies.

What we can do is try to buy from companies or organizations which promote equitable and conscientious development.

Another matter for concern is animal welfare. You can avoid meat that has been raised by intensive farming methods, and cosmetics and toiletries that are tested on animals.

Principles

Green Consumerism

A Green Consumer Week was held in Britain in 1988, launching the original *Green Consumer Guide*. There is much to be said for "buying green"—that is, choosing CFC-free aerosols, energy-efficient appliances, and organic produce. However, this approach doesn't tackle some fundamental ecological and economic issues. The main problem is simple—we consume too much. Buying green is not going to affect that; we might even feel so virtuous that we will buy more.

Neither does green consumerism concern itself with the question of our dependence on a few large firms and the vast multinationals, whose primary interest is and will always be profits. As environmentally conscious consumers we need to be aware that the power of industry and of the multinational corporations is not easily challenged and brought into line with our principles. Exerting pressure at the checkout counter is important, but to some extent we need to step away from the stores themselves.

Durability

It's natural to want pretty things, and to want new and different things. But the cycle of buy and throw away and buy and throw away has reached dizzying proportions. We feel slightly sick when we read about the thousands of pairs of shoes Imelda Marcos left behind when she fled the Philippines, but perhaps don't think so much about just how many pairs are cluttering up our own closets. Certainly, there's a big difference between 500 and 15. But where does need turn into desire, and desire turn into greed and dependence?

A big part of the problem is that so much of what we can buy is of such poor quality that in a couple of months a new pair of shoes is looking shabby. And they often aren't made of materials which can be touched up or repaired. Who could repair them anyway—and wouldn't you be told that they weren't worth mending?

There's a curious contradiction here: good quality, expensive items, from shoes to umbrellas to shaving brushes, tend to be made of natural materials which, when they do eventually find their way into the trash, will gently break down and disappear, while inexpensive items which will last only a couple of years at best are made of synthetic materials which will not biodegrade.

A really good piece of clothing might last 50 years. This may sound crazy in these days of cheap and cheerful clothes and ever-changing fashion silhouettes, but quite a few of us have a vintage tweed jacket or a Victorian nightdress. Furniture, assuming that it is well made in the first place, can last for centuries.

Buying more costly items is an incentive to choose carefully and to make things last. A fountain pen will outlast dozens of plastic ball-points, and be a pleasure to write with. A good one will last a lifetime. (If you cannot trust yourself with an expensive pen, try to be frugal with ordinary ball-points, and use refills.)

Most household mugs and glasses are easy to break, and you'll get better wear by buying things designed for restaurant and hotel use. One excellent source is the Vermont Country Store, which sells hotel-grade bath towels weighing 1-1/2 pounds each (an inexpensive towel might weigh a third of that) and many other products which will last for years.

Think about durability and repairability when you shop. This doesn't necessarily mean spending more. Good quality secondhand furniture is often a far better buy than new showroom items, and a reconditioned vacuum cleaner may give many more years of service than a bright new plastic one.

Sympathetic Materials

While plastics last virtually forever, cluttering up the planet, natural materials like paper, cloth, wood and silk will disappear into the soil in a year or so, and actually enrich it. To see this, bury a variety of household items in your compost heap or in a deserted patch of ground: a milk bottle cap, an old beach shoe, a piece of natural cellophane, a cereal box and plastic liner, a worn out polycotton shirt, a glass jar and a tin can. Which will disappear first? Which items will outlive you, and your grandchildren? If you choose natural materials—sisal door mats, a wooden file box, leather shoes—they will not pollute the earth long after you've left it.

Sympathetic materials come from natural sources, do not create other environmental or social problems, encourage local enterprise and small firms, and do not have an excessively high energy cost.

Natural materials have another important advantage. As Edith Schaeffer says, in *The Hidden Art of Homemaking*, "synthetics seem a step away from the basic simplicity of the production of wool, cotton, linen and silk: a step away in somewhat the same way as a highway, a car or a building separates man from experiencing the earth." By choosing materials which come from the earth, we become more conscious of our connections with it, and more appreciative in our use.

Building Materials

The authors of *A Pattern Language* suggest that good materials must be ecologically sound: biodegradable, low in energy consumption in production and in use, and not based on depletable resources. Nor should making them pollute the environment.

When you start building or decorating, look for natural, unprocessed materials. This means wallpaper made of paper rather than plastic; wood, cork, or tile floors; and wool carpets or cotton rugs. Many people choose these things because they are inherently more pleasant to live with, and in many cases wear better than synthetics. When they do wear out, they won't be lingering in a landfill site for hundreds of years. You'll get lots of ideas from David Pearson's *The Natural House* (Simon and Schuster, 1989).

If you are restoring an older home, what could be more appropriate than to use original materials, most of which are biodegradable and nontoxic? There are many sources of both secondhand "salvage" and good reproductions, virtually all of which will be in natural materials and designed to last. *The Old House Journal* is a good source of information.

Local Shopping

Shopping centers have taken shopping from our neighborhoods to centralized sites which are geared to car owners. This needs to change. Doing your shopping near home saves time, transportation costs and fuel, and by keeping your neighbors in business you enrich your own locality.

Architects at the Center for Environmental Structure in Berkeley, California, write: "We believe that people are not only willing to walk to their local corner groceries, but that the corner grocery plays an essential role in any healthy neighborhood: partly because it is just more convenient for individuals; partly because it helps to integrate the neighborhood as a whole." (Alexander et al., *A Pattern Language*). In fact, neighborhood stores are one of the most important elements in our perception of an area as a neighborhood.

Everyone needs a local convenience store for spur-of-the-moment purchases, a carton of milk or pound of butter or the Sunday paper, but many of us ignore nearby specialty stores and give our real allegiance to the giants. Instead, we should get to know the specialty stores near our homes and use them whenever we can. Of course you won't find the same range of goods at small independent grocers, but they can often obtain things for you if you ask. The much vaunted choice we are offered in big stores can be misleading, and dazzling variety is a spur to overconsumption. Just as our diet should emphasize locally grown food, we ought to choose other goods which have been produced or crafted locally when this is possible.

Craftsmanship

John Seymour wrote in the January/February 1985 issue of *Resurgence*: "Slowly and steadily, I am ridding my home, as far as I can, of mass-produced rubbish, and either learning to do without certain things or replacing them with articles made out

of honest materials by people who enjoyed making them and who, by long diligence and training, have qualified themselves to make them superbly." This is a constructive approach which we can all adopt to some degree or other.

In any given city there are hundreds of small businesses and craftspeople who sell their goods direct to callers as well as by mail order, and often at fairs and street festivals. Prices are relatively low because there are no middlemen, and it's satisfying to know that your money is going to the person who has actually made the thing you are going to use. The contact is delightfully personal, too, compared with going to a department store, and you won't find yourself wearing the same sweater as a quarter of a million other people.

Ask around—there may be a potter who lives down the road, or a skilled seamstress a few doors away. This principle means using a local carpenter instead of going to a large building contractor, and buying prepared food for a party from a local vegetarian caterer instead of from a big chain store.

To find these people, ask friends and check the classified

columns in newspapers and magazines, especially around Christmas. The small ads in many green journals and newsletters are full of fascinating offers. Debra Lynn Dadd is a great source of recommendations—her books list hundreds of mail order catalogs and her regular newsletter, *The Earthwise Consumer*, mentions new suppliers.

Do It Yourself

When your child asks for a dollhouse, do you go to the toy store or do you look around the house to see if there is an old washstand which could be converted? When we buy everything readymade, our creativity and inventiveness is stifled. We become incapable of seeing the potential in the things around us. Preparing for Christmas becomes simply a matter of choosing the right gifts, spending days fighting through crowds, utterly depending on what the stores offer.

Think of all the people who trained at art college or loved woodwork classes but have let their talents grow rusty through disuse. Everyone has some creative ability. Using and cultivating whatever skills and talents we have will contribute to a richer, more interesting environment in the home, and reduce our dependence on commercially produced goods.

This does not mean shabby, inadequate substitutes for store goods, but things which are better than what you could buy—in quality, perhaps in materials and workmanship, and certainly in *soul*—even when made by a novice. We don't need to measure what we make against industrial products, which are bound to be perfectly square and absolutely regular. In fact, manufactured goods sometimes have simulated irregularities (machine-made yarn, for example, is made to imitate the look of hand spinning). I once heard a man say that he would rather get someone else to lay his new kitchen floor because if he did it himself he would always notice the mistakes. Try not to take that attitude! Think of any slight flaws as adding character—and allow time to do the job to whatever standard will satisfy you.

Making things yourself can take as much or little time as you have, depending on whether you knit, make candles, carve furniture for a dollhouse, or decide to build a studio at the end of the yard.

Simply making your own greetings cards is a constructive

step. There are dozens of different ways to decorate the front— if you have buried artistic talent here's your chance to put it to use—and you might want to learn some calligraphy to letter the inside. Even if you just use cutouts from other cards and a colored felt tip to write "Happy Birthday Dad," the result will be far more interesting than most of the cards one can buy.

Look around the house for odds and ends which can be put to good use in your artistic endeavors. Good materials are essential, no matter what craft you choose—try to go to professional suppliers instead of to a hobby shop. Get your children involved, or a friend. To share planning and making something— a set of painted wooden blocks or a woven arbor for the garden— adds an immensely satisfying dimension to relationships.

Ethical Investment

Socially responsible investment funds have shown tremendous growth in the last few years. These funds avoid involvement with companies that produce tobacco, alcohol, or armaments, that are involved in gambling, the fur trade and cosmetic research with animals, or which have links with oppressive regimes. They seek investment in companies with good records in employee welfare, environmental awareness, and community involvement. The criteria vary from fund to fund; South Africa and tobacco are the most common exclusions.

People who take a moral tone about political and social affairs sometimes see their investments in the stock market as something unaffected by normal values and ethical judgments. I know a woman whose husband had died of emphysema and who is extremely conscious of how deadly smoking is; she was dumbfounded to hear that she was enthusiastically investing in a multinational tobacco firm.

You can invest in responsible businesses and use an ethical credit card, Working Assets VISA (part of the worldwide VISA network). Every time you use it, five cents go to an organization such as Greenpeace or the Environmental Defense Fund.

Saving Money

If you are extremely short of money, you may be limited when it comes to a few of the ideas in *Home Ecology*, but creativity is far more important than cash. Saving money is very often also ecologically sound—buying secondhand goods, refinishing an old chest of drawers, cooking with real potatoes instead of buying frozen French fries. Growing your own fruit and vegetables and reusing everything from yogurt cups for freezing leftovers to wine corks (saw them in half lengthwise and fix them on a leftover board with wood glue to make a practical and charming bulletin board) are excellent ways to keep expenses down. Basic nontoxic cleaning supplies are cheap, especially compared with aerosol products.

Organic vegetables cost up to twice as much as their chemical counterparts. But another way of looking at the money question is to ask how much food your money is buying. What is a soft drink, for example? Sugar, water, flavoring, and several dubious chemicals. What about those packets of whipped dessert? Sugar and hydrogenated fat, with a substantial dose of additives and coloring.

When your choice means that you are not contributing to pollution or to the exploitation of coffee pickers in the Third World, you may decide that paying more is a fair social contribution. Paying more for better quality products, which will last longer, is ecologically and financially sound.

Although green consumption may mean higher prices, it can help to avoid some of the potential catastrophes which now face us, including the loss of irreplaceable forests, wildlife, and genetic stock. If we continue to pollute the earth, the cleaning bills are hard to imagine.

SECONDHAND STRATEGY CHECKLIST
Buying secondhand goods is an excellent way to "precycle" and you can save loads of money, too. If you are not an experienced secondhand shopper, these tips may help:

❑ Quality varies considerably. It's worth getting to know good stores and popping in regularly to look at new stock.
❑ Garage sales have the lowest prices. The best garage sales tend to be in reasonably prosperous areas. Take your own bags and small change. Garage sale helpers are likely to get first chance at the better articles, something to consider when you are asked to lend a hand.
❑ Remember that goodwill stores do not exist to give you a

bargain but to raise money for an organization's projects. Prices, however, vary a great deal. While a Salvation Army store in the country might charge 50 cents for a skirt, you might see a similar garment in downtown Dallas for $5 or more (due, presumably, to higher rents and rates).

❑ Don't be too squeamish. To find treasure—and it's there— you will probably have to wade through piles of stretched-out synthetic jumpers and horrendous polyester pants suits.

❑ Vintage clothes which sell at high prices at market stalls sometimes turn up for next to nothing at yard sales.

❑ Surplus stores are full of peculiar things, some of which can be very useful. Military and other work gear is designed for rugged use and will wear well. I've seen a wide variety of kitchenware as well as heavy ex-army cotton sheets which would make excellent tablecloths, napkins or curtain lining.

❑ Factory seconds are sometimes available direct to the public at factory outlet stores, and are everywhere during annual sales. Buying goods with slight flaws is good domestic management and makes ecological sense.

❑ Check the advertisements on local bulletin boards. Better yet, place your own, asking for the things you want.

❑ Some areas have lots of junk-cum-antique and resale stores —worth a browse.

❑ Resale shops in many towns also sell good quality used clothing on consignment, with the shop taking a percentage of the sale price; some sell very expensive designer garments at a considerable reduction.

❑ For household items there are auctions and salerooms, ranging from cheap and seedy to very exalted indeed.

❑ Remember that antiques are second, if not fifteenth, hand. People often feel conscience-bound to confess if something they are wearing is secondhand, especially if they are complimented on it. If you want to make a point, or crow over the bargain, fine. Otherwise, say "thank you" and leave it at that.

Pooled Labor and Tools

Anyone who has seen the Amish barn raising in the film *Witness* will have some idea of the way small rural communities traditionally share labor. No money needs to change hands and the work is a social event which binds the community together. Some version of this is possible even in modern urban neighborhoods. Why not help a friend draftproof his house in return for a hand with laying a new floor in your children's playroom? Or have a housewarming and painting party—everybody wears old clothes, and you provide plenty of hot food and cold beer.

Sharing equipment and tools is another way to save money. A modern home is full of gadgets, many of which are seldom used. Why not think about what you'd be happy to share and see that friends know about it (which will encourage them to do the same in return).

Creative Acquisition

I once stayed with friends in a tiny New York apartment. They were designers and wanted their home to display their talents, but had little money. I was astonished to hear how many of their things had been scavenged from the street—a pretty chair, several lamps and an area rug. It was usual to put things you didn't want out on the sidewalk on Saturday mornings, and a scouting trip early in the morning was almost certain to turn up something useful.

There are always people looking furtively into the builders' dumps which abound in areas being gentrified. If you want to discard large items, why not make it easier for them by setting out any potentially useful item with a sign offering it to anyone who wants to carry it away?

Builders' dumps are good sources of firewood and scrap lumber for building a compost bin, and you can also find anything from old bricks to bathtubs on them. We once carpeted an apartment with beautiful wool carpet from a dump in front of a London embassy (the carpet needed cleaning but was virtually unworn).

Keep your eyes open. Our local library replaced its wooden bookcases with adjustable metal shelves a couple of years ago. We talked to the workmen as they were breaking up the old ones, and were able to carry home beautiful hardwood shelves which would have cost hundreds of dollars.

Good Wood

Wood is a satisfying material to work and live with, but the choices we make when we buy wood have substantial environmental consequences. You may have bought a rosewood salad bowl, or pans with teak handles without having the slightest idea that you were contributing to the destruction of the earth's precious rainforests. How will you know what to buy next time?

Rainforest activists would like to see us using sustainably produced North American lumber and avoiding tropical hardwoods such as iroko, mahogany, teak, rosewood, and ebony. Temperate hardwoods include maple, cherry, oak, alder, apple, aspen, beech, birch, elm, hickory, and black walnut. Temperate softwoods include pine, spruce, hemlock and Douglas fir. Ask for wood which has not been treated with pentachlorophenol (PCP), lindane, TBTO, or dieldrin.

Dioxins in Paper

An environmental and practical problem has been raised by recent research into the bleaching process used for virtually all paper products—from paper towels and milk cartons to disposable diapers—and was highlighted in a report produced for Greenpeace in 1987, *No Margin of Safety.*

The Environmental Protection Agency (EPA) has concluded that the chlorine used in the bleaching process is a source of dioxin contamination of water—which has a serious impact on water life around paper mills—and of the paper products themselves. Dioxins have been found in facial tissues, kitchen towels, paper plates, sanitary napkins and tampons, as well as in milk and long-life juice cartons. Research is being done on the way the dioxin migrates into food or into the body through contact, but tests have already found dioxin in coffee made with paper filters (a prominent scientist doing research on this has switched to a metal filter).

We need to stop using chlorine and its derivatives for bleaching. In Sweden and other European countries, consumer consciousness has made available unbleached paper products, sold as chlorine-free. Changes in pulping technology, such as the use of oxygen bleaching and the extended cooking of paper pulp, can greatly reduce the use of chlorine. Sweden has already reduced its discharge of organochlorines by 80 percent, and is talking about zero discharge by 2010.

Unbleached paper ranges from the brown envelopes we are all familiar with to the gray-beige of some recycled toilet paper. We have learned to associate white with cleanliness and purity. When it comes to paper, white means danger. Many of us have made a similar psychological leap, switching from white to brown bread. In a statement to the Canadian House of Representatives, Renate Kroesa said: "Greenpeace will not be convinced that consumers, when made to understand the real tradeoffs between breastmilk contamination and the color of their toilet paper, will not make a wise choice when given one."

Safe choices are few and far between, but this will change. In addition to choosing unbleached paper products, consider switching to some of the reusable items suggested below.

Beyond Disposables

Many common articles have been specifically designed to be disposable—disposable cameras are an infamous example. Most of these products are made from paper or plastic, placing unnecessarily heavy demands on natural wood and oil resources. There are occasions when modern disposables are handy, but try some of the following items.

CLOTH TOWELS

Use terry towels for your hands and a dishcloth for the countertop and spills. Drain fried food on brown paper grocery bags or newspapers. What about an old-fashioned roller towel?

SPONGES

Cellulose sponges are a good (biodegradable) choice. Dishcloths last much longer than sponges—my mother knitted me some with scraps of cotton yarn.

DISPOSABLE CLEANING CLOTHS

Accumulate a good supply of cotton cleaning rags, cut from old sheets or clothes. Linen is good for windows. Cleaning expert Don Aslett (*Is There Life After Housework?*—see Sources, Chapter 10) suggests making super-efficient cleaning cloths by folding an 18-x-18-inch square of cotton terry cloth in half and sewing up the long side to form a tube. All the edges will need to be hemmed, unless you start with outgrown cloth diapers. Refold the cloth and use both sides, then turn it inside out for another four fresh surfaces.

CLOTH NAPKINS

Cloth napkins are far nicer to use than paper napkins. For every day, choose a sturdy cotton fabric which does not need to be ironed. Many readymade napkins are made of synthetics (useless on sticky fingers) or linen (too much trouble for daily use), so you may want to buy a suitable fabric and make your own. Terrycloth works well. A good shortcut is to buy textured cotton teatowels in a suitable pattern, cut them in half and hem the cut edges.

A personalized napkin ring for each family member saves washing—when the napkin is still clean, tuck it back into the ring and put it aside for the next meal. Plain wooden rings or curtain rings can be painted and attractively decorated by gluing on seashells.

COFFEE FILTERS AND TEA BAGS

Use a percolator or a drip coffee maker—lots of connoisseurs prefer coffee made in a jug anyway. Other options include unbleached paper filters, reusable cotton filters, and permanent goldplated or nylon models. Buy loose tea instead of teabags. Instant coffee is not the answer because it is an energy-intensive product.

PLASTIC TRASH LINERS

Use paper bags from the grocery store or a piece of newspaper—your trash will be dry if you compost food scraps.

STORAGE KITCHEN BAGS

Wash and reuse plastic kitchen bags, or store food in reusable containers. You can get natural cellulose food storage bags by mail order from Seventh Generation—buy half a dozen and give some to friends.

SHOPPING BAGS

Buy a durable canvas shopping bag. French string bags are great to tuck into a handbag or pocket, although they seem to have disappeared from most stores. If you find some, buy a half dozen and give them to friends.

DIAPERS

Garbage magazine proclaimed "Disposable, degradable, recyclable. . . . Get a load of this, folks: they're garbage unless they're cloth." For more about switching to cloth diapers, see Chapter 15.

FACIAL TISSUES

There are times when these are essential—when the whole family comes down with a cold, for example—but cotton handkerchiefs are a nice alternative.

TOILET PAPER

While there is no satisfactory alternative, unless you don't mind using newspaper, look for toilet paper made of unbleached, recycled paper. Your natural food store may carry it, or you can order from the Seventh Generation catalog (see Sources). Supermarkets are beginning to carry toilet tissue made from recycled paper, but a lot of this is made from high grade mill offcuts which could be put to better use.

RAZORS

Disposable plastic razors are cheap, but an appalling waste of raw materials—and we use over two billion a year. While you might consider switching to an old-fashioned open razor, a reasonable compromise is to use a razor for which you only need to buy refill blades.

SANITARY AND PERSONAL CARE PRODUCTS

When you buy supplies like cotton balls, cotton pads and tampons, look for those made from biodegradable materials: paper and 100 percent cotton. The presence of synthetic fibers in tampons increases the growth rate of the bacteria which cause Toxic Shock Syndrome—another good reason for choosing cotton. Choose tampons with cardboard, not plastic, tubes. As unbleached products become available, buy them.

PANTYHOSE

Millions of pairs of pantyhose are sold each year in the United States. Since this is a disposable article of clothing, you might think about going barelegged, wearing more socks or switching to cotton stockings. This is a good health move, anyway, as nylon tights are associated with persistent infections.

BATTERIES

Batteries contain a wide variety of toxic substances, including zinc, mercuric chloride, lead and cadmium, and we go through two and a half billion a year! Manufacturing batteries takes 50 times more energy than they produce. Avoid buying battery-powered toys, and choose equipment that can run on house power. Buy rechargeable batteries (cheaper in the long run)—you can get a solar recharger from Seventh Generation. In Japan batteries are deposited at gas stations for separate toxic waste disposal.

SHOPPING CHECKLIST

❑ Be a thoughtful buyer, not merely a consumer.
❑ Shop locally.
❑ Buy from goodwills, garage sales, friends, and neighbors.
❑ Choose beautiful, functional, durable items made by craftspeople.
❑ Look for natural, sympathetic, nontoxic materials.
❑ Take your own shopping bag.
❑ Select goods with the least packaging.
❑ Buy products in recyclable containers.
❑ Buy from companies with a good environmental record.
❑ Pay more for better quality, longer lasting products.

Sources

Books

Blueprint for a Green Planet, John Seymour and Herbert Giradet (New York, Prentice Hall Press, 1987).

The Fate of the Forest, Susanna Hecht and Alexander Cockburn (Oxford, Verso, 1989). Available from Marston Book Services, P.O. Box 87, Oxford OX4 1LB.

A Forest Journey, John Perlin (New York, W. W. Norton, 1990).
The Furniture Doctor, Revised Edition, George Grotz (New York,
Doubleday, 1983). A terrific book about restoring old furni-
ture, which contains a useful description of many types of
wood.
The Green Consumer, John Elkington et al. (New York, Penguin
Books, 1990). The general information in this book will help
you make shopping decisions, but Dodd's *Earthwise Con-
sumer* is better for sources and specific products.
The Hidden Art of Homemaking, Edith Schaeffer (Wheaton, IL,
Tyndale House Publishers, 1985).
No Margin of Safety, Greenpeace, 1987 (brochure).
A Pattern Language, Christopher Alexander et al. (New York,
Oxford University Press, 1977). One of my favorite books.
It's expensive, but worth saving your pennies for.
Home Economics: Preserving Wilderness, Wendell Berry (Berke-
ley, North Point Press, 1987).

Catalogs
Lehman Hardware and Appliances, P.O. Box 41, Kidron, OH
44636. Catalog $2.
Seventh Generation, 10 Ferrell Street, South Burlington, VT
05403. (800) 456-1177. Free catalog which includes string
bags.
The Vermont Country Store, P.O. Box 3000, Manchester Center,
VT 05255. Free catalog.

Magazine
The Old House Journal, 435 Ninth Street, Brooklyn, NY 11215.
(718) 788-1700.

Newsletter
The Earthwise Consumer, Debra Lynn Dadd, P.O. Box 1506, Mill
Valley, CA 94942.

Organizations
The Other Economic Summit (TOES), 1442 Harvard Street NW,
Washington, DC 20009. (202) 667-4659. An international
forum for the development of a sustainable and just society.
Every year TOES presents the Right Livelihood Awards,

sometimes referred to as the alternative Nobel Prize.

The Rainforest Action Network, 301 Broadway, Suite A, San Francisco, CA 94133. (415) 398-4404. Organizes scientific symposiums, media campaigns, consumer boycotts, and public protests to help save the tropical rainforests. Send SASE for information and a list of woods that come from the rainforests.

Save A Tree, P.O. Box 862, Berkeley, CA 94701. Carry one of their Save A Tree canvas shopping bags.

4
RECYCLING

What poverty makes poor countries do—value their resources too much to use them only once—rich countries must learn to do as a matter of ecological good sense.

—Richard North, *The Real Cost*

Introduction

In the early 1970s, when my father was making ecology runs into the California foothills, recycling was a virtuous activity adopted by a few eager souls. Today it has become part of many people's daily lives, an economic necessity and a civic virtue.

Recycling generally means the reprocessing of an industrially-produced material like glass or metal. But a more cost-effective form of recycling is to reuse things. Containers can and should be designed for reuse. If you're over 40 you will probably remember returnable milk bottles. In Britain, milk is still delivered every day, and each bottle is filled an average of 25 times.

Long dusty summers at my grandparents' home in Iowa always included daily trips to the store for icy bottles of soda, which we financed by combing the roadsides for discarded bottles. Each kind of soda came in a different bottle. In France, the system is simpler and cheaper because most beer is sold in identical bottles—brands are distinguished by the paper labels. This means that returned bottles can be taken to the nearest factory.

After a period during which deposit containers nearly disappeared, today nearly half the states have bottle bills. Cutting litter is a consciousness-raising exercise which those of us who grew up in the throw-away society can do with.

We don't like to think about garbage. When there was plenty of landfill space and little publicity about leakage of toxic chemicals, we were able to ignore our garbage. Times really have changed. Garbologists appear on television talk shows, and there's a bright new magazine on newsstands called *Garbage,* about sewage systems, composting, and disposable diapers.

Americans are world leaders in garbage. The average New Yorker is responsible for nearly 1,500 pounds of municipal waste every year—compared to a West German's 750 pounds and the 400 pounds of an Indian. We can no longer afford to be squeamish about garbage. It doesn't sound as important as education or law enforcement, but next to these it is the most expensive item in many local government budgets.

Because landfill sites are filling up, rich countries including the United States are sending their waste abroad, and poor countries have accepted not only domestic rubbish but also toxic waste, in spite of the long-term risks to their own citizens. Fortunately this is changing; Nigeria recently forced Italy to reload a nightmarishly hazardous cargo which had been dumped on open ground near a river which provides washing and drinking water for the local population.

Although recycling centers operate successfully in many communities, these depend on stalwart individuals bundling their newspapers, bagging their cans, boxing their bottles, and taking them to the center in their cars. Many communities now offer curbside recycling, often by popular demand. One solution, first used in Santa Rosa, California, is to provide each household with a set of brightly colored, stackable containers for storing cans, bottles and paper. These can be kept in a convenient kitchen cupboard or in the garage, and carried out to the curb for collection.

What does this mean for you? First, find out what the recycling facilities are in your community by telephoning the city hall. Remember, every telephone call about recycling will emphasize its importance. Second, work out a neat, convenient system for sorting types of waste.

Try to arrange things so that you can separate and store everything, except perhaps bulky newspapers, in one spot. The kitchen sink is a central place in many homes, but you may find a utility room or back porch more convenient. Once you get used to sorting, the idea of tossing everything into the same container will seem messy and unpleasant. And when you see how vigorously your garden grows with compost made from kitchen scraps, you won't dream of dropping coffee grounds into the same container as newspapers and last night's wine bottle.

Recycling is a second step, an essential adjunct to careful buying habits. First, we need to rethink our buying, and particularly the way we expect goods to be packaged. Become a canny shopper. Try not to buy things you don't need or want. If you're not sure, try a sample or buy a small size. Go away and think about the purchase for a couple of days, particularly if it is a major one.

This approach not only saves money but makes recycling at home much easier, because there just isn't so much to deal with.

Packaging

Next time you unload your weekly shopping, take a good look at how much packaging there is. Cardboard boxes, plastic and styrofoam trays, plastic film, plastic bags, foil packages, tin cans, aluminum cans, plastic and glass bottles. If you were given a luxurious box of glacé fruits last Christmas, there were probably three, four or even five separate layers of wrapping. Microwave meals are infamous: a microwavable soup-and-sandwich snack which won Package of the Year award from a packaging industry magazine has six separate layers of packaging, five of them plastic.

Packaging performs a number of functions. It protects the product during transport and storage; keeps it dry; enables it to be boxed or stacked neatly; displays it to advantage; makes it easy to carry or easy to use; and carries information. But the packaging of an item can vary a great deal, and you can make constructive choices.

Some manufacturers box and bag and wrap their goods so thoroughly that you have to empty the garbage before you can start cooking. Organic food at the supermarket seems to be packaged more than the conventional produce. For example, some organic fruits are wrapped in plastic to differentiate them from chemically grown produce. I have seen attractive organic lunchpacks sold on plastic trays with plastic wrapping. The food is wholesome and environmentally desirable, but the packaging is a disaster.

Sympathetic Packaging

What makes for "sympathetic" packaging? The minimum necessary to protect the goods inside, it should be reusable, recyclable, or biodegradable. Plastics are the least desirable, and the people of Suffolk County, Long Island—who sent the infamous garbage barge on its abortive voyage—have banned all nonbiodegradable packaging because of the waste disposal problem it represents.

An old stock-in-trade direct action technique is to leave unnecessary packaging at the checkout counter. I used to find this idea pretty obnoxious, but it now seems like a good way to make a point. Don't lumber the checkout clerk with a bunch of bags—ask for the manager. It might be a good idea to bring a letter with you explaining why you are refusing the packaging.

Of course we want to avoid buying overpackaged food in the first place. This will be more effective if a group of people do it together, perhaps to accompany a day of action outside stores in your neighborhood. You could offer information sheets about the problems of packaging and local recycling services.

REDUCING PACKAGING CHECKLIST

❑ Buy in bulk
❑ Buy in returnable/refillable containers
❑ Buy loose items
❑ Choose paper wrapping over plastic
❑ Carry your own shopping bags, and use boxes
❑ Ask stores to take their own-label bottles and jars back
❑ Cut down on canned and bottled food

Keep several mugs in the car. Why hasn't someone developed a lightweight, nonplastic drinking container for cars? For cold drinks you could keep one of those little collapsible cups in your bag.

A natural food store in Santa Barbara, California, displays this sign: "To help keep our deli prices down as well as to encourage individual environmental awareness, please feel free to bring your own containers when purchasing our food."

Hazardous Waste

It isn't just big industrial plants that generate hazardous waste. Sixty percent of the hazardous waste dumped by households is made up of batteries, oven and drain cleaners, toilet cleaners, mothballs, brake and transmission fluids, antifreeze, pesticides, and paint and paint products. These products don't belong in our sewers, in our backyards, or in ordinary landfills. Try to eliminate them from your home, and ensure that any toxic trash goes to an appropriate disposal site.

Used motor oil can be recycled, and if you have leftover paints, varnishes, or hobby products which you no longer need, why not try to find someone who could use them instead of just throwing them away? A local scout troop or school might be delighted to have your leftover paint.

There are a number of organizations which will advise you about hazardous waste and collection programs in your area (see Sources), and Chapter 10 gives many suggestions for nontoxic household products. In general, hazardous wastes are disposed of in special landfill sites, where they are less likely to contaminate groundwater supplies. Eventually, we need recycling schemes to enable materials like the mervury and cadmium in batteries to be recovered and used again.

Paper

When I was in high school I incited the other members of my history class to share a single sheet of paper to take our daily quiz, so we each turned in a scrap of paper about an inch square. Our teacher had a sense of humor, fortunately, and seemed to appreciate our attempt at being ecologically conscious.

Over a third of the waste in the average landfill site is paper, although this is an excellent material for recycling. Paper production consumes large quantities of energy and water, and the bleaches, dyes, and other chemicals used contribute to air and water pollution, as well as posing a danger to human health when we use bleached paper. The plantations of fast-growing conifers which provide most of our paper pulp are a uniform kind of reforestation, able to support far less of a variety of wildlife species than natural woodlands.

Newspaper Nexus

The price paid for low-quality paper by recycling buyers makes it difficult even for voluntary organizations to justify the time and money required to collect, sort, and bundle old newspapers. While numerous towns and groups do recycle newsprint, U.S. markets for old newspapers currently seem to be well-nigh saturated. Asking that your newspaper be printed on recycled paper is as important as recycling old papers, but the time may have come to concentrate on alternatives too.

You might consider cutting down on the number of papers you buy—some modification of your reading habits. How many of us claim never to have time to read a book, but spend many hours each month reading the paper, perhaps one each morning and evening, as much for entertainment as for news? Books are also a lot easier to handle on a train or bus than a full spread of newspaper.

Newspapers can be used as firelighters, for making paper hats and boats, paper patterns, homemade "peat" pots, underlay for carpeting, or as a disposable doormat. You can turn them into papier mâché. They can be spread on a newly washed floor to protect it, on the table while you prepare vegetables for soup (the whole bundle goes into the compost bucket), or under the table where a toddler is eating.

I use newspapers as a weed-smothering mulch on my garden. Perennial weeds like crabgrass and dandelions will eventually die if deprived of light, so you simply cover the ground with opened newspapers—at least six sheets thick, but the more the better— making sure there are no gaps between them. Hold them down with earth or small stones, or with a layer of another mulch material like straw. For more on gardens and mulching, see Chapter 13.

Paper Waste

You shouldn't have to make many trips to the office supply store if you reuse as much paper as possible. Much of what we write, from shopping lists to interoffice notes, could easily be done on scrap paper.

An easy source of jotting paper is envelopes. Open incoming letters with a paper knife and stack the envelopes, face side down, next to the phone or in a small basket on your desk. This soon becomes second nature, and is particularly handy for shopping lists because you can put coupons or a swatch of fabric to be matched inside the envelope.

Make use of the paper which comes through the door or passes through your hands at work. Cut attractive cards in half and use the front as a postcard next time you need to drop a note to a friend. Save sheets of paper which have been used on one side for drafting notes or for children to draw on. I was once given some out-of-date letterhead bearing the title Histopathology, and a friend's children spent days writing out lists of words they could make from the letters.

Eliminate at least part of the problem at the source—and save yourself constant aggravation, especially if you are one of the many people who loathe junk mail—by having your name removed from solicitation lists. Write to Mailing Preference Service, Direct Marketing Association, 6 East 43rd Street, New York, NY 10017, to have your name removed from most large direct mailing lists. However, this won't stop everything. Why not prepare a photocopied note saying that because you are concerned about the environment and paper waste, you do not want your name sold to any other firm? Enclose a copy whenever you join an organization or subscribe to a magazine.

Recycled Paper

One of the most important things you can do to stop the unnecessary cutting down of trees is to buy products made from recycled paper. Although paper production is only one of the causes of the world's increasing shortage of trees, the potential savings from recycling paper are very important. Trees play an essential and irreplaceable role in the earth's ecological systems, and their destruction is a factor contributing to the greenhouse effect.

Most recycled paper requires no new raw material, cuts energy consumption, and reduces air and water pollution by up to 50 percent. It creates jobs and saves money on waste collection and disposal.

Until recently, recycled paper was often coarse. The quality has, however, improved by leaps and bounds, and you can now get fine stationery, photocopying and art papers, and glossy board made from recycled paper. Choose recycled paper whenever you can, but watch out. One fast food chain has printed "recyclable paper" on some of its packaging next to the international recycling symbol. That is, it is not made from recycled paper but could be recycled—just like any other paper! This is the equivalent of labeling food edible.

Making Things Last

REPAIRS CHECKLIST

❑   Buy things which can be repaired and for which you can buy replacement parts. Ask about servicing when you buy.

❑.   Learn to do basic repairs yourself. Everyone should be able to replace buttons and to sew a straight seam, for example. Something as simple as replacing the inner filters in a vacuum cleaner can add years to its life.

❑   Patch early. You know where certain things are going to wear out, so protect them from the beginning. My mother used to sew patches on the knees of our jeans

before we wore them. Carefully placed rugs will protect the carpet.

❏ Build in sections. Work can be done gradually, and it is easy
to replace the damaged corner of a brick patio, whereas a
concrete patio would have to be relaid.

Love Your Tools

A cook's spoon, a carpenter's hammer, and a gardener's
trowel are essential tools, as is the word processor I've used to
write this book. Tools help us to accomplish and create, but
most of us are pretty feeble when it comes to looking after them.
Think how you envy people who are good with their hands, and
how much in demand a handy man or woman is. I know the breed
well, having grown up with a father who could do everything
from electrical wiring to building a house, and lived with a man
who thought the best way to fix anything was to take it completely to pieces and then put it back together—and who does
this successfully.

Think of the amounts of money we pay to have our machines
serviced. And of how often we call out the repair service only to
find that one of the kids had unplugged the machine. Mechanical
ineptitude—which I suffer from too—leads to a great deal of
waste. Learn to love your tools and take care of them:

❏ Buy sturdy, well made tools, from a specialist shop rather
than the nearest superstore, and keep them in good condition. There should be a copy of the *Whole Earth Catalog* on
your reference shelf; published since 1969, it is subtitled
"Access to Tools."

❏ Read the instructions. These are sometimes rather freely
translated from the Japanese or German, and not very
inspiring pieces of literature, but it's well worth coming to
grips with their terminology and structure.

❏ Before calling for help, make an effort to solve the problem
yourself. Don't be intimidated by dials and lights; try to
think of reasons for the problem.

❏ Read *Zen and the Art of Motorcycle Maintenance*, by Robert
Pirsig, if you want to explore the subject in exquisite depth.

DISPOSAL CHECKLIST

❑   Cut waste to a minimum by buying only what you need and by avoiding excess packaging.

❑   Avoid plastics, plastic-wrapped products, and synthetic fabrics.

❑   Buy recycled products (stationery, for example) and returnable packaging (beer in glass bottles) whenever you can.

❑   Compost kitchen scraps—for details see Chapter 13. This is extremely satisfying, and you won't need to buy commercial fertilizers or manure for a small garden once you get a compost bin going.

❑   Reuse envelopes, paper, jars, and other containers. Fabric scraps can be turned into quilts, rugs, or dolls' clothes.

❑   Have worn articles repaired or restored whenever possible, either doing the work yourself or having it done professionally.

❑   Give things you no longer want to friends or a local charity.

❑   Paper, wood, and cardboard scraps can be used as tinder, if you have a suitable woodburning stove. Telephone directories—an enormous volume of waste in major metropolitan areas—are a prime candidate here.

❑   At present you may have no choice but to put plastics out for the garbage collectors, although plastics recycling is beginning in some communities.

❑   Toxic wastes, including used batteries, old paint, and paint thinners, need particularly thoughtful disposal. Used motor oil should be taken to a garage which collects it. Some Sears automotive shops collect used oil; you might check with the local store.

DONATION CHECKLIST

Many charitable organizations and voluntary groups welcome donations of clothes, books, and miscellaneous articles, which they resell to raise money. If you have things to get rid of, please don't put them in the garbage! Here are some guidelines:

❑   Pin sets of clothing, and bag articles which should stay together.

❏ Do not remove buttons!

❏ Ensure that anything you pass on is clean and still useful. Really worn clothing is better turned into dust cloths.

❏ If you give away an appliance or an old record player, attach a note to say whether or not it works.

❏ Some groups will collect garage sale items from your home. Telephone charity stores to find out when they accept donations.

❏ Playgroups welcome a wide variety of household items, such as yogurt cups and egg cartons.

❏ Our local doctors' office was delighted with a large bundle of fairly current magazines.

❏ Disaster appeals do not take used clothing, because it would need to be fumigated and is often inappropriate for the countries in need. Inquire before donating any large items.

To find out about your local recycling center or curbside program, look under Recycling in the Yellow Pages, or dial 1-800-CALL EDF to get help from the Environmental Defense Fund.

Waste Separation

Separation of different types of waste is crucial to any recycling program, whether in your home or nationwide. The problem is being tackled in some areas of North America with legislation forcing businesses to separate biodegradable and nonbiodegradable waste. In some schemes residents are provided with different colored bags while in others there are collections on different days, for different sorts of household garbage. At home, you'll need to develop a system too.

My mother had a laundry cart which was divided into three sections, labeled whites, colored, and delicate. A similar principle is involved here. Once you get used to sorting things rather than putting it all into the garbage can, and get a system going which works for you, the battle is won. For advice, designs, and up to the minute information, *Garbage* magazine (see Sources) will give you the latest scoop. It's also a great source of information for dinner party conversation.

CONTAINER CHECKLIST

❑   bucket for compost, lined with newspaper
❑   if you have pets, some scraps can go to them (see Chapter 14)
❑   cardboard box for glass—if you have a lot, use three boxes (clear, green and brown)
❑   box or bag for aluminum cans and foil
❑   box for other metal cans, if you have a way to recycle them
❑   your regular garbage can, for plastics (and perhaps metal cans), lined with newspaper rather than a plastic liner
❑   basket by the woodstove for paper and cardboard
❑   shelf for jars and reusable plastic containers
❑   somewhere to stack newspapers and other recyclable paper
❑   box or shelf for garage sale items and other donations

This is easier in practice than it sounds. Recycling shouldn't take over your life or your home. You'll find that you think twice before you buy, once you start taking responsibility for disposing of the trash.

Label the boxes to make it easy for your family. If you have a small kitchen—and most separation will go on there—use small boxes and move them out frequently.

HOUSEHOLD RECYCLING CHECKLIST

❑   Vegetable and fruit trimmings and food scraps go into the compost bucket. Line this with newspaper for easy emptying. The newspaper will not add nutrients to the soil but is a fine source of garden fiber. For neat vegetable preparation, spread a sheet of newspaper on the countertop for peelings and trimmings. When you are finished put the vegetables aside for rinsing and it's easy to scoop up the leavings, in the newspaper, into the compost bucket.

❑   Meat scraps can be offered to pets. Birds like fat (mix it with stale cereal or leftover rice). Some garden books advise against putting any meat scraps on the compost because it could attract rats, and a whole carcass would probably be a bad idea, but the tiny amounts which we have left over have never been a problem. Bury them well, of course. Use bones for soup, then add them too.

❏ Some people have large amounts of frying fat to dispose of. The easiest and healthiest solution is to cut down on frying. Dripping and chicken fat from free-range animals is a perfectly good cooking fat and adds flavor. Otherwise you'll have to put it in a can or bottle and throw it in the garbage.

❏ Small amounts of paper can go into the compost heap, and newspapers can be used as a mulch (see Chapter 13).

❏ Some paper and cardboard wrapping can be reused. The waxed paper lining from breakfast cereal boxes is useful for wrapping sandwiches. Cereal boxes can be used at home or a local playgroup for children's cutouts and drawing. Paper bags from the supermarket can replace paper towels for draining fried food. If you have a woodstove, no doubt you already save paper scraps for tinder.

❏ Plastic bags can be used many times. Try to keep them clean, because it's a hassle drying them and they clutter up a small kitchen. Stick them over an empty wine bottle or a whisk in your drainer to dry, or buy a swinging towel rack to dry them on.

❏ Yogurt cups and other plastic containers can be used for storage and freezing, although you may find it frustrating to see three identical ones and not know which is leftover curry, which parsley, and which macaroni salad. (Glass jars are better for identification purposes.) Labeling them is probably unrealistic so try to stick to casual divisions of the fridge—leftovers go on the top right hand shelf, for instance. This system breaks down when you have guests staying, or if you share with a number of people, but otherwise works fine.

❏ Glass jars and bottles can be reused—if not by you, ask around for an enthusiastic jam maker. They are terrific for kitchen storage: seeds, chunks of Parmesan, or chopped parsley in the fridge. Large jars make permanent containers for flour and grains and beans—they look nice and are easier to cope with than plastic bags. A painless way to clean bottles for the recycling center (if they contained something messy, which could smell) is to fill them with warm soapy water—from your dishwater—and leave them overnight. Pour out half the water, put the lid back on, give it a good shake, and rinse. With bottles for recycling, throw lids away and remove any metal or plastic; paper labels are okay.

❏ Aluminum is a valuable metal. Recycling not only saves 95 percent of the energy needed to produce aluminum but reduces the amount of land, often in tropical rainforests, being destroyed to mine the bauxite ore it comes from. Use as little aluminum as possible, and do not let it come into contact with food (particularly acidic dishes)—aluminum has been associated with Alzheimer's disease. Drink cans and their pull-tabs, aluminum foil, trays, and pie plates can all be washed and taken to your nearest recycling center. Large aluminum items, like window frames, can be recycled, too.

❏ Other cans are harder to recycle because they contain several metals, which have to be separated in processing. Try to avoid buying canned food.

❏ There is considerable interest in recycling PET (polyester terephthalate) plastic—this is the hard plastic in which many kinds of soda and cola are now sold—but it is likely to be some time before this is widely done. Nonetheless, environmentalists agree that *recycling* is far more important than the development of so-called "biodegradable" plastics. Don't burn plastics, as the smoke they give off is often toxic.

❏ Keep one or two mesh shopping bags folded in your purse or briefcase or backpack.

❏ Another thing to think of when throwing garbage away is the potential danger to wildlife. Animals can be caught in plastic netting, and deer have been known to die as the result of swallowing plastic bags. The plastic rings which hold packs of beer and soft drinks cans together can be lethal too. When spending a day outdoors, take your garbage home with you!

❏ Tie newspapers into bundles with natural fiber string, or pack them in paper bags or cardboard boxes.

❏ You may want to keep a small container in the bathroom for compostable material. Personally, I end up trailing out to the kitchen with damp bits of cottonwool balls. Once you become enthusiastic about composting—after seeing the good results in your garden—everything goes in the compost bucket: hair trimmings, cotton (100 percent) balls, even nail clippings.

❏ Some bottles can be washed and taken back to be refilled—

natural food stores sometimes offer this service.
❏ Pump-top and spray bottles are useful for homemade
cleaners or for repackaging products bought in large containers. Save any you have, or beg them off friends—but be
careful about labeling.

The Future

In the long term, we should look for a return to returnable,
rather than recyclable, containers. Glass is far better reused
than recycled, and this would become easier for both consumers and manufacturers if there were standard sizes for all bottles
and jars.

The Environmental Protection Agency estimates that returnable bottle legislation nationwide could save an annual
500,000 tons of aluminum, 1.5 million tons of steel, and 5.2 million
tons of glass—and in turn 46 million barrels of oil.

Development of sympathetic packaging is slow, but as
disposal problems and demand for landfill sites grow more
intense, there will be more public and legislative pressure for
alternatives.

We should all adopt a more appreciative, frugal attitude
toward the things which pass through our hands—to start
seeing them as resources, not garbage.

Sources

Books
50 Simple Things You Can Do to Save the Earth, The Earth Works
Group (Berkeley, Earthworks Press, 1989).
The Real Cost, Richard North (Chatto & Windus Ltd., 1986). A
fascinating survey of the real costs of products ranging
from coffee to cotton. Order from Books for a Change.
Zen and the Art of Motorcycle Maintenance: An Inquiry into Values,
Robert Pirsig (New York, Morrow, 1974). To say that this
book is just about tools and motorcycle maintenance is like
saying that *Henry V* is just about war.

Catalogs
Earth Care Paper Company, P.O. Box 3335, Madison, WI 53704. (608) 256-5522. Free catalog and lots of information.

Seventh Generation, 10 Ferrell Street, South Burlington, VT 05403. (800) 456-1177. Free catalog with a range of recycled paper products.

Whole Earth Access Mail Order Catalog, Ten Speed Press, P.O. Box 7123, Berkeley, CA 94707. (800) 841-BOOK. A superb sourcebook. Ask the folks at Ten Speed to send a catalog of all their books.

Magazine
Garbage, The Practical Journal for the Environment, published by Old House Journal Corp., 435 Ninth Street, Brooklyn, NY 11215. (718) 788-1700. A bright new magazine—about a dirty old subject!

Organizations
Hazardous Wastes from Homes, Enterprise for Education, 1302A 3rd Street, Suite 202, Santa Monica, CA 80401.

Environmental Protection Agency Hotline to find out about hazardous waste collection program for your area (800) 424-9346, or call your town or county environmental officer.

Mailing Preference Service, Direct Marketing Association, 6 East 43 Street, New York, NY 10017. Write to have your name removed from most large direct mailing lists.

Paper Recycling Committee, American Paper Institute, 260 Madison Avenue, New York, NY 10016. (212) 340-0600. Free pamphlets.

5
ENERGY FOR LIFE

The return to designing buildings in response to climate, and employing "passive" or "natural" methods of heating and cooling, may be as healthy for us as it is for our planet. It not only conserves fossil fuel and reduces pollution but also reintegrates us with climatic cycles, both physiologically and mentally.
—Carol Venolia, *Healing Environments*

Introduction

My father used to stomp round the house, turning off lights and shouting about saving energy. He would call all five of us kids together and demonstrate the startling fact that light switches could be turned off as well as on, with caustic remarks about this being the result of careful industrial design.

We weren't very cooperative. Saving energy seemed so mundane. Now, as we enter the 1990s, our energy habits are threatening us with catastrophe, and the decisions and changes we need to make look a lot more interesting, if undeniably daunting. It is encouraging to know that there are many things we can do to cut our personal use of energy, and that new technologies are being developed which have astonishing potential for reducing overall energy use.

Perhaps you want to know if it really matters—after all, oil prices fell in the 1980s. But as in a horror movie just when you begin to feel safe, the worst is yet to come. The low price of energy hides the long-term costs we will eventually have to pay for our lavish use of fossil fuels. There is a lot you can do to turn this around, but before looking at the practicalities of home conservation, insulation, and simple solar energy, we need to consider the issues surrounding our use of energy.

Problems with Power

Climate Change

Fossil fuels—coal, oil, and natural gas—provide most of the world's commercial energy. Supplies of these are limited, likely to last from 20 to 300 years, depending on the fuel. When they are burned, carbon dioxide (CO_2) is released. CO_2 is transparent to incoming radiation, but it creates a "greenhouse effect" by impeding the escape of heat (infrared radiation) from the earth. This heating effect is amplified by a roughly comparable amount of heating owing to a build-up of other trace gases: methane, chlorofluorocarbons (CFCs), and nitrous oxide.

The amount of CO_2 in the atmosphere is now more than 15 percent higher than in pre-industrial times and could easily double within the next 50–100 years. According to the Worldwatch

Institute, "Climate change looms as the ultimate environmental threat. Its impact would be global and, for all practical purposes, irreversible" (*State of the World 1988*).

No technical solution to this problem is known except reduced combustion of fossil fuels, which account for four-fifths of global energy use. Energy efficiency is the most important way to cut our use of fossil fuels and thus limit the temperature rise. Predictions vary and no one knows for certain, but even conservative estimates suggest a rise of about 35°F in global temperatures. The main impacts will be on weather patterns and global water levels.

The cutting of tropical rainforests is making a substantial contribution to the greenhouse effect, both because there are fewer trees to use available carbon dioxide and because unused plant material, burned or left to decay when forests are cleared, releases CO_2. Another suspected factor is a reduction in the oceans' photoplankton caused by marine pollution.

Everything we can do to prevent the release of more carbon dioxide into the atmosphere—from insulating our homes to buying recycled paper—is an important contribution to controlling the greenhouse effect.

Acid Rain

No doubt you've heard about acid rain. But do you know what it is? I didn't. When fossil fuels are burned—to generate electricity, power our car engines, or run the factories which produce steel—a number of chemicals are released, in addition to the carbon dioxide which is causing the greenhouse effect, and these cause acid rain.

Approximately 100 million tons of sulphur dioxide are released into the atmosphere each year. This sulphur forms a dilute sulfuric acid solution in rain water, and the resultant acid rain is killing plant and animal life in lakes across Europe and North America. It has already damaged or destroyed more than 20 percent of Europe's forests, and is now dissolving the surfaces of buildings and historic monuments. Many lakes in Scandinavia and in the United States are dead, completely empty of aquatic life.

It is possible to filter the sulphur in a properly designed power station, but the policy of recent U.S. administrations has been to resist these changes—an attitude not appreciated by Canadians, whose forests are being killed by the sulphur emissions from our power stations.

Nuclear Power

We are still encouraged to think of nuclear power as the great hope for clean energy in the 21st century. More than that, we are told that without it we will soon find ourselves living in dark mud huts, chewing on bark for supper.

Nuclear power is being phased out in many countries, and is at a standstill in the United States, where no nuclear power stations have been ordered within the past decade, and all orders since 1974 have been canceled. Its "technical, economic, and political problems now appear severe enough to rule out substantial expansion" (*State of the World 1988*). British Nuclear Fuels won the Friends of the Earth "GreenCon" award for 1990, with their advertising slogan, "Just how green are you about nuclear power?"

One of the main problems with our present energy path is the threat of nuclear weapons proliferation that goes along with the spread of nuclear power. Nuclear reactors produce substantial quantities of plutonium, a material which is needed to make nuclear weapons. A report from the World Resources Institute of Washington, DC, *Energy for a Sustainable World* (1988), stated baldly, "If a nation without nuclear weapons acquires plutonium recycling technology, it thereby acquires nearly all the technology and materials needed to make nuclear weapons quickly." This risk is much less if plutonium recycling is not readily available, but without recycling only about one percent of the energy in uranium can be utilized in present reactors.

The only way to reduce this risk is by limiting the overall level of nuclear power—by regarding it as the energy source of last resort. Most environmentalists would say that nuclear power should eventually be eliminated altogether, and replaced with renewable energy supplies.

The day-to-day health threat from nuclear power stations is discussed in Chapter 11, but it is interesting to note that even the government is not happy with safety standards at a number of power stations. These problems are forcing early closure of some stations, the cost of decommissioning is uncertain, and there is still no solution to the question of radioactive waste.

The disposal versus storage debate is a misnomer; nuclear waste is not disposable. The question is simply one of where it is to be stored, whether at processing stations, buried, or in deep sea storage.

I hadn't given nuclear power a second thought (frankly, it was the last thing I wanted to think about) until a couple of years ago when I came across *Race to the Finish? The Nuclear Stakes* by a favorite travel writer, Dervla Murphy. This coincided with the birth of my first child, making the nuclear issue of special poignancy. Murphy writes for nonscientists, and points out that the staggering potential danger of this industry, and its dependence on and inextricable connection with the weapons industry, makes the fact that it is in some senses cleaner than coal or oil irrelevant. As Murphy says, "This unique danger presents a unique challenge to human wisdom. A new technology has never before been abandoned and it goes against man's exploratory nature to seem to retreat from the Fissile Society just because unprecedented difficulties have arisen. But the nature of those difficulties makes retreat essential."

Western Waste

It is good news that we in the West are using no more energy now than we were 15 years ago, contrary to even the most optimistic forecasts made at the time. But there is still considerable potential for cutting down the amount of energy we use, personally and nationally.

As long as we use more than we generate or can renew, conventional sources of power won't last for more than a few generations; in financial terms, we are living on capital, instead of interest—and, as *State of the World 1988* explains, as long as "consumers have neither the means nor the information to make cost-effective investments in energy efficiency, we will continue to squander our remaining fossil fuels."

Part of the cost of each item we buy is the energy which has been used to make it. Potato chips have to be fried. Iron ore has to be smelted to make steel for bicycle chains. Chemical farming techniques are energy-intensive because of the equipment used and because man-made fertilizers and pesticides are produced from petroleum derivatives. Added to these is the energy needed for packaging and transport.

Worst of all, we waste a prodigious amount of heat. Strange as it sounds, this heat is a form of pollution. Water is used in industrial cooling (just as you might cool a boiled egg by filling the saucepan with cold tap water), and the resultant hot water is generally pumped into neighboring rivers and streams, where it harms water plants and animals.

A cheap energy supply has enabled us to be wasteful; *State of the World 1988* points out that "energy prices in most countries reflect neither the true replacement cost of nonrenewable resources nor the environmental damage that their use can cause." Attitude changes, including willingness to pay more for our energy supplies, are essential—as is the proviso that any price rises or "climate protection taxes" do not hurt the poor.

The Other Energy Crisis

In the Third World, the most serious energy crisis is the shortage of firewood. This has led to overcutting and deforestation, and causes soil erosion, flooding, and food shortages. People in need of fuel burn animal dung and agricultural waste which would otherwise be used to enrich the soil.

Effective aid must take this into account. If you are wondering about where to give money to help with a current disaster in the Third World, consider sending some to an organization like Intermediate Technology (see Sources) which is helping to develop things like efficient cooking stoves which can be made by the people who will use them from locally available materials.

Human Health

No one who lives or travels near busy roads can be unaware of air pollution caused by vehicles; the problem is compounded by emissions from power stations and industry. There are short-term effects on human health like emphysema, bronchitis, asthma, and upper respiratory disease. Deaths from these causes have been reduced in many places over the past twenty years, but there remains a second major health concern: human cancers caused by air pollutants. In a 1980 report, Wilson et al. estimated that "general air pollution in the United States alone is responsible for 53,000 deaths annually" (*Health Effects of Fossil Fuel Burning*, quoted in *Well Body, Well Earth*).

Think of this as you reduce the number of miles you drive, insulate your home, and choose organically grown food. A sensible, discriminating attitude towards energy conservation will have many indirect benefits, for your family as well as for society as a whole: a better diet, more exercise, and cleaner air and water.

Energy Solutions

Imagine a central heating system which also provides electricity for lights and domestic appliances, using natural gas as fuel—a miniature combined-heat-and-power station. This technology would reduce our dependence on enormous, inefficient power stations, and would mean lower domestic energy consumption and carbon dioxide emissions. The system, based on the stirling engine (invented by Robert Stirling, a nineteenth-century Scottish clergyman) could revolutionize the energy world. The prototype engine was developed in Sweden, and is being promoted as an energy-efficient, environment-friendly alternative to the internal combustion engine.

This is just one example of the technologies we need to solve today's energy problems. Donella Meadows, adjunct professor of environmental studies at Dartmouth College, has pointed out that the changes we need to make to reduce global warming are exciting opportunities to improve our quality of life. She insists that every measure that will reduce greenhouse gas emissions is worth doing anyway, has other benefits, and can be cost-effective. Here is the list she gives:

❑ Use energy more efficiently and step up the transition to solar, wind, hydro, and biomass energy supplies.
❑ Phase out CFCs completely. CFCs are destroying the ozone layer and are powerful greenhouse gases.
❑ Shift fossil fuel use away from oil and coal to natural gas, which produces less carbon dioxide and is less polluting.
❑ Stop deforestation and start planting trees.
❑ Reduce waste and increase recycling.
❑ Support low-input, sustainable agriculture.

Efficiency First

Four international energy experts claim in a 1987 report (*Energy for a Sustainable World*) that by making full use of presently available energy-saving technologies, global energy use can be stabilized—allowing us time to switch to alternative fuel sources and largely enabling us to avert the crises which threaten us—while providing sufficient energy for everyone throughout the world to enjoy a standard of living equivalent to that in Western Europe.

Super-efficient fridges, long-life lightbulbs, and cars which can run at nearly 100 mpg are some of the technologies they have in mind. Today's buildings are wasteful of energy, but architects are increasingly conscious of energy-efficient design and there are now model building projects in which energy use is as low as a quarter of that in similar but conventionally built houses. With good insulation, the right materials, and careful orientation, remarkable savings are possible. Imagine cutting your fuel bill from $160 per month to $40—and cutting down on your contribution to carbon and sulphur in the atmosphere at the same time.

Individually, we can choose energy-efficient appliances and products. We can also adopt, in practice, the idea that ways of saving energy—"negawatts"—are a better buy than energy generation. Energy efficiency has other things going for it: very efficient cars should be regarded not just as attractive consumer products but also as indirect deterrents to war, because of a reduction in the global insecurity which results from the West's overdependence on Middle Eastern oil. This assessment has a special poignancy as we go to press in August 1990.

They conclude their report by saying, "The energy future we have outlined here is not the ultimate answer to the world's energy problems. Eventually, the world will need economical and environmentally benign renewable energy sources—the development of which will take time and ingenuity. But this future would give our children and grandchildren a world free of draconian energy-production regimes and, we hope, a world sufficiently prosperous and peaceful to allow them to work out long-term solutions to energy problems. It should give them a little breathing space and some room to maneuver."

Renewability

The coal and oil supplies we are so rapidly using up were laid down millions of years ago. Renewable energy sources, on the other hand, can be indefinitely sustained. Potential sources include sunlight, wind, flowing water, wood, and plants. Some would have to be managed with care so as not to be used up more quickly than they replace themselves (that is, one would use only as much wood from a stand of trees as grows each year). Renewable energy generation will reduce smog, oil spills, and toxic waste disposal problems.

Renewable energy technology has made remarkable strides over the past decade, even without anything like the measure of support enjoyed by conventional and nuclear power industries. They are particularly suitable for small scale, local projects—a shift which would be welcomed by many energy researchers. Small does not mean inefficient. In fact, huge electricity generating plants have turned out to be far less efficient than their creators envisaged back in the 1940s and 1950s. In some areas, small generation and renewable energy projects are already selling power to public utility companies.

What Fuel?

Using electricity for low-grade energy such as domestic heating and hot water is wasteful because it is produced in power stations which burn large quantities of coal or oil and, which are, at best, only 35 percent efficient. An open coal fire, by contrast, is 20 percent efficient (i.e., 80 percent of the heat goes up the chimney), and a gas furnace is about 70 percent efficient. According to one estimate, when we heat by electricity we lose over 90 percent of the fuel's primary energy because of the inefficiency of the transmission systems and electrical appliances—on those figures, electricity is even less efficient than an open fire. In some countries, notably Sweden, the waste heat from power stations is used to heat whole districts.

Gas and coal are the best fuels for space heating and hot water, which make up 80 percent of home energy use. A better long-term energy source for this purpose is the sun, and very simple systems are available which will provide hot water and space heating throughout much of the year. A well designed wood or coal stove is a good space heating option, and pleasant to live with.

Electricity is suitable only for high-grade energy needs: lighting, and powering electronic equipment and motorized appliances. In England a few years ago the Central Electricity Generating Board (CEGB) extensively advertised electricity for heating and hot water, in order to even out expensive power station plant load. John Bennet, a former engineer for the Yorkshire Electricity Board, wrote: "The current promotion drive will obviously contribute to a higher demand during the winter peaks, thus helping to fulfil the CEBG's 'prophecy' of electricity shortages—shortages which they blame on the planning delays caused by public resistance to their nuclear power programme" (*The Ecologist,* January/February 1988). Think about this the next time you see your local utility advertising on television.

According to Debra Lynn Dadd, (see Sources) who specializes in alternatives to toxic household chemicals, it was better home insulation that led to awareness of the dangers of combustion byproducts, which include formaldehyde, nitrogen dioxide, sulphur dioxide, and a host of other vapors and gases. For people sensitive to petrochemicals and those with health problems including emphysema, asthma, and angina, this can be a matter for concern. Robert Matthews wrote in the *New Scientist* (December 5, 1985) that "epidemiological studies, such as that of over 8,000 children in the U.S. in 1980, hint that gas cookers in the home can increase susceptibility to serious respiratory illness."

Be especially careful to ensure that gas appliances have plenty of ventilation while in operation. They must be correctly adjusted in order to burn efficiently; if they burn inefficiently there will be unnecessary fumes given off. Your gas company can provide advice and service.

Wood

Everyone loves an open fire, but people concerned about the environment and worried about toxic emissions are looking at their fireplaces and wondering whether they ought to leave the summer display of dried flowers in place throughout the year.

The hearth is the traditional center of the home. Television, which seems to have taken its place in western culture, has certain qualities in common with a fire: both form complex, moving patterns which engage the eye and provide a certain shared experience. But the noisy, commercial insistence of television has a very different effect on social life. Architect Christopher Alexander and co-authors explain: "The need for fire is almost as fundamental as the need for water. Fire is an emotional touchstone, comparable to trees, other people, a house, the sky" (*A Pattern Language,* see Sources, Chapter 3).

But should we burn trees, which counteract the greenhouse effect by locking up carbon? Wood, made into a table, can efficiently store carbon for hundreds of years. If trees are sustainably harvested, the cut wood can be burned while an equal amount of carbon is retained in the new growth, with no net increase in greenhouse gases.

Wood is a primary fuel for many people in the United States, and it will continue to be the primary heating and cooking fuel for most people living on the earth. As a fuel, it has the advantage of being renewable, and in rural areas much of it comes from dead or dying trees, and from thinnings.

As Stewart Boyle and John Ardill point out in *The Greenhouse Effect*, with the right stove, burning wood is as efficient as other sources of heat. You can buy highly efficient, clean-burning stoves, which meet tough EPA regulations. Some have glass fronts, so you can see the fire. I know this isn't the same as a log burning on an open hearth, but we need to find ways of combining romance with the practical exigencies of the 1990s.

Renewable Supplies

If you are itching for a new project, you could tackle something like solar panels or a wind generator, and there are plenty of books and organizations to help. But the simplest, cheapest form of renewable energy, available to all of us, is passive solar heating. This means making maximum use of the sunlight which falls on your home, and works on a few simple principles. If you are building a house, get professional advice on design. You'll need large windows on the south-facing side of the house and smaller windows in north-facing rooms.

My editor lives on the south side of a hill at 8,000 feet outside Boulder, Colorado. His home was built with a combination active and passive solar heating system. A twelve-panel array includes two panels for passive solar heating that keep the house toasty during the day, and 10 panels for active hot air collection where the heated air is pumped into a rock storage area. Warm air from the heated rocks is circulated through the house as the day gets cooler. Additionally, the heated rocks preheat water going to the water heater. "The only time we need to go to backup electrical heating is when we have two or three days of snow, and long snow storms like that only happen three or four times a year," he says.

Here are some points to keep in mind.

❑ The orientation of rooms, as well as of the whole house, determines how much solar energy you can use. Chapter 12 gives many ideas about maximizing the natural light in your home.

❑ Leave drapes and blinds open or shades up throughout the daylight hours and close them promptly when it gets dark.

❑ Don't use net curtains, especially on south-facing windows.

❑ Remember that dark colors absorb sunlight (and heat), while light colors reflect it.

❑ Take advantage of the thermal inertia of building materials. A brick floor will absorb heat from the sun during the day and give it off through the evening, just as a brick garden wall is perfect for espaliered fruit because it retains warmth.

❑ Conservatories (attached greenhouses) are an ideal source of passive solar heat, and can make a substantial contribution towards warming your home, as well as providing an extra space. If you are a gardener, it's much easier to nurture seedlings in February if you don't have to tramp down a muddy path to get to them.

Practical Steps

The rest of this chapter consists of energy-saving ideas and techniques. As you read, check off the ones you want to try. There are many books and publications available which give detailed advice on materials and methods. Your local library will have some and the utility company may be able to help. The suggestions are ways of making the best of what you have now, and do not depend on special technology or equipment.

Energy conservation may be the easiest step to take in home ecology, because you can judge your success so directly. The lower your bills, the better you're doing. For regular information, subscribe to *Home Energy* magazine (see Sources).

TRANSPORTATION CHECKLIST

Getting around is discussed at length in the next chapter, but it is worth reminding ourselves that using less gasoline is an essential part of overall energy savings, since 40 percent of our fuel is used for transportation. Keep these tips in mind:

❑ Improve your car's fuel efficiency.
❑ Consider switching to a smaller, more efficient vehicle.
❑ Walk or ride a bicycle whenever you can.
❑ Buy locally made goods and patronize local stores.

DRAFTPROOFING CHECKLIST

❑ Find out where the drafts are. On a cold, windy day, close all doors and windows. Light a stick of incense, and walk around your home. The smoke trail from the joss stick will enable you to see where the drafts are.

❑ Stuffed draft-excluders—those dachshund- or snake-shaped bolsters—are an easy and cheap way to prevent drafts under doors.

❑ Fold newspaper into long thick strips and use them to fill gaps between sash windows and frames on windows which you don't plan to open through the winter. Hold the strips in place while you shut the window.

❑ Commercial draft strips are useful, but choose the expensive, durable kind instead of adhesive foam, which disintegrates after a year or two and is a pain to remove. Hardware stores have a wide range—you may want to consult a reference book before you buy.

❑ Drapes are nearly as effective as double-glazing at cutting drafts. The longer they are, the better. Floor-to-ceiling drapes are particularly good for draftproofing.

❑ Open doors as infrequently as possible in cold weather.

❑ Try to arrange some sort of airlock on doors that are used a lot. The idea is to prevent gusts of wind blowing straight through the house when the door is opened. You do this by having two doors; the outside one is closed before the inside one is opened, or vice versa. This can be done fairly easily in a house or apartment with a narrow front hall, by putting in a solid or glazed interior door. A porch or small conservatory will serve the same function.

❑ If your front door opens into a living room, you can increase comfort and save some heat by using a large screen or room divider to prevent direct drafts on people sitting in the room.

❑ Chimneys have to be well ventilated in order to draw

properly. You can tell that you've overinsulated if your chimney stops drawing—you'll get a house full of smoke. But an unused fireplace can be very drafty. Either install an efficient stove, brick up the fireplace—incorporating air bricks as required, or block it with a fitted frame covered with board, with holes to allow some air through. Arrange half a dozen potted plants or a large vase of dried flowers on the hearth.

INSULATION CHECKLIST

❑ Fitted double-glazing is expensive, inflexible, and resource-intensive. Heavy drapes and insulating blinds are just as effective. Secondary double-glazing (detachable in case of fire) is cheaper. A more attractive and permanent solution is using double-pane glass in existing window frames.

❑ Heavy drapes are cheaper than double-glazing, easier to maneuver, and look elegant. I've seen good ones in auction rooms, and you can make them yourself (see Jocasta Innes's *The Pauper's Homemaking Book*). The bigger and thicker, the better. Curtains can also be used over doors and at the top of drafty stairs. You can buy special lining fabric (aluminum or plastic-coated) for extra insulation. Drapes should be drawn as soon as it gets dark for maximum heat retention.

❑ Shutters are even more effective, and provide a good measure of security too. They are often boarded over in older houses, and it's worth taking a look in case you have some. If they have been removed, you can replace them with appropriate ones from a salvage firm or with new ones made up by a carpenter. You can add shutters to modern windows—get a copy of *Thermal Shutters and Shades* (see Sources).

❑ Attic insulation is a good way to cut both heating and cooling costs by up to 15 percent. Use vermiculite, mineral fiber, or cellulose fiber (made from recycled newsprint) rather than synthetic materials.

❑ Cavity wall insulation is suitable for some homes. Mineral fiber is a better ecological choice than polystyrene beads.

❑ Hot water tanks need a warm jacket, and as with attic

insulation, the payback period on this is only a couple of months. Get a large size and fit it over the old, thin one. You can also pad it with the same mineral fiber used in the attic, before putting the jacket on, and a layer of old blankets or clothes salvaged from the garage sale bag would be a cheap additional layer of insulation. Water pipes should be wrapped too.

❏ Floors are insulated by carpeting and sheet flooring, but you can improve on this with fiber underlay or a layer of newspapers.

❏ Exposed suspended timber floors are best insulated with an under-floor layer, but this is a big job to tackle. Eliminate drafts by filling cracks with an appropriately tinted filler; papier mâché works well.

Ventilation

It's no good insulating so well that bad smells, solvent fumes, and moisture in the air have nowhere to go. A high-tech, super-insulated building will need mechanical ventilation, and indoor air pollution control will be essential. Avoiding toxic chemical products is increasingly important as we improve building standards.

Exhaust fans in the bathroom and kitchen can be automatically controlled by a "dew stat" or timer. Opening a window a little bit is an alternative, as long as you remember to close it as soon as the moisture or smell you want to get rid of has cleared.

In the summer ceiling fans help to keep the place cool, and in winter they circulate the warm air which would otherwise rise to the top of the room and stay there. More elaborate devices for circulating warmed air around the house are available too.

Condensation

Internal damp is usually combatted by turning up the heat or by opening a door or window, both wasteful solutions. Condensation occurs when warm, moist air comes into contact with cold surfaces—when you turn the heating on in a cold house, for example. To avoid this:

❏ Use natural materials and fabrics, which absorb moisture and slowly release it back into the air.

❑ Cut the amount of water which gets into the air: cover cooking pots and don't dry clothes inside.

❑ Constant low heating can cost no more than occasional (morning and evening) heating and has the advantage of eliminating the main cause of condensation by keeping surfaces and air on even temperature.

HEATING AND HOT WATER CHECKLIST

❑ Use a timer. New ones with electronic programming allow you to choose different settings for different days, and to separately time heating the house and heating water.

❑ Heat only the rooms that you use, when you use them. This is standard advice, but in fact you may be better off with a different approach—see below.

❑ As an alternative to timers and electronic programming, continuous low heating is more effective, comfortable, and less expensive than the intermittent heating that most of us use, taking advantage of the thermal inertia of the building. Experiment for a week with a constant, 24-hour a day heating at 62°F, keeping track of the readings on your gas or electricity meter. This may be a particularly good idea if you have fine wood furniture or antiques, which can be damaged by fluctuations in temperature.

❑ You may find that you can heat your home more flexibly and efficiently with space heaters.

❑ With forced air systems, change air filters once a month. This applies to all systems—keeping them in good working order will cut fuel bills and save energy.

❑ Fit thermostatic valves to radiators, and use room thermostats. The hot water heater needs a thermostat too. Get the family to agree on acceptable temperatures!

❑ Look for systems with a spark ignition rather than a pilot light. These are safer (because the flame cannot blow out) and do not burn gas 24 hours a day.

❑ Radiators should be placed on interior walls—contrary to the usual pattern, which is intended to warm drafts before they enter the room. Draftproof your windows and this becomes unnecessary. If you have radiators on external walls, paste sheets of aluminum foil (shiny side facing you)

onto the wall behind them with heavy duty wallpaper paste
or glue.

❑ Shelves above radiators will direct warm air into the room
rather than allowing it to rise to the ceiling: a layer of
aluminum foil on the underside of the shelf makes this more
efficient; you can purchase ready-made reflective shelves.

❑ If your ceilings are very high, consider building a platform
area to take advantage of the warm air near the ceiling and
increase your living space at the same time. A ceiling fan or
heat recycling pump will circulate the warm air.

❑ Try moving your living rooms upstairs, at least in winter,
to take advantage of rising heat.

❑ If you have a hot water tank, insulate it properly.

❑ Turn your water heater down to 130°F (or even 120°).

❑ Avoid letting hot water go down the drain, when possible.
Allow bath and dish water to get cold before pulling the
plug—its heat is given off into the room.

Radiant Heat

Many people complain of the stuffy, dry atmosphere in centrally heated rooms, and compensate for this stuffiness with humidifiers (or, in my apartment, with wet towels hung over the radiators). Winter colds and flu seem to increase when central heating is on because the dry air affects the protective membranes of the respiratory system.

According to the *National Trust*, which is responsible for many historic structures in Britain, central heating has become perhaps the largest single factor in causing damage to the contents and even the structure of houses. Relative humidity (RH) of 50 to 60 percent is ideal—for people as well as bookcases—but the RH sometimes drops as low as 20 percent in centrally heated houses. The ideal situation is an even, low temperature of not more than 60°F, which can be an energy-saving measure, too.

In *Healing Environments*, architect Carol Venolia discusses the way we have become engrossed in creating "thermally stress-free environments" (central heating in winter and air-conditioning in summer) assuming that constant temperature is desirable. In fact, a thermally stress-free environment lessens sensory input and is actually bad for us, mentally and physically.

Everyone has a different comfort zone, depending on time of day, season, and state of health, but in general the most comfortable heating for human beings is a combination of convected and radiant heat. The authors of *A Pattern Language* suggest that this is biologically built into us by our evolution in the open air, with plenty of sunlight. Examples of this combination are sitting in warm sunshine on a mild spring day, or in front of a glowing fire in a fairly cool room.

According to architects at the Center for Environmental Structure in Berkeley, the *radiant* temperature (that is, the average temperature of all surfaces) should be 2 degrees higher than the *ambient* temperature (that is, the air temperature). Since windows and outside walls will be much cooler than the indoor air temperature, you need some surfaces which are much hotter. This could mean old-fashioned radiators (the kind you can sit on are wonderful), a woodstove, or a fireplace. Traditional European stoves were the center of the household, a source of warmth as well as a place to prepare food. Some even had beds on top of the massive tiled structure.

STAYING WARM CHECKLIST

❑ How warm you feel depends on your metabolism, your body fat, your biological rhythms, and on how much exercise you get. Do a little running in place to warm yourself up on cold mornings.

❑ Hot food and drinks are a great help. And you can use a mugful of coffee or vegetable broth to warm your hands.

❑ Dress with lots of layers. Tights or long underwear are good under pants. Wool and cotton are warmer than synthetics, but it can be useful to wear a thin synthetic layer next to your skin when it's very cold, with a cotton shirt outside it and whatever collection of sweaters seems necessary. Perspiration "wicks" through the synthetic fabric and into the natural material, where it slowly evaporates while the layer next to your skin stays dry. Remember to keep your feet warm.

❑ Use and enjoy good, old-fashioned warming methods like afghans and shawls when you are sitting at home in the evening.

❑ In bed, a hot water bottle is very comforting. We used to have an electric underblanket, but got rid of it after reading about the effects of electromagnetic radiation. Use of electric blankets has been linked to cancer and miscarriages.

❑ Thick cotton flannel sheets make the bed feel warmer—by comparison, polycotton sheets feel like sliding into a plastic bag. A flannel comforter cover can be made from a pair of winter sheets. Flannel—or 100 percent cotton—is soft and pleasantly absorbent in cool or hot weather. A wool blanket under the sheet seems to help the bed warm up too.

❑ Warm clothing at night certainly helps—socks, a sweater over your pajamas, even a nightcap. Most heat loss is from your head.

Air-conditioning

In many parts of the United States, air-conditioning throughout the summer is as much a fact of life as heating in winter. The 1988 heat wave led to series of power outages because of high energy demand. Air-conditioning is energy-intensive, dangerous bacteria can grow in the units, and some people are sensitive to sterilizing chemicals used in them. It also cuts us off from natural light and air and does not allow or encourage our bodies to adapt to heat. Changes in temperature are a form of natural stimulation which we need to stay tuned to the environment around us and to stay healthy.

KEEPING COOL CHECKLIST

❑ Dress for the heat in loose, light clothing. A sheer dress is more comfortable than tight shorts—think of a sari.

❑ Avoid synthetic fabrics. Cotton and linen may wrinkle, but you will be infinitely more comfortable.

❑ Spray yourself with spring water, sprinkle water on your head, wet your clothes, or go swimming.

❑ Drink cool drinks (or hot ones, if you are one of those who believe that a cup of tea is cooling).

❑ Open windows at night and close them during the day. Keep the curtains closed too while sun is shining directly on the windows. Outdoor planting can provide welcome shade during warm summer months.

❑ Ensure that there is plenty of air movement, either by ventilation or an electric fan.

❑ Use a hand fan. A collection of exotic fans is beautiful arranged on a wall, and you can offer them around at a party.

KITCHEN ENERGY USE CHECKLIST

❑ Use an automatic switch-off electric kettle and heat only as much water as you need, or heat water over a gas stove. Upright plastic kettles make it possible to boil a single cup of water, but there is some concern over the fact that minute traces of plastic will inevitably dissolve into the water. Scale deposits will make your kettle less efficient, so clean it with a strong vinegar solution from time to time. Filtering water can remove the minerals which cause scale.

❑ Put extra boiling water from the kettle into a thermos for later, or use it to start soaking a pan of beans. This is a money-saving move if you use filtered water for drinks and cooking.

❏ Improve your health and save energy by eating more raw food, salads, and fresh fruit.

❏ Cover cooking pots to cut cooking time and save energy (you know, a watched pot never boils—put the lid on).

❏ Let the fire fit the pan: flame licking up the side of a small saucepan is wasted.

❏ Use a pressure cooker (stainless steel rather than aluminium) to cut cooking time drastically. Useful for beans which you haven't remembered to soak.

❏ Fill the oven. For example, bake a pan of apples on the lower shelf while a nutloaf or pot roast is cooking, then put in a tray of meringues before turning the oven off and leave them overnight.

❏ Toaster ovens use less energy when you are preparing a single portion.

❏ Cut vegetables, including potatoes, into small pieces: they cook much more quickly.

❏ When preparing foods which take a long time, cook more than you need and save the rest for another meal. Cooked beans and grains keep for about a week in the fridge, and are excellent in salads.

❏ A tiered steamer will hold several vegetables at once, and you can use the bottom pan of a double boiler to simmer eggs or steam rice while you stir a curry sauce in the top.

❏ Gas is a more efficient cooking fuel than electricity, so use it if you can. It's also more responsive to your cooking needs. Careful ventilation is important.

❏ Refrigerators gobble energy—choose an energy-efficient model, keep the seals clean and place it as far as possible from any heat source, especially the stove.

❏ Chest freezers are more efficient than upright models, though less convenient to use. If you have a freezer, defrost regularly and try to keep it full. Keeping it outside, in a garage or cellar, cuts energy costs, or you can put foil on the wall behind it to reflect waste heat into the room.

LAUNDRY ENERGY CHECKLIST

❑ Wash full loads, and keep the cycles as short and cool as possible. Clothes can be rinsed in cold water, but a hot wash is probably preferable to using large amounts of detergent.

❑ In dry weather, even in winter, hang clothes outside to dry (they'll smell wonderful), or on racks indoors; if necessary, tumble dry for a few minutes.

❑ A spin dryer can halve the time and energy needed to dry a load of clothes, even after they have been spun in a washing machine. It makes drying clothes on racks much faster too.

❑ Iron in bulk rather than one piece at a time, and use a heat reflective cover or cut a piece of aluminium foil to fit under your cloth ironing board cover.

LIGHTS CHECKLIST

❑ This may be too obvious to state, but I know my father would want me to point out that lights should be turned off when they are not needed!

❑ Use low-energy, long-life bulbs when you can find them. *The Green Consumer* is good on these.

❑ Switch to low-wattage bulbs where only a small amount of light is needed—hallways, for example. Friends of mine with a new baby switched to 25- and 40-watt bulbs upstairs because it was pleasanter for night feedings, and they found that the soft lighting also made getting up in the morning less of a shock to the system. Just be careful about matching socks! And always make sure you have enough light for safety and to avoid eye strain.

❑ See Chapter 12 for more on home lighting and our need for natural daylight.

Appliances

Over the past ten years appliance efficiency standards have been developing in the United States, and by the year 2000 these are likely to have saved $28 billion worth of electricity and gas and kept 342 million tons of carbon out of the atmosphere, according to the Worldwatch Institute. You can easily save money and cut your contribution to the greenhouse effect by choosing efficient appliances.

An additional step you can take is to reduce the number of electrical appliances in your home. If you already have many electrical appliances, consider how you use them.

Of the major domestic appliances, only refrigerators, washing machines, and vacuum cleaners seem essential to me, but everyone will have different feelings about this. With a decent-sized freezer compartment in your fridge, a separate freezer is only necessary if you have a garden, or parents-in-law with one, or do a lot of cooking ahead. Otherwise it may just encourage you to buy frozen pizzas. However, wholefood cooks often find a freezer invaluable for avoiding processed commercial foods.

A dishwasher saves time for a large family and certainly keeps the kitchen a lot tidier, but there are sound arguments against having one. You need more dishes, have the hassle of rinsing and loading and unloading, and miss out on companionable chats over the suds. They require strong detergents and use large amounts of hot water, as well as considerable amounts of energy for drying. If you have a dishwasher, choose the economy setting and turn the machine off when it gets to the dry cycle—open the door and pull the racks out. Since the dishes are already hot, they will dry in very little time.

Christina Hardyment argues in *From Mangle to Microwave* that supposedly time-saving appliances, and their manufacturers' substantial advertising budgets, have created impossibly high housekeeping standards—that they have, in fact, made the homemaker's lot harder, not easier. The same might be said of modern miracle cleaning products.

New equipment shouldn't be a substitute for adequate assistance from the entire family. In *Living More with Less*, Doris Longacre points out that although labor-saving devices are not all bad, neither is labor. Like Christina Hardyment, she observes that people with lots of machines are not less harried—in fact, Americans spend more time on housework now than they did in the 1920s.

APPLIANCE CHECKLIST

❑ Think of any appliance as a long-term investment. Buy good quality models and keep them in working order by following manufacturers' instructions (except that you can halve the suggested amount of washing powder), and by having them serviced regularly.

❑ Do you really need a dishwasher/video machine/second television (or even a first television)? Don't get one just because your friends have one. If possible, borrow or hire one for a month or so, to see if you really make use of it.

❑ Doing without a TV can free a surprising amount of time, and maybe your mind too. Watch important programs at a friend's house.

❑ Look for equipment made of metal rather than plastic—which can release fumes, especially when heated. Try buying reconditioned models, or secondhand ones through the ads in the local paper. Debra Lynn Dadd says older models provide high-quality nontoxic materials at significant savings, and buying them keeps useful equipment in circulation. Unless you can ensure that the CFCs in your old fridge will be recycled, avoid buying a new one.

❑ While you want to make good use of your appliances, don't let having a food processor tempt you into blending/processing everything. Some chefs complain that food processors spoil the texture of food. I find mine invaluable, but Henry Fairlie of the *Washington Post* wrote that chopping is a "concentrated physical effort, it is a skill, it is always thoroughly enjoyable, and I can probably chop a leaf vegetable very fine as quickly as any. If I left this to an electrical gadget, I would have to take my fingers jogging."

❑ Look for hand-operated models. Carpet sweepers are great, especially if you like to give the main areas of wear a quick going-over every day. Carpets last longer if they are swept or vacuumed frequently.

❑ A pantry can expand your cold storage considerably; unrefined oils, wholegrain flours, seeds and nuts should be kept cool.

❑ For hot food, there's the option of slow cooking with a haybox: a pot of stew or soup is put into a box, packed with hay, which works like a vacuum flask to maintain the heat. You can build an urban version with some leftover polystyrene packing, as long as you ensure that there is a good layer of newspaper or towelling between it and the hot pan.

The Future

Changing government and international energy policy is a task to which we can contribute in various ways: by donating money to research and campaigning organizations, writing letters to our representatives, choosing our fuels with care, and showing willingness to pay higher prices when appropriate.

Sources

Books
Cut Your Electric Bills in Half, Ralph Herbert (Emmaus, PA, Rodale Press, 1986).

Energy for a Sustainable World, Jose Goldemberg et al. (New York, Wiley, 1988).

From Mangle to Microwave, Christina Hardyment (Cambridge, MA, Basil Blackwell, 1987). A fascinating survey of the history of domestic work.

The Green Consumer, John Elkington et al. (New York, Penguin Books, 1990).

Healing Environments, Carol Venolia (Berkeley, Celestial Arts, 1988). A lovely book which will give you new ways to look at your living and working spaces.

Living More with Less, Doris Longacre (Scottdale, PA, Herald Press, 1980). This book is enlightening because it contains comments from people from other cultures.

More Other Homes and Gardens, Jim Leckie et al. (San Francisco, Sierra Club Books, 1981). Distributed by Random House, New York. Geared toward the self-sufficiency buffs, with lots of design ideas.

The Passive Solar Energy Book, Edward Mazria (Emmaus, PA, Rodale Press, 1979).

The Pauper's Homemaking Book, Jocasta Innes (London, Penguin, 1976).

Race to the Finish? The Nuclear Stakes, Dervla Murphy (John Murray, 50 Albemarle Street, London W1X 4BD, 1981).

State of the World 1988, A Worldwatch Institute Report on the Progress Toward a Sustainable Society, Lester R. Brown (New York, W.W. Norton, 1988).

Thermal Shutters and Shades: Over 100 Schemes for Reducing Heat Loss through Windows, William Shurcliff (Andover, MA, Brick House Publishing, 1980).

Well Body, Well Earth, Mike Samuels and Hal Zina Bennett (San Francisco, Sierra Club Books, 1983). Distributed by Random House, New York.

Catalogs
Seventh Generation, 10 Ferrell Street, South Burlington, VT 05403. (800) 456-1177. Free catalog. Lots of energy conserving products.

Magazine
Home Energy, 2124 Kittredge Street, Berkeley, CA 94704. (415) 524-5405.

Organizations
American Council for an Energy Efficient Economy (ACEE), 1001 Connecticut Avenue NW, Suite 535, Washington, DC 20036. (202) 429-8873. Collects and publishes information about energy efficient technologies. Send SASE for a list of their publications.

Elemental Enterprises, Larry Weingarten, P.O. Box 982, Monterey, CA 93942. (408) 394-7077.

Intermediate Technology Development Group NA, 777 United Nations Plaza, New York 10017. This organization puts some of economist E. F. Schumacher's ideas into practice by providing support for Third World projects using local skills and resources.

Massachusetts Audubon Society, Educational Resources Office, South Great Road, Lincoln, MA 01773. They publish a series of eight practical leaflets about saving energy. Send stamped, self-addressed envelope for a price list.

National Appropriate Technology Assistance Service (NATAS), P.O. Box 2525, Butte, MT 59702. (800) 428-2525; in Montana,

(800) 428-1718. Funded by the Department of Energy, NATAS will give free advice on energy efficiency and renewable energy sources. Give them a call!

Nuclear Information and Resource Service (NIRS), 1424 16th Street NW, Suite 601, Washington, DC 20036. (202) 328-0002. Information about nuclear power, radiation and human health, and alternative energy sources.

Rocky Mountain Institute, 1739 Snowmass Creek Road, Snowmass, CO 81654. (303) 927-3128. Write for a copy of their comprehensive publications list, which includes the *Resource-Efficient Housing Guide* by Robert Sardinsky, 1989.

Worldwatch Institute, 1776 Massachusetts Avenue NW, Washington, DC 20036. (202) 452-1999. International environmental information gathering organization and think tank.

World Resources Institute, 1750 New York Ave NW, Washington, DC 20006. (202) 638-6300. Advise public and government on energy issues and economic development.

6
TRANSPORTATION

Excessive reliance on cars can actually stifle rather than advance societies. The very success of mass motorization has created conditions that cannot be ameliorated simply by making cars more efficient and less polluting.

—Michael Renner,
Rethinking the Role of the Automobile

A Look at the Automobile

The car dominates our way of life so profoundly that it is difficult to get a clear look at how it affects our lives, our health and the health of our society.

Car ownership is one of the statistical measures of a society's affluence and increases in mobility are generally considered a desirable thing; mobility is equated with independence. But social health requires a certain degree of dependence—or, rather, interdependence. Complete independence leads to social alienation. Everyone is affected by the social problems cars create. Let's take a look at them.

Air Pollution

As we saw in the last chapter, the burning of fossil fuels, including gasoline, has a range of serious environmental consequences, including acid rain and global climate change—the greenhouse effect. Car engines emit a number of pollutant gases including nitrogen oxide, carbon monoxide, hydrocarbons, and sulphur dioxide. Worst of all, because it is completely avoidable and because it has well documented consequences for children, is lead.

Most of us have felt the effects of these pollutants, while waiting for a bus by a busy road or while stuck in a traffic jam. Headaches and smarting eyes and throat are common complaints, but long-term damage is far more serious and ranges from respiratory problems like bronchitis and asthma to lung cancer.

Noise

Traffic noise is an insidious pollutant, perhaps most striking in its absence—for example, when snow blocks the roads. Many people hesitate to open windows because of the roar of traffic outside their homes, while others have trouble getting to sleep at night because of cars and motorcycles zooming past. Trucks with diesel engines are largely responsible for unacceptable noise levels, and emit eight times more smoke than the equivalent vehicle run on gas.

Danger

This is a problem inherent in the nature of cars: they are large, heavy objects which travel at high speeds in close proximity to pedestrians and cyclists. Only careful road and town planning, with restrictions on cars in residential and shopping areas and an overall reduction in traffic volume, can alleviate it.

Space

Cars and their infrastructure (roads and parking lots) take up approximately one-third of all land in an average city. Congestion on the roads makes crossing more difficult for pedestrians and parked cars frequently block sidewalks. Interstates cut swathes through large stretches of the country, obliterating everything in their path; many valuable and beautiful wildlife sites have been destroyed already.

Ill Health

You may think first of the effects of pollution as a cause of ill health, but more important is the simple fact that driving requires no physical effort. Some of us make up for this with regular exercise, but many people do not. Cutting down on car use—switching to bicycles or foot for short journeys—could substantially improve health.

Social Consequences

Architects at the Center for Environmental Structure in Berkeley, California, suggest that cars may "cause the breakdown of society, simply because of their geometry" (*A Pattern Language*). This is an important—and neglected—aspect of car use and requires some explanation.

A person in an automobile takes up approximately 100 times the amount of space required by a person on foot, and cars have the overall effect of spreading people out, and keeping them apart. Rather than meeting people as we go about our business, to and from stores and school and work, generally we see each other in well defined indoor places. Shopping in a supermarket miles from your home is a different social experience than walking to a nearby grocer, and increased dependence on the car is likely to prevent what these architects call "the collective cohesion people need to form a viable society."

An interesting aspect of this can be seen by observing the way people behave in cars. Behavior which is the social equivalent of slamming a door in your face is not uncommon on the road, although that driver would never consider doing such a thing if you were not separated by a mass of steel and glass.

In addition, neighborhood identity is seriously affected by heavy traffic. The more traffic there is in a particular area, the less likely are residents to know their neighbors and to think of it as home territory. According to a study by Donald Appleyard and Mark Lintell: "All aspects of perceived livability—absence of noise, stress, and pollution; levels of social interaction, territorial extent, and environmental awareness; and safety—were found to correlate inversely with traffic intensity" (*The Environmental Quality of City Streets: The Residents' Viewpoint*). The inner city regeneration we hear so much about needs to take this factor into account.

Another social factor is the way motor vehicles have taken over common land—the space between houses and workplaces which used to act as a meeting ground. Streets with motorized traffic are noisy and unsafe, and it is possible that this may be a reason for the emotional disorder called agoraphobia (literally, fear of the *agora,* or marketplace) which appears in modern cities. Sufferers are afraid to go outside for any reason. It may be that this disorder is reinforced by an environment in which people feel they have no right to be outside their own front doors (*A Pattern Language*).

The only way to solve these problems is to give higher priority to social criteria in traffic planning, and to cut down on the total amount of traffic while moving more of it out of residential neighborhoods and onto major roads.

The Natural World

The less contact we have with a place, the less we care about it. If you drive everywhere, you may rarely go anywhere on foot in your own neighborhood, let alone further afield; driving doesn't provide any real contact with blooming cherry trees or wildflowers or frolicking squirrels. When you read about urban decay or that the countryside is under threat, it won't mean much to you if you are always protected from these realities. The inside of your car turns into a little home away from home, with stereo, telephone, and other technological comforts.

Urban children may spend little time on foot or bicycle—and this is bound to affect their attitudes towards the world we live in.

Cities for People

Instead of clinging to the "independence" cars give us—worryingly reminiscent of the way some people insist that carrying firearms is essential to their freedom—we should be thinking about what we need access to. Most people need to do the shopping, to get to school and work, to see friends, and to go to the movies, theater, baseball games and so on, but we do not need limitless mobility.

If we could do the things we need and want to do, and at the same time cut car use, everyone would benefit.

All of us suffer the effects of traffic to some extent, but it is often people who do not own cars who suffer most from heavy traffic and badly planned traffic systems: children, the elderly and disabled, and mothers pushing strollers.

Individually, we need to rethink the way we use our cars, recognizing that that overemphasis on this particular form of transport is lowering the quality of life for everyone. Rather than plan for more cars, why not look at ways of making us less dependent on them? Local shops, post offices, hospitals, and schools increase a sense of neighborhood identity, lessen our need to travel long distances for basic facilities, and make life easier for people who do not drive.

When it comes to controlling the car, Friends of the Earth U.K. suggests four principles in their Kids Alive campaign:

❑ Reduce the amount of traffic. Residential streets can be made unattractively awkward for rat-racing motorists by adjusting traffic priorities at junctions, and installing road closures and ramps. These systems help to limit traffic to local residents, and careful planning (including plenty of trees and shrubs, which help muffle noise and improve the air) can make residential streets far more attractive.

❑ Reduce vehicle speed. Traffic bumps, width restrictions, and street "furniture" all slow cars down and make roads safer for everyone.

❑ Create special bicycling facilities. Bicyclists can be exempted from one-way restrictions and road closures, and provided with special bicycle paths and turning lanes. This extra convenience and safety will encourage more people to use bicycles.

❑ Increase pedestrian facilities. Wider and higher sidewalks increase pedestrians' security, and a sidewalk extended straight across the road at a junction forms a clear pedestrian crossing and a traffic hump for motorists. Special footpaths and pedestrian shopping areas are other examples.

If all this leaves you anxiously clutching your car keys, please stop for a minute and imagine your neighborhood without so many cars. Would you be more likely to stroll over to the park or to a friend's house—or stretch your legs with a bike ride? Do some digging in your front garden? Or just sit outside, enjoying the peace and quiet with the Sunday papers?

Bicycles

When I mentioned that I was thinking of getting a bicycle to two male friends, both regular bike riders, they were horrified. A passing bus would blow me over—*It was not safe.* There's no doubt that the main problem for a bike rider is the sheer mass of metal which threatens you every time you venture out, and in a collision the person on the bike is always the one at risk. Many drivers behave appallingly badly to bike riders, while others are simply oblivious of us; the few who are courteous probably have bikes themselves.

Nonetheless, cycling is a convenient, efficient, and enjoyable way to get around—much faster than walking or rush hour driving, and eminently suited to short journeys. While weather is sometimes a problem, safety is the most important deterrent for most people.

A transport strategy giving high priority to bicycles would change everything. How wonderful it would be to have separate bicycle paths, plenty of marked bicycle routes, and counter-flow lanes on one-way streets. In the long-term, measures like these are essential to getting lots of people onto bicycles, which the Worldwatch Institute calls "vehicles for a small planet."

There are some places where people *do* function without cars. Some examples are Mackinac Island, where visitors are charmed to find everyone gets around on their pins or on bikes or in buggies; Faneuil Hall area of Boston, where a large area is closed to traffic; Dickens-On-the-Strand festival in Galveston, where many city blocks are closed to cars and the area seems positively Victorian as a result; Pueblo Indian communities in Arizona and New Mexico; Living History Farms at Des Moines; and Amish communities. All these places have a special magic feeling because of the absence of cars.

The more people there are who cycle, the safer all bike riders are, because this gives us a higher profile in drivers' eyes: they get used to looking for us. As it is, if you want to start bicycling but feel nervous, stick to local journeys and streets you know are quiet until you develop the skills and confidence to cope with traffic. Going out with a friend can be a great help.

The fact that you bicycled all the time when you were a child doesn't mean you have the necessary skills to deal with today's traffic the first time you get on a bike again.

Many people wonder whether the exercise and transport benefits of bicycling are not outweighed by the stress of traveling in traffic and the damage that exhaust fumes do to your lungs, not to mention your face, which gets rosy but filthy. Cyclists are especially vulnerable to smoke particulates because they are breathing deeply, and some choose to wear masks. But the exercise makes you fit, and therefore less likely to suffer from other health complaints. Nonetheless, the only way to really get away from these problems is to get away from cars.

Children

Cycling is the ideal way for older children and teenagers to get around. Walking, by comparison, is very slow, while public transport can be inconvenient, especially for very short journeys. Safe bike routes are even more important for children than for adults.

This is well worth considering, because one study found that 24 percent of the car journeys made by families with children under the age of 15 were escort journeys—to and from school, sports activities, and music lessons or to friends' houses —and this applies nearly as much to able-bodied 13-year-olds as to small children.

If you are nervous about your child bicycling because of traffic, sit down and work out routes to frequent destinations. Ride them together once or twice to assess your youngster's skill and concentration.

If you use a bicycle for local shopping, get a childseat for small children (up to 40 pounds)—you can even buy a child-size helmet. Some parents use a tricycle or a trailer seat, which is very practical for shopping too.

Your Bicycle

Buy a secondhand bike if you can, through a store or the classified ads, or by word of mouth. A relative may have an old bike in the garage which you can resuscitate. You may want to move up to a fancier model when you get hooked and start planning trips over the Rockies, but any bicycle which is the right size and in decent condition will manage journeys around town.

If you decide to buy a new bicycle, go to several stores. They can be intimidating to the uninitiated, full of athletic young staff wandering around in cycling sweatshirts and those funny black shorts, and you may feel self-conscious about flabby legs or asking for a new tire for the battered Raleigh a friend has given you.

Explain that you want a bicycle and intend to use it for commuting/shopping/touring or whatever, have about so many dollars to spend, and ask for a recommendation. You're looking for friendly, intelligent assistance. Make some notes, and compare not only price but the quality of information you get. Do they talk about the cotterless cranks without explaining that this means the bits the pedals go on? What about a guarantee, accessories, and service?

Do not think that you have to get a smart touring or racing bike. An old-fashioned upright bike can be more practical around town. An alternative is the mountain bike. These sturdy conveyances look like adult versions of a child's first bike and are designed to cope with any terrain. City versions are slightly less rugged but their thick, heavy-tread tires can handle roadways strewn with fragments of broken glass and death-dealing potholes better than a touring bike's narrow wheels. They are also good for going up and down curbs.

Try to get some help and advice from an experienced rider, especially if you are spending a lot of money. And resolve that you will get to grips with the nuts and bolts of your bicycle, so that you in turn become an experienced and knowledgeable rider.

A lightweight bike is easier to carry up and down stairs, but quality matters a lot more than lightness. At low speeds, up to about 14 mph, weight matters more than air resistance, but the difference between a heavy and a light bike is only a small proportion of your combined weight. You're probably not worried about trimming 10 seconds off your home-to-work speed.

Make sure the bike fits you, and adjust the seat to the correct height. A rule of thumb is that with the saddle half extended on its pin, you should be able to touch the ground with both feet, without being on teetering tiptoe. This is important for back and knees, as well as for speed.

CYCLING CHECKLIST

❑   A copy of *Richard's New Bicycle Book*, by Richard Ballantine, is the best investment you can make before you start.
❑   Low-profile, high-pressure tires will help you get around with least effort. Check the pressure weekly.
❑   Get a repair kit and a spare inner tube. You may want to carry the kit and a small tire pump with you.
❑   Good lights and reflective gear are essential if you will be riding in the dark. A helmet can save your life.
❑   Decide what you are going to do about rain, in advance. The right gear makes it easy to cope with light showers. Remember that really bad weather not only makes roads slippery and visibility poor, but makes you far less visible to drivers. If in doubt, switch to public transportation.
❑   Good locks are essential—check at your friendly local bike shop. Finding a secure place to lock your bike can be a problem. Parking meters and stout metal railings are ideal. Use U-shaped solid locks—Kryptonite or Citadel, for example—if you want the bike to be there when you get back.
❑   Check tires for fragments of glass and tighten all nuts and bolts every week. *Richard's New Bicycle Book* will take you through most maintenance procedures. Try to tune in to

your bike so that when something isn't quite right, you hear it. A regular monthly tuneup—just 10 minutes on a Sunday afternoon—will make a big difference in reliability.

❏ If you feel unable to cope with even the simplest maintenance, you'll want to develop a good relationship with one of the folks at your bicycle store. A bicycle which isn't looked after can be dangerous as well as inconvenient, so be willing to spend a little money keeping it in good repair.

❏ If you commute to work, perspiration is almost certain to be a problem during warm weather. Bicycling in town also gets clothes dirty. If you can change when you get to work, get a neat riding ensemble together (sweatsuit or t-shirt and shorts and a pair of jogging shoes would be basic) and carry your work clothes. Getting in early makes this much easier. Think how fresh you'll look when everyone else turns up.

If you can't change upon arrival, wear as light a shirt as possible and open a few buttons while you are cycling. You may have to wipe down with damp paper towels in the restroom. A fresh shirt, rolled or folded inside your saddlebag or left in a desk drawer, is good insurance.

A few lucky people work for companies that provide changing and shower facilities.

❏ Cycling can be rough on shoes (even without toeclips), and a pair of pretty Italian high heels will not give you sufficient grip on the pedals for safety or speed. Running shoes work well—carry office shoes or stick them into a desk drawer at night.

❏ Buy reflective bands or clips for your trouser legs, or make do with rubber bands. Tucking the pants legs into your socks doesn't look very elegant, but it also does the trick. A bicycle chain can chew through expensive fabric in seconds —use a chain guard for commuting. Skirts are hard to manage on a bicycle and can be dangerous.

❏ Fit a plastic flap at the bottom of your front mudguard to keep feet dry and clean.

Finding Routes

Car drivers who turn to bicycles may find themselves on the same traffic-clogged routes they used to drive. Once you establish a normal route it can be quite difficult to try something new, although you think about it every time a truck cuts you off at the traffic light and cloaks you in its foul black exhaust.

Bicyclists can be far more flexible than drivers and alternative routes, using quieter residential roads, make traveling less stressful, safer, and faster.

To work out a new route, spread a large-scale map on the table and mark your home, workplace, or other destination. Go via parks and take advantage of any cycle lanes. It may be worth planning a route which takes you past a good food shop or market, so you can pick up something fresh for lunch or do some of your shopping on the way home. This is an undervalued benefit of traveling by bicycle. A new route will take longer for a few days, depending on your memory and map-reading skills, so allow extra time.

Walking

Most people in the world travel on foot because that is the only means of transport available to them. Many car owners never walk anywhere. Walking can be a great pleasure. You notice changes in the trees, watch the restoration being done on a dilapidated but beautiful old house, enjoy the tangy smell of newly turned earth or the luxurious scent of a bank of honeysuckle. The fresh air and light are good for your body, and walking gives one time to think, a precious commodity in our hectic lives.

Don't think of walking solely as a leisure activity. It should be part of daily life and part of your transport strategy. Are we really so short of time that we cannot walk? Traveling by car frequently means fighting through heavy traffic and trying to find somewhere to park, but because we are inside the car we may not count the time spent there.

Country dwellers have the advantage when it comes to pleasant places to walk, but even in urban and suburban areas it is possible to find interesting routes which keep you clear of the traffic and noise of the main roads. Wildlife groups have helped to turn abandoned railroad lines into attractive pedestrian and cycle paths.

In the city, a walker can explore back streets and parks. You may find that it is worth a longer walk to avoid main roads, or to go to a shop which sells homemade Greek specialities or where you enjoy a chat with the owner.

I used to love taking long walks in historic parts of London, but of late cars seem intrusive almost everywhere. This is a great loss. Piccadilly Circus was once an exciting spot, but the volume of traffic makes it very uncongenial these days.

Have you ever taken a stroll under a cavernous underpass, where there used to be a pleasant wood with riding trails? As you drive down a freeway—delighted by how quickly you can get to Aunt Margaret's—give a thought to the effect heavy motor transportation has on rural communities and landscape. We city dwellers can be extraordinarily insensitive to the consequences of our demands on nearby stretches of countryside, and let our convenience overshadow the destructive impact of more roads on the towns.

A small backpack is more practical than carrying a bag. Comfortable shoes are essential. Put your high heels in the pack and change when you get to your destination. Personal security is a thorny question, and one which women face continually. If in doubt, do not walk. Get a bus or cab or ask a friend for a ride.

Brisk walking is nearly as good for your heart as jogging and it's also good for losing weight. Many people now walk for fitness. Not just a five-minute stroll down to the store, but a vigorous 30 or 40 minutes—you might even be able to walk to work.

Public Transportation

Both city and country dwellers need a good public transportation network. Closure of rural bus routes and train lines has left people in many towns and country areas isolated, or increasingly dependent on cars. We should support public transport, with our votes and by using it whenever we can. Join public pressure groups as well as any local association which campaigns on traffic issues. Think about the personal benefits of not driving: time to read, doze, or meditate, with no worries about parking or about having a drink. An intriguing point for drivers to consider is that the best way to speed up car travel is to improve public transportation.

Using public transportation requires somewhat different planning than travel by car, and the following ideas may make you more likely to choose to take the bus or train.

PUBLIC TRANSPORTATION CHECKLIST

❑ Set aside a shoebox for bus and train schedules and maps, and go out of your way to assemble a complete collection. Put information numbers in a prominent place by the telephone, and write them on the top of your shoebox. There may also be a number you can dial to get up-to-the-minute information on cancellations and delays.

❑ Get whatever reduced price fares or cards you are entitled to.

❑ Get details of last buses and trains and night buses for your area. The number of a reliable cab company won't go amiss either.

❑ Allow yourself enough time to catch the right train without killing yourself with a last minute dash to the station. This is a hard habit to get into if you are used to stepping out of the door and into a car. A book is invaluable when waiting for a delayed train.

❑ A backpack and an easily collapsible stroller will make all the difference if you have to manage large parcels or a small child.

❑ Working on flexitime makes it possible to travel off-peak, avoiding packed buses and trains and sometimes saving money too.

Using a Car

Giving It Up

Grab a piece of paper and make a list of the reasons for choosing to drive on a local journey to the stores or to a friend's place, instead of using some other form of transport. There are all kinds of factors, from not wanting to put on a coat to avoiding crowds, the fact that it's raining or you're late, or you don't feel safe outside after dark.

If you didn't have a car, how much extra time would you have to spend walking to the bus stop or the station? Perhaps 20 minutes a day, enough to keep you in reasonable shape.

Maintaining a car is time-consuming and expensive. If you don't have a car, is this a conscious choice or are you simply waiting until you can afford the monthly payments? Taking cabs occasionally and renting a car now and then works out considerably cheaper than keeping your own vehicle, and may be a happy choice for you.

Another possibility is using a moped or motorbike. These use little fuel, do not add much to traffic congestion, and are easy to park.

Driving as if People Mattered

I was talking to a friend about traffic systems when her son piped in, "If it was the future and cars were alive, everyone would think they were much more important than people."

He was right, unfortunately. Those of us who drive should do some soul searching about just what matters: getting to the supermarket as quickly as possible or letting pedestrians cross the street without fear.

If you have a car and never go anywhere without it, the first step toward increasing your awareness of pedestrian problems is to spend an hour or two walking around your own neighborhood. There are always a few places where it is virtually impossible for pedestrians to cross, and other places where people hover in the middle of a busy road, waiting for a gap in the traffic.

Apart from supporting local and national pressure groups to improve traffic conditions for everyone, there are a number of things drivers can do immediately to make the roads safer and pleasanter.

DRIVER'S CHECKLIST

❑ Do not drink and drive. How many times does this need to be said? (Be careful about drinking and bicycling too, especially if you have to ride home through heavy traffic, where you need fast reflexes and all your faculties.)

❑ Slow down. Speed kills. At 15 mph there is only a 3 percent chance of death for a pedestrian hit by a car, while at 40 mph the risk rises to 90 percent.

❑ Don't let common courtesies disappear when you get behind the wheel. Let people cross the street, slow down when there are children around, and do not rev your engine to hurry pedestrians at a crossing. Stop when the lights turn yellow instead of streaking through, especially when there is someone waiting to cross. A calmer driving style will be good for your blood pressure—and bank balance!

❑ Learn to drive well. This means not only handling the vehicle well, but also paying attention to what's going on, and staying alert. Passing the driving test does not make you a good driver. Be responsive to other drivers' signals and to the needs of pedestrians and bicyclists.

❑ Don't get angry at pedestrians or cyclists just for being there. Watch out when you open your car door or back up, instead of assuming that anyone not in a car will always look out for you.

❑ Don't be bullied by other drivers into driving too fast or dangerously.

❑ Slow down to 20 mph in residential districts, including your own.

DRIVING CHECKLIST

❑ Think before you drive—don't drive if you can avoid it. A bike is a great way to get around. Think of walking down to the store as a pleasant outing. A walk or a bicycle ride is a good way to get some exercise, fresh air, and your daily dose of sunlight.

❑ Shop, work, and play locally whenever possible.

❑ Plan ahead. Make one trip instead of three, and swing by the recycling center on your way to the shops.

❑ Don't drive alone. Try carpooling to work if you cannot use public transport, share driving the children to school, and why not do your weekly shopping with a friend?

❑ Slow down to save gas. Consumption is highest in start-and-stop town traffic and at over 55 mph on the highway.

❑ Driving technique affects mileage per gallon. Avoid slamming on the brakes, use gears to slow down, and don't rev the engine. Aggressive driving uses 20 percent more gas.

❑ Keep your car in good repair and regularly tuned. Keep fuel filters clean. Rust prevention is vital to keeping cars alive as long as possible.

❑ Other ideas include fitting an electronic ignition and using steelbelted radial tires, properly inflated, balanced, and rotated. Tires should be recycled.

❑ Remove roof racks when not in use; wind resistance means increased gas consumption. Lighter loads make for better mileage, so empty out the trunk.

❑ Support public transportation. The greater the demand, the better the service which can be provided.

❑ Recycle your used motor oil. You can buy a recycling kit at some automotive stores.

When You Buy a Car

We had a 1966 Volkswagen van for several years, and sometimes felt smug when friends talked about their new cars. There are advantages and disadvantages to maintaining a vehicle that old. We undoubtedly saved the van from the junkyard, and therefore did not contribute to the extraordinary waste of resources involved in replacing cars. On the other hand, older vehicles weren't designed to be fuel efficient, and we had to use leaded gas every fifth tank to keep the engine from an early grave.

The lifespan of any car can be greatly extended by good maintenance and, most of all, by rust prevention. Almost 21 million cars were sold in the United States in 1988, while some 8 million were discarded. Since the manufacture of a car requires enormous inputs of energy and raw materials, keeping cars alive is ecologically sound. Buying a new one every time you have the old one paid for is not.

When you do buy, think about these points:

❑ Look at secondhand cars, and get impartial advice if you feel you cannot judge yourself. Take a really knowledgeable friend with you, or pay a mechanic $20 to look a vehicle over for obvious problems. Most dealers will allow you to take a used care to a mechanic.

❑ Get a car you like and will be happy to drive for many years. Buy the right size, not only for your family but for your frame. *The Green Consumer* has a lengthy section about choosing a new car (see Sources, Chapter 5).

❑ Improving the efficiency of our cars is crucial. *Gas Mileage Guide,* a free Department of Energy/EPA booklet, is available from the Consumer Information Center, Pueblo, CO 81009.

❑ Do not choose a diesel engine—these are often sold as ecologically sound, but the fact is they produce far more particulate pollution than standard engines. Technical improvements are needed before they become a good buy; stricter regulation of diesel buses and trucks is essential, too.

❑ Optional extras like air-conditioning, power steering, and automatic transmissions soak up a lot of energy, and increase pollution. Anything that adds to a car's weight will increase fuel consumption. See what you can do without.

Vacations

How many people come back from a vacation feeling more exhausted than when they left home, with only a pile of photos, credit card bills, and a few amusing stories for the office to serve as reminders of that year's trip?

The importance people attach to vacation plans might be seen as a sign that many of us are not too happy with life at home. Next time you sit down with a pile of glossy holiday brochures it's worth taking stock of what you really want to get out of this year's weeks away, especially when you consider just how much those weeks cost. Perhaps you simply want to enjoy some sunshine and get away from the commitments of home life. Nothing wrong with that. You may want to travel in a new part of the world and see famous sites for yourself.

Tourism can be seen as a sort of pollution, something which destroys the thing it loves. You've probably heard someone talking about Cancun or Acapulco "before it was spoiled." Hotel complexes line the seafront in popular mass market resorts, catering standards degenerate to ubiquitous hamburgers, and the real life of the region disappears. Added to this is the extremely serious effect tourism has on the ecology of many wild areas.

Tourism in the Third World has heavy social and cultural prices, borne by local people. Unfortunately, the notion that we can bring jobs and prosperity to poor regions by traveling there is not confirmed by recent studies, which have found that at least 80 percent of the money spent on vacations in the Third World comes back to home countries, in the form of foreign staff salaries, foreign-owned hotel profits, travel agency commissions, payment for imported food and other items, insurance, and interest on loans. Most of the remaining 20 percent goes to a few wealthy locals and government officials.

Dervla Murphy, who has traveled in a number of Third World countries by bicycle and on foot, writes: "The distortion of human relationships, rather than the building of hotels or the sprouting of souvenir stalls, is the single most damaging consequence of Third World tourism. And let no one believe that those children's families would be better off if Antsirabe were 'developed.' They would not. But a lot of already rich Malagasy would be even richer" (*Muddling Through in Madagascar*).

The tourist industry generates only unskilled jobs—responsible positions tend to go to foreign employees—while causing a disruption of local life. Customs and religious rituals are transformed into spectacles, and traditional crafts become souvenirs.

One of the main reasons we go on holiday is to have a break from routine, to recharge our batteries. A camping trip or walking holiday may sound strenuous and tiring, but can do more to energize you than two weeks at a crowded resort. Edith Schaeffer says, "Man does not have the same healthy refreshment for his nervous or his physical system if he never gets his feet on the earth, and his eyes, nostrils, and taste buds free from the sights, sounds, flavors and smells of machine, concrete, exhaust and other non-natural things" (*The Hidden Art of Homemaking*). She emphasizes the refreshment one gets from walking, bicycling, skiing, and swimming away from man-made things.

Doris Longacre comments that we need wilderness as a check-point, so we can see where development is taking us, and, essentially, "to give us the humbling experience of leaving something alone" (*Living More With Less*).

VACATION PLANNING CHECKLIST

Here are some things to think about while you plan next summer's trip:

❑ How will you travel? Walking and cycling are good for you and put you in contact with the places you visit. When Dervla Murphy bicycled around Belfast, researching her book *A Place Apart,* she often arranged a tire puncture when she wanted an excuse to stop and have a chat with the locals.

❑ You may be able to travel by train instead of car. In Europe, cars can go on the train—getting you somewhere quickly and pleasantly. In many places a bicycle, whether hired or brought from home, will do as well.

❑ Where will you go? Instead of "doing" sights, or towns, or countries, choose a spot which holds some genuine interest for you or your family and stay there. Read up about it in advance. This will not only make your visit more rewarding but will help you to fit in while you are there.

❑ Try to avoid package tours, which have been described as mobile ghettos because they give the tourist no contact with anyone who is not servicing tourists.

❑ Instead of looking for a home-away-from-home, think of vacations as a chance to experience something different from your regular way of life. Interesting options may include bicycling vacations, Outward Bound, and working weekends on organic farms.

❑ If you are concerned about the impact of tourists on other countries, you may want to contact one of the groups listed below. Respect for other people's feelings and customs is the most important thing you can take with you, whether you stay in the United States or leave the country.

The Future

Technological advances are making cars more efficient users of gas, but this fuel efficiency will eventually reach some practical limit. We need to develop public transportation networks, and to give more thought to the way our towns and neighborhoods are designed. Building strong, self-sustaining local economies is an important part of improving the quality of life in America. Local food production and energy generation will help to reduce the greenhouse effect. Frieght should be moved by water and rail. If these ideas interest you, contact the Institute for Local Self-Reliance, which works with urban and rural communities to develop "closed-loop systems [where] goods and services would be produced locally, from local resources, for local consumption."

Social pressure is a potent force. Using a car for short journeys or for traveling to work should eventually become as unacceptable as smoking in public.

Sources

Books

The Environmental Quality of City Streets: The Residents' Viewpoint, Donald Appleyard and Mark Lintell (Berkeley, CA, University of California, 1971).

The Hidden Art of Homemaking, Edith Schaeffer (Wheaton, IL, Tyndale House Publishers, 1985).

Living More with Less, Doris Longacre (Scottdale, PA, Herald Press, 1980).

Muddling Through in Madagascar, Dervla Murphy, (New York, The Overlook Press, 1989).

A Place Apart, Dervla Murphy (Greenwich, CT, Adair Publishers, 1980).

A Pattern Language, Christopher Alexander et al. (New York, Oxford University Press, 1977).

Rethinking the Role of the Automobile, Michael Renner (Washington, DC, Worldwatch Institute, 1988).

ington, DC, Worldwatch Institute, 1988).

Richard's New Bicycle Book, Richard Ballantine (New York, Ballantine, 1987). This is a terrific book, whether you are a novice or an expert.

Organizations

Centre for Responsible Tourism, 2 Kensington Road, San Anselmo, CA 94960-2905. (415) 258-6594.

Global Exchange, 2940 16th Street, #307, San Francisco, CA 94103. (415) 255-7296.

Institute for Local Self-Reliance, 2425 18th Street NW, Washington, DC 20009. (202) 232-4108.

7
AIR

"This most excellent canopy, the air, look you, this
brave o'erhanging firmament, this majestical roof
fretted with golden fire, why, it appears no other thing
to me but a foul and pestilent congregation of vapours."
—Shakespeare, *Hamlet*

Introduction

The sharp, cold scent of a new Christmas tree. The sweat-
and-chlorine smell of a locker room. Our sense of smell plays a
vital role in our consciousness and memory—smells can bring
places, events, and people we've known clearly to mind. An
evocative smell—gingerbread baking—can make you feel that
you are back in your grandmother's kitchen, hungry and happy.

But smell is a neglected sense. We get little information
about a modern city environment through our noses. We tune

out noxious odors because we have little control over them. Indoors, we smother ourselves in artificial fragrances.

What a loss. Our sense of smell is controlled by the primitive part of the brain, closely connected with the parts of the brain which control emotion, mood, and personality, and it plays a key role in sexual attraction. A baby's nose is its first source of information about the world, but few adults have finely attuned olfactory senses—although there are people who can sniff out truffles as pigs traditionally do, and wine specialists develop an acute sense of smell.

Smells signal danger—a gas leak, for example, or rotting food—and give us knowledge about the world, as well as being a source of considerable pleasure. Part of the reason many of us have a dull nose may be sensory overload, which starts from a very early age. Scented baby lotions, powders, and even disposable diapers will interfere with our olfactory awareness.

I suspect that one reason we use our noses so ineffectually is that modern life bombards us with unpleasant odors and we tune out in self-defense. For example, I used to use nail polish remover frequently. Now that I use few chemical products, I find the smell of acetone so unpleasant that I cannot bear to have it in the house. The same is true of the harsh synthetic fragrances in many cosmetics and shampoos, though they are supposed to smell good.

Move to an open window or go outside. Close your eyes and take several long, deep breaths. Fill your lungs all the way down to your stomach. Can you remember times when breathing has been a conscious pleasure? Shallow, inadequate breathing is characteristic of sedentary people, and perhaps our heedless pollution of the air around us has something to do with the fact that we don't use it with appreciation, and pleasure. One of the many benefits of getting fit is a sharper awareness of the environment.

Air Pollution

What most of us think of as air pollution—that acrid, brown haze which lies over every large city—is the result of burning fossil fuels, from automobile exhaust and industrial emissions. Clean air controls in the industrialized West have cut many of these emissions over the past 30 or 40 years, but air pollution remains a serious problem throughout the world, causing the crumbling of historic buildings, damage to trees and wildlife, illness, and death.

Air pollution affects human health in a number of ways. It damages the delicate linings of the nose, throat, and lungs, causing a variety of respiratory complaints. While in the lungs it can enter the bloodstream and reach other parts of the body. More subtly, air pollution suppresses the immune system by reducing lymphocyte and antibody production, making us more susceptible to illness. Some of the chemicals in typical urban smog have been found to alter DNA in individual cells, which can cause cancer and birth defects.

The Ozone Layer

We've heard a great deal about the CFCs used as propellants in aerosol cans, and manufacturers have responded to considerable public pressure by agreeing to start switching to alternative gases. This is a great success, but it is disappointing to think that environmentalists have been warning about the danger to the ozone layer since the mid-1970s!

The Montreal Protocol, agreed upon in September 1987 by 35 countries, states that CFC production must be cut by 35 percent of the 1986 level by 1999, and manufacturers are scrabbling to find suitable and safe substitutes. This is a step, but Friends of the Earth has concluded that an immediate 85 percent reduction in CFCs is necessary to stabilize the ozone damage at its current level, and a complete ban on CFCs should be in effect as soon as possible.

This switch poses a formidable problem for the foam industry, and they are looking for viable and safe alternatives to CFCs. Manufacturers of air-conditioning equipment are looking for ways to conserve or recycle the CFCs they contain. This has not been done before because it was uneconomic, but is likely to be highly economic in the future.

You can help by not buying CFC-propelled aerosols, foam packaging, or new refrigerators and freezers. If possible, do not allow an old fridge to be junked—sell or donate it.

Aerosols, whether CFC-based or not, are a source of indoor air pollution. Because they disperse their contents as an extremely fine mist, products which contain toxic ingredients, such as hairspray and insecticide, can be inhaled and easily enter the bloodstream. The American Lung Association advises against their use. You can always find a nonaerosol equivalent: pump action, liquid, or cream products work very well. Certain propellant gases are themselves lung irritants and depress the central nervous system.

Toxic Clouds

Michael Brown is the reporter who helped bring the Love Canal toxic dump story to the attention of the world. In a recent book, *The Toxic Cloud*, he argues that the dangers of airborn chemicals present a far greater threat than has been realized.

In 1982 the Environmental Protection Agency found high levels of toxaphene (a highly carcinogenic insecticide), PCBs, dioxins, and DDT byproducts (more nasties) in an isolated part of Lake Superior in the northern United States. Toxaphene was never used in significant quantities by farmers in that part of the country, and researchers concluded that the poisons must have traveled by air from the cotton fields of the southern United States, 1000 miles away.

Brown claims that this toxic fallout, made up of solid particles, invisible gases, and aerosol mists, may be responsible for thousands of cancers and genetic mutations. Aside from the known hazards related to individual chemicals, there is the unpredictable danger of what those chemicals could do in combination, or of what the cumulative effect will be as they build up in the atmosphere. Our experience so far with CFCs doesn't give a good prognosis.

You may think that severe air pollution is confined to large urban areas, but the fact is that some people have to move into the city in order to get away from agricultural chemicals. Modern agriculture is a source of the most dangerous chemicals in use, because they are specifically designed to kill living organisms. Many do not break down in the environment. Country folk, from farm workers to weekending stockbrokers, face problems with nitrate fertilizers and agricultural chemicals in drinking water, and dangerous and debilitating contamination from aerial crop spraying.

CLEAN AIR CHECKLIST

❏ Buy organically grown food (Chapter 2).
❏ Conserve energy (Chapter 5).
❏ Drive less and choose unleaded gas (Chapter 6).
❏ Do not buy CFC aerosols (and, preferably, no aerosols at all).
❏ Use non-toxic domestic products (Chapter 10).
❏ Plant trees (Chapter 13).
❏ Write to your Congressional representative about particular concerns.
❏ Support anti-pesticide campaigns.

PERSONAL CHECKLIST

❏ Spend as much time as possible outdoors, preferably in clean air spots (these become increasingly difficult to find, but include mountains, beaches, and some parts of the countryside).
❏ Increase ventilation at home.
❏ Avoid synthetic materials.
❏ Stay away from smokers.
❏ Carry or wear a silk scarf which you can use to cover your mouth and nose when necessary. Bicyclists may want to try this.

Indoor Air Pollution

People are exposed to more potentially harmful pollutants indoors—at home, in the office, and in the car—than outdoors. . . . Researchers found average indoor levels for 11 chemicals were 2–5 times higher than the average outdoor concentrations. . . . The greatest effect on toxic chemical concentration did not come from living close to a chemical plant but rather the building materials, consumer products, and personal activities of the people living inside the house. . . . The worst household dangers identified so far include smoking, living with a smoker, using air fresheners, moth balls, aerosol sprays and storing paints and solvents.

—From a 5-year study by the
Environmental Protection Agency,
Los Angeles Times, November 9, 1986

Our increasingly energy-efficient houses are leading to more air pollution because concentrations of gases from building materials and domestic products are allowed to build up to dangerous levels. We also spend an increasing amount of time indoors, some 90 to 95 percent, on average.

U.S. Army doctors at the Walter Reed Army Institute found that colds and flu are less likely in drafty buildings. They attributed this to a build-up of viruses in well sealed buildings, but it may be that fresh air is needed to keep our immune systems functioning effectively. Many people find themselves suffering from regular colds as soon as the central heating is turned on and the windows are closed in the autumn. The dry, stuffy atmosphere of centrally heated buildings affects our respiratory systems and makes us more vulnerable to whatever viruses are around.

Sick Office Syndrome

Minor health problems are common in modern office buildings, affecting up to 70 percent of staff. This will come as no surprise if you work in one of these buildings. A friend told me that in her office, "someone is always sick and we all get headaches—a couple of people are being treated for migraines."

Symptoms range from headaches, especially above the eyes and at the base of the neck, to fatigue and depression. These sometimes disappear when the employees leave the building, but may affect the way they feel all the time.

Of course some people's jobs leave them feeling depressed anyway, but studies have been done between people doing similar work with the only difference being the type of building they work in. The reasons for sick office syndrome vary, but the primary problem seems to be lack of natural ventilation. Buildings with air-conditioning and centralized heating allow a build up of various toxic gases in the air. Arbitrary temperature control is also hard on people, and in many offices it is impossible to open a window or turn the heat down.

Old photocopying machines give off ozone and many building products give off formaldehyde, a potent allergen. Air-conditioning systems are excellent breeding grounds for bacteria and viruses, which are then dispersed into the air. Biocides used to kill algae in the equipment can be dangerous too. More subtly, the electromagnetic fields from large amounts of electronic equipment can affect human perception, and artificial lighting has a deleterious effect on many people.

Modern offices simply intensify problems which all of us face in our homes, shops, and schools. Recently built colleges are often similar in design to modern office blocks, and I wonder whether this is affecting student performance.

Cleaning Products

Debra Lynn Dadd (*The Nontoxic Home*) has described these as "among the most toxic substances encountered in one's everyday environment, causing health problems ranging from rashes to death." Homemakers are most at risk! While packages often give lengthy warnings about avoiding ingestion and contact with the skin, they do not always mention the hazards of breathing the volatile fumes given off by many products. If chlorine bleach and ammonia, both extremely common household cleaners, are mixed, they produce a gas which can cause death within minutes.

You can make your own inexpensive cleaning products, or buy a number of commercial products which are safe for you, for children and pets, and for the environment (see Chapter 10).

Decorating, Hobby, and Office Products

Many of these contain hydrocarbon solvents, which are so toxic that they can cause death by inhalation. Take great care when using them, use as little as possible, and choose alternative products when you can.

Your nose is a good guide. As adhesives dry, they emit various chemicals in gas form. Sealants which stay soft will continue to do this for years. Even paint can cause problems for sensitive people—stay away from new paint or varnish until the smell has disappeared, or at least keep windows open. In any case, circulating air speeds drying more effectively than heat.

In general, the best choice is materials which are hard or which dry hard (brittle rather than soft plastic, for example), and which have no perceptible smell.

Pesticides

Avoiding chemical insecticides is crucial inside your home. Indoor plants can be raised organically (see Chapter 13). Organic pest control methods are quite safe, but if you are spraying for aphids with diluted onion juice, it is advisable to move the plants outdoors for treatment!

Don't use fly sprays, which contain dichloros, tetramethrin or d-allethrin. Certain plants repel flies—hang bunches of bay leaves, mint, pennyroyal, or eucalyptus by your doors. Old-fashioned sticky flypaper is safe and effective, if gruesome. Make your own by soaking strips of heavy brown paper in a thick sugar syrup. Let them dry until just sticky to the touch, then hang them in out of the way places. You can put the following mixture into little cloth bags and hang them on or above doors: equal parts of dried and crushed bay leaves, pennyroyal, ground cloves and eucalyptus leaves, very slightly dampened with eucalyptus oil. Citrus oil is another repellant. And fly swatters are effective.

Mothballs simply add to indoor air pollution. Avoid using them by taking these precautions: wash clothes before storage and air regularly. Tumbling in a dryer will kill moth eggs. Put small bags of lavender, rosemary, peppercorns, or cedar chips into drawers with woollens.

Air "Fresheners"

Some commercial preparations disguise bad smells with another strong scent, while others work by coating nasal passages with a fine oil film, or by releasing a chemical which deadens your olfactory nerves. They are potentially dangerous and certainly unnecessary.

Beware of products like the "potpourri" air freshener I saw the other day. The plastic case of potpourri decorating the front covered a disc containing paradichlorobenzene, which mothballs are made of. When you want to add a pleasant scent to the air, or to disguise the smell of burned toast or a new puppy, use one of the natural air fresheners suggested in Chapter 10.

Heating and Humidity

Electrical appliances give out no fumes, but they are less effective as a source of domestic energy than gas appliances and there is considerable scientific concern about the effects of living with high levels of electromagnetic radiation.

In a draftproofed house it is especially important to see that gas and wood fires are properly vented. Gas ranges should burn with a blue flame—if yours has orange flames ask the gas company to come and adjust it—and the kitchen needs a vent or fan to remove combustion by-products.

The American Lung Association advises against the use of any unvented gas or kerosene heater, and they are illegal in some states. If you use this form of heat, consider alternatives, and in the meantime ensure that there is plenty of ventilation.

Central heating creates a dry atmosphere—some people have trouble with sore throats when the central heating is switched on, and the low humidity is hard on plants and furniture.

One solution to this problem is a humidifier, but acquiring an energy-hungry appliance to counteract the effects of an unsatisfactory method of heating seems silly. Humidifiers can also have the bacterial growth found in air-conditioning systems. Combination heating is probably the best solution: using radiant heat sources whenever possible and saving the central heating for very cold weather. A well-insulated house doesn't need a great deal of heating in milder weather.

Humidity can be increased by keeping bowls of water around—the speed at which they evaporate will give you a clue as to just how dry your home gets; and by having plenty of plants inside. Plants suffer at least as much as we do from central heating, but can be arranged in such a way as to add moisture to the air—see Plants, below.

Artificial Materials

Many plastics emit gas in tiny quantities throughout their use. You won't be conscious of this except with something like a brand new shower curtain, which you can smell outgassing, but it still adds to the total level of air pollutants.

Synthetic fabrics continually give off fine fibers into the air. This has been associated with the rise in juvenile asthma and allergies; perhaps you know someone whose child cannot sleep on synthetic materials.

Needless to say, you are not going to throw away everything you have that is not made of natural materials. But when you next replace your carpets or buy new sheets, seriously consider choosing natural materials.

Improving the Air

My grandfather smoked cigars continually, and when he died after 40 years in the same house, my mother wondered how anyone else could possibly live in it, with the odor of his cigars so deeply ingrained in every room. If you've bought a house from a smoker you will know how the smell lingers, and how much work it is to remove the yellow stains on the walls and ceiling. The smell of dogs or cats can be pervasive and intractable too.

Some people live near factories which provide continuous background odor—a sensory pollutant—and the emissions from chemical plants and busy roads are actually dangerous. Most of us do not have such substantial problems to contend with, but we still want to improve the air we breathe at home.

FRESH AIR AND VENTILATION CHECKLIST

In the summer you can throw the windows open, but during the colder months the following ideas are especially important.

❏ Declare your home a no-smoking zone. If you don't feel you can go quite that far, establish that smokers can only use a particular room, and see that it is one which can be aired easily. Some people simply ask that smokers step outside with their cigarettes.

❏ Research into sick office syndrome has found that still air feels stuffy—we need air movement, though we want to avoid direct drafts.

❏ Still air, like still water, encourages bacterial growth. Open strategic windows for a daily airing. Various essential oils, including lavender and tea tree, are said to have antibacterial properties.

❏ Don't overheat your home. Steady background heat together with specific sources of radiant heat may be the best solution to the problem of stuffiness.

❑ Use bowls of water to humidify the air. If you do this, and keep the temperature moderate, a humidifier will be unnecessary.

Ionizers

Air-conditioning and heating systems, cigarette smoke, electronic equipment of all kinds, and synthetic carpeting change the balance of ions in the air. Air near running water is refreshing and invigorating in part because of its negative ion charge; a positive charge is associated with increased susceptibility to illness, including hayfever and migraine headaches.

Using fewer electrical appliances and more natural materials in your home, along with good ventilation, may solve part of the problem, but an ionizer, which creates a negative charge in the air, makes a perceptible improvement in the indoor environment for many people.

In offices, they have been found to increase alertness and productivity. People who spend a great deal of time in front of a video display terminal (stock brokers and journalists as well as secretaries and data-entry clerks) are exposed to some 50 times the positive ion charge of someone who does not use a VDT. The screen repels positively charged particles onto the face and into the lungs of the user—a likely reason for the increase in bronchial and skin disorders and conjunctivitis amongst VDT operators.

If you use an ionizer, point it at you, as the effect is directional. Turn it off during the day if you use it at night, or vice versa—the change in ion concentration is important for the metabolism. Ionizers are relatively inexpensive and use very little power.

Plants

Plants and vases of flowers give off water and oxygen, so both will improve the air—and fragrant flowers or foliage will add their scent too. The common spider plant (*Chlorophytum*) and golden pothos (*Scindapsus aureus*) are said to reduce indoor toxins, but all plants will improve the quality of the air you breathe.

Plants stay healthier if they are grouped together. This

increases the humidity of the air around them. An easy way to see that their atmosphere stays moist as well as increasing the general level of humidity is to stand them on trays of gravel which you keep topped up with water. The plant pots should not be in the water—many plants will die if their roots are waterlogged —but just clear of it.

Scientists are trying to develop special air filtering systems, and suggest that you may one day keep a banana tree on your desk, in a soil bed reactor which can filter smoke and other pollutants from the air.

Natural Air Fresheners

The best freshener, of course, is fresh air. Frequent and thorough airing of the house was always a part of the household routine.

But throughout history people have used the scents of herbs and flowers to enhance the atmosphere in a room, as well as to disguise unpleasant odors. Potpourri means "rotten pot": potpourris were originally moist, fermented mixtures of flowers and herbs. The potpourri many of us are familiar with today is a dry blend based on rose petals and lavender. This looks pretty but usually does not have a strong aroma. An occasional stirring releases the fragrance, and adding extra essential oils from time to time will increase its effectiveness. Blends vary, and you can make your own with garden flowers or purchased ingredients.

More potent mixtures are fermented with salt, and need to be kept in covered potpourri jars—they smell delightful but are not as attractive to look at.

Essential oils can be used in small pottery burners as natural alternatives to chemical air fresheners. Some scents— ginger and patchouli for example—are said to have aphrodisiacal properties, so you might keep those in the bedroom.

A fast trick, which smells delightful and is useful if you've just burned something in the kitchen, is to boil a few pieces of orange or lemon rind in a small saucepan of water. Cinnamon and cloves work equally well.

Encourage Your Nose

After you have gotten rid of unpleasant or noxious smells, encourage your olfactory sense with good things. Baking bread will make everyone think your home is the nicest place in the world. Freshly ground coffee is nearly as good. Perhaps as our food has lost its taste, our noses have lost some of their acuity. As you eliminate harsh chemical and artificially scented products from your life, you may find that your nose becomes much more sensitive.

Modern hybrid flowers rarely have the rich smells of their predecessors. In fact, it is quite possible to raise a garden full of flowers which have no smell at all, because they have been bred for show, not scent.

Grow a scented garden, concentrating on old-fashioned roses, night-scented stock, and plants with aromatic leaves. Put scented plants in raised beds or near seats in your garden. Some municipal parks have put in gardens for the handicapped, with beds raised to wheelchair level and filled with interesting leaves and fragrant flowers for the blind. There is no reason why the rest of us cannot benefit from this use of our senses, too.

Herbs have aromatic leaves. Plant them where you will brush against them or where you can run your hand over them. In John Aubrey's *Brief Lives*, he mentions how "Sir John [Danvers], being my Relation and faithfull Friend, was wont in fair mornings in the Summer to brush his Beaver-hatt on the Hysop and Thyme, which did perfume it with its natural Spirit; and would last a morning or longer."

Sources

Books

Nontoxic and Natural: How to Avoid Dangerous Everyday Products & Buy or Make Safe Ones, Debra Lynn Dadd (Los Angeles, Jeremy P. Tarcher, 1984). Distributed by St. Martin's Press, New York.

The Nontoxic Home: Protecting Yourself & Your Family from Everyday Toxics & Health Hazards, Debra Lynn Dadd (Los

Angeles, Jeremy P. Tarcher, 1986). Distributed by St. Martin's Press, New York.

The Toxic Cloud, Michael Brown (New York, Harper & Row, 1987).

Booklet

Protecting the Ozone Layer: What You Can Do, a $2 booklet available from the Environmental Defense Fund, 257 Park Avenue South, New York, NY 10010. (212) 505-2100.

Organizations

American Lung Association, 1740 Broadway, New York, NY 10019. (212) 315-8700. An association of health care professionals and laymen interested in the prevention and control of lung diseases.

Friends of the Earth, 218 D St. SE, Washington, DC 20003. (202) 544-2600. Publishes a newsletter about the ozone layer called *Atmosphere*.

8
WATER

We came from the water; our bodies are largely water; and water plays a fundamental role in our psychology. We need constant access to water, all around us; and we cannot have it without reverence for water in all its forms.

—Christopher Alexander et al.,
A Pattern Language

Introduction

A tragedy of modern life is that not only are most of us cut off from the sources of our water, but we pollute them individually and corporately in such a way that clean, fresh water is almost entirely a thing of the past.

Our earth is the water planet, with some 75 percent of its surface covered by water. Human beings are largely made of water too, as any schoolchild should be able to explain. A drink of water can be an exquisite pleasure—after a hard game of football or a long run or a walk in the mountains when you finally find a small stream and kneel to drink from cupped hands.

Rivers, lakes, and oceans have been dumping grounds for millennia. But when the world's population was smaller and the types of waste less toxic, the water—full of animals, plants, and bacteria—was able to render it harmless. Much modern waste, however, is not only nonbiodegradable but highly toxic, and the ocean's natural cycles cannot clean it up.

Industrial chemicals, toxic materials of all sorts, oil, and even nuclear waste is ignominiously dumped into our streams and rivers, and into the sea. Rosalie Bertell (*In No Immediate Danger*) describes the U.S. dumping of radioactive nuclear wastes off the American coasts, which went on for some 25 years after the end of World War II. When canisters failed to sink, sailors shot holes in them! Some were dropped into the San Francisco Bay because seas were rough. A study estimated that 36 percent of the nuclear waste drums were damaged.

Accidental spills of sulfuric acid and other chemicals wreak havoc on water life. Oil spills at sea are common, and it is thought that some five tons of highly toxic polychlorinated biphenyls, PCBs, were released into the North Sea when the Piper Alpha oil platform exploded in 1988.

Few people see any connection between what they pour down the drain or flush down the toilet and reports of animal deaths on the news—let alone the water they drink the next week. Yet we all contribute to the pollution of the earth's water—and our own water supplies.

Water Pollution

In many areas, people can tell that there is something wrong with their water by the fact that it smells and tastes so bad. But most of the 700 or so known chemical contaminants in public drinking water are not detectable to the nose or eye or taste. Just because your water looks all right doesn't mean that it is good for you. The following is a summary of the major problems facing our water supplies.

Fertilizers

Nitrate fertilizers are probably the most serious threat: 11 million tons are used in the United States every year. Of this, approximately half is taken up by the crops (there are increasingly high levels of nitrates in agricultural produce), and the remainder is washed out of the soil, into our water.

In rivers and lakes, nitrates contribute to excessive algae growth, which tends to choke other plant and animal life. The nitrates slowly seep into deep boreholes and formerly pure groundwater, and there is concern that our water supplies contain higher nitrate levels than ever before.

The nitrates in the water we are drinking now were probably applied to the land 20 to 40 years ago. Since nitrate use has been much heavier since the 1960s, we can expect the problem of nitrate contamination to worsen, even if we drastically cut nitrate fertilizer use now.

In the body, nitrates are reduced to nitrites (also used as preservatives in meat products) and nitrosamines, both of which have been strongly implicated in stomach and esophageal cancer. They are also thought to cause the potentially fatal blue baby syndrome. Another worry is that water which contains a high level of nitrates is almost certain to contain agricultural pesticides as well.

Pesticides

If you consider the vast amounts of toxic chemicals which are used each year to kill insects and weeds, it is not surprising that a substantial amount should reach us via our water supplies. A switch to organic farming methods will cut pesticide use, and in the meantime we can have little choice but to drink whatever happens to be in our domestic water supply. Some filtration systems, however, will remove a high percentage of pesticides from drinking water.

Slurry

Perhaps you had a grandfather who used to race out into the street if a horse had left a sign of its passing. He was right, of course, and even gardeners who use considerable amounts of chemicals realize the benefits of old-fashioned manure. Getting hold of it is the city gardener's biggest headache.

Modern farming is usually done on a single crop basis: pigs or wheat or potatoes. This does not lend itself to farming practices that take advantage of ecological basics—on a traditional mixed farm animals grazed on rough grass and ate plant stalks, while providing fertilizer for the next crop.

Intensively reared, factory-farmed animals—pigs and cattle, as well as chickens—produce manure, but it is frequently treated as a disposal problem instead of as a rich source of fertilizer, and the waste slurry can contaminate water supplies. Moreover, routinely administered antibiotics enter the soil and water in this way.

Detergents

Detergents are made from petrochemicals, and have a number of serious effects on the environment. As you'll see in Chapter 10, The Nontoxic Home, eliminating them from your home—or at least making a big reduction in the amounts you use—is one of the basic steps of home ecology.

"Eutrophication" is a daunting word which is used a lot when talking about water pollution. It simply means to become rich in food, but is having disastrous effects on water life. When the water in a lake or stream becomes too rich in nutrients, thanks to our input of phosphates from detergents and nitrates from fertilizers, there is excessive growth of algae. As a result other forms of water life, including fish, die.

Switzerland has banned phosphates because of concern about lakes, and other countries should follow suit. Switch to low-phosphate or phosphate-free cleaning products. You can make your own, and there are several excellent commercial ranges available.

Plumbing

Most people know that lead water pipes were common in homes built before 1900, and many of these pipes have been replaced. But what many of us are unaware of is that the joints in our new copper pipes are sealed with lead solder (as are tin cans), and these too are a source of lead.

A 1981 Water Research Council report advised against the use of lead solder for pipes carrying drinking water. At present, the alternatives are mechanical rather than soldered fittings, or a special 95/5 solder made for heating systems, which contains only a tenth as much lead as the standard 50/50 solder.

The leaching of lead into water is accelerated by the presence of chlorine and other chemicals, soft water will dissolve more heavy metals than will hard water, and hot water more than cold. Researchers suggest that you flush the toilet or let the water run for several minutes first thing in the morning, and use only water from cold faucets for drinking.

Water can also be contaminated by polyvinyl chloride (PVC) pipes. Vinyl chloride, which they contain, is a potent carcinogen, and Debra Lynn Dadd mentions that a 1980 study sponsored by the California Health Services Department showed a wide variety of toxic and carcinogenic substances leaching from pipes into the water (*Nontoxic, Natural and Earthwise*). Once again, use cold water for cooking and drinking, and let water run for a little while first thing in the morning.

Toxic Chemicals

The waste from manufacturing products is often disposed of by pumping it into the nearest river or ocean. Major aquifers are now contaminated by effluents from industrial waste, and these problems have led to legislation about dumping and landfill in some industrialized countries, particularly the United States, and precipitated the new international market in domestic and industrial waste.

Waste disposal is a growing problem, and according to the authors of *Well Body, Well Earth,* solid waste disposal sites are the single most important source of groundwater contamination. We are inevitably going to have to put our house in order by cutting the quantities of waste we generate and by finding new ways of dealing with what is left.

Toxic chemicals get into our water in other ways, too. In San Jose, California, there was a sudden increase in the numbers of miscarriages and birth defects in a small area, and it was eventually discovered that the water supply to these homes had been contaminated by leakage from underground chemical storage tanks. What made this particularly surprising is that the area, Silicon Valley, is known for its clean industry—there is no smoke belching into the sky from the semiconductor plants. The leaked chemicals were trichloroethane (TCA) and dichloroethylene (DCE)—mutagens and suspected carcinogens—which are used as solvents to remove grease from computer microchips.

Similar leakage from gas storage tanks is not uncommon, and in the same area some residents need filters to remove gas from their drinking water.

Drugs

There have been questions raised about the danger of cytotoxic cancer drugs entering the water supply through patients' urine and excreta. Although this fear is countered by claims that treatment and dispersal would reduce even large quantities of the drugs to below detectable amounts, and that we can therefore assume there is no risk, the quantities of chemicals or drugs which pose a risk to human health depend a great deal on individual tolerances, and studies of risk differ greatly. And we don't know about the effects of even minute quantities of hazardous drugs in combination.

The drugs we consume are eventually excreted and flushed away, and one is advised to dispose of unused drugs by dumping them down the toilet, to prevent their getting into the hands of children; both seem good reasons to cut down drastically on use of drugs. The Women's Environmental Network in Britain is concerned about water supplies being polluted with estrogen, a human hormone, from birth control pills.

Sewage

In the past, human waste was garnered by farmers as carefully as animal waste. In China, attractive roadside outhouses were even provided, in the hope of enticing passersby to add to the farmer's stock of fertilizer. The soil produced food, and everything was returned to it in a beneficial and sustainable system. But as people have moved into cities, human waste has become a disposal problem instead of a recycling material.

In towns and cities there is not much alternative to a centralized system, but this could be designed to make use of waste rather than treat it as a nuisance. One advantage to a centralized system is that sewage can also be used to produce energy in the form of methane gas.

Composting at the source is an even better choice because pipes and tanks and transport are unnecessary. Anyone with land can use one of the modern composting systems (instead of a septic tank, if that's what you have now) which use both kitchen/household scraps and toilet waste to make a rich, safe fertilizer. If you feel squeamish about this, you probably don't want to know just where the water which went into your coffee this morning came from!

In dry climates, low-water toilets and cutting down on bulk water use are important not only to environmentalists but to every citizen.

Water Conservation

We tend to equate the water that pours from the sky with the water that comes from the faucet. The former is an abundant natural resource, whereas the latter has undergone considerable processing, with a wide range of ecological and environmental consequences.

In *Blueprint for a Green Planet,* John Seymour and Herbert Girardet point out the ways in which we affect the earth's natural water cycles. Water comes from rivers, reservoirs, and from deep underground aquifers. Valleys are flooded and villages and woods are lost in order to make reservoirs to supply drinking water for us. Lowering of the water table is a problem in some parts of the United States and in many other parts of the world.

It's not a pleasant thought, but much of the water we drink has been reprocessed from effluent, the water and sewage we use and send down the drain. All our water, not just the water we drink or bath in, is expensively purified, and questionable chemicals are added to it in the process.

Seymour and Girardet suggest that the current single pipe system should be replaced with a dual water system. This may not be as expensive as it sounds, because many older water systems are due for renewal. Drinking and washing water would come from underground boreholes and springs, and would not need the addition of chlorine. It would taste good! All other water, for industrial use, watering the garden, washing the car and flushing the toilet, would get a minimal filtering.

This is one possible solution, and worth keeping in mind. In the meantime, as we have to make do with an inefficient and

potentially hazardous system, let's think about the ways in which we can use water wisely, both for our health and for the health of the environment.

There are a number of easy ways to reduce the amount of water you use without the slightest inconvenience.

WATER CHECKLIST

❑ Turn off faucets.
❑ Stop leaks.
❑ Adjust the toilet to take less water on each flush—the arm of the float can be bent, or put a plastic bag full of water into the tank. Plastic bottles work well. Displacement bags can be had free from some utilities or cheaply at a plumbing supply store.
❑ Install a low-flush or ultra low-flush toilet
❑ Take showers instead of baths.
❑ Aerate your faucets and install a low-flow shower head. Showers account for 32 percent of home water use—these shower heads cut consumption by 50 percent.
❑ Run the washing machine with a full load.

❏ Wash dishes by hand.
❏ Save rainwater and use it in the garden or to wash the car—or bicycle. The easiest way is to run water from gutters into a barrel or water trough, which must be carefully covered to prevent animals or children from going for a dive.
❏ Use plants that don't need to be watered frequently.
❏ Don't water outside during the heat of the day, when the water will evaporate. Occasional deep soakings, rather than frequent sprinkles, save work and water. Mulch will cut watering to a minimum.

Personal Health

Anyone who has been on a diet will know that the standard advice is to drink lots of water because it fills you up and flushes you out. Eight glasses a day is a suggested target. That's about three pints. How much do you drink?

Bottled waters can be delightful, but they are bad news, ecologically: to package and transport water around the world is wasteful and should be unnecessary. I remember ordering a bottle of Perrier in a Sydney bar, and thinking how strange it was to be drinking a mineral water which was fashionable in California and on every supermarket shelf in Britain.

Water bottled in plastic absorbs a certain quantity of possibly carcinogenic polymers and it is preferable to choose glass bottles when you buy mineral water. A local source of fresh spring water in returnable bottles would be a good alternative.

Water Filters

For many of us, there is little choice at present but to filter our drinking water if we are concerned about its quality. This does not remove all impurities, but gives a safer, more palatable beverage at a reasonable price.

There are a number of filtration systems on the market. The cheapest is a plastic jug which holds a disposable filter. These are easy to use and reasonably effective, but less than ideal because of the plastic and the filters. You need at least one filter a month, and probably more often as they are dangerous if overused, releasing the filtered heavy metals and possibly bacteria back into the water.

There is a travel water filter which fits straight onto the faucet, and a number of plumbed-in systems are available—expensive initially but probably cheaper in the long run, and with fewer disposable parts.

Effectiveness and the chemicals and pollutants that each type removes vary a great deal. Prices range from a few dollars to a $1,000 or more. There are three basic methods of filtration, and the type appropriate for you depends on your water supply.

ACTIVATED CARBON

Activated carbon is inexpensive and removes chlorine, pesticides, and organic chemicals, but not fluoride or nitrates. A carbon block filter may also remove heavy metals. Choose a granulated rather than powdered carbon filter as it is less prone to bacterial growth.

REVERSE OSMOSIS

Reverse osmosis (R/O) uses a fine cellulose or plastic membrane to filter water under pressure, and removes asbestos, bacteria and viruses, fluoride, aluminium, heavy metals, minerals, salts, and nitrates. R/O removes all minerals, even desirable ones like calcium and magnesium (which contribute to the pleasant taste of a good mineral water), and the output water is said to be very acid.

DISTILLATION

Distillation is promoted as being closest to nature because rainwater, too, is distilled. The natural water we would drink by choice, however, is spring water, which is filtered through many layers of rock, absorbing valuable minerals and flavor. Distilled water is pure but insipid, and it requires a great deal of energy to produce. On the other hand, distillation is extremely effective at removing contaminants—although care has to be taken to ensure that organic chemicals are not condensed along with the steam.

You should get an analysis of your local water supply from the water or health department before deciding on a system, and insist on having laboratory test results from any supplier, especially if you are buying one of the more expensive systems. Enquire about how best to avoid bacterial growth in the filter— the most important thing is to change the cartridge as directed. As public concern about water supplies increases, unscrupulous manufacturers are bound to get into the filter market. They can easily make unsubstantiated claims. Check the Earthwise Consumer for details.

Water Softening

Calcium and magnesium salts make water hard. They can also make it taste good, and provide needed minerals. But it is harder to get lather in hard water and the limescale deposits in your kettle make it less efficient. The scum on tea is not dangerous, but it isn't very pleasant either. If you use a mechanical water softener, try to have it plumbed to the hot water supply, and then drink from the cold. You should not drink softened water because of its high sodium content.

Bathing

You can save water and energy by having a shower instead of a bath, but bathing has a place in our lives, too. The bath is a sensual experience—ideally one to be shared. In Japan, the bathing room is a social center. You wash in a small bucket of water, and get into a large communal bath of hot water to soak and relax.

In *A Pattern Language*, Alexander et al. suggest that rather than having several small and separate bathrooms, we design our homes to incorporate a single large bathroom designed for joint bathing. This would fit beautifully into an ecologically conscious home: with biodegradable soap and shampoo, the used water could go to the garden (see Chapter 13).

Filtering the entire water supply to our homes would be very expensive, but some researchers believe that 50 to 60 percent of soluble contaminants that we absorb enter the body through the skin while bathing.

A report on the American Chemical Society's 192nd national meeting, as quoted in the *L. A. Times* on September 11, 1986, explained:

Julian B. Andelman, professor of water chemistry at the University of Pittsburgh, found less chemical exposure from drinking contaminated water than in using it to wash the clothes or take a shower.

Experimenting with a model shower and common water pollutants, Andelman found that the toxic chemicals evaporated—or volatilized—into the surrounding air. Increased concentrations of the chemicals build up in the shower and spread through the home, he said.

The amount of the chemicals that vaporizes increases with longer and hotter showers, the scientists found.

"I tell my friends to take quick, cold showers," Andelman said.

The Future

Water authorities acknowledge that substantial improvements to our present water systems will be needed to provide clean, safe, and palatable water into the next century. This will entail substantial costs, but we must do something now, if we want to continue to drink the water which comes from our faucets. There are no easy answers, and public resistance to paying more for something which we think should be free as air (and even clean air has its costs, these days) makes changes difficult.

Filtering our water and using biodegradable detergent powder are important steps to take, but in the longer term we need to reassess entirely our attitude to water and make substantial changes in the way it is used to fulfill our needs, including the needs of industry, without damaging its quality and adversely affecting human health. Our relationship with water is explored in Michel Odent's book, *Water and Sexuality*. Water is a potent symbol in our culture; we should not use the world's oceans and rivers as garbage dumps.

In *A Pattern Language*, Christopher Alexander et al. suggest: "Our lives are diminished if we cannot establish rich and abiding contact with water. . . . As marvelous as the high technology of water treatment and distribution has become, it does not satisfy the emotional need to make contact with the local reservoirs, and to understand the cycle of water: its limits and its mystery."

Alexander proposes that water be brought back into the environment: "Natural streams in their original streambeds, together with their surrounding vegetation, can be preserved and maintained. Rainwater can be allowed to assemble from rooftops into small pools and to run through channels along garden paths and public pedestrian paths, where it can be seen and enjoyed. Fountains can be built in public places. And in those cities where streams have been buried, it may even be possible to unravel them again." This sounds idealistic, but a new and appreciative attitude toward the water around us is a vital step in stopping our pollution of it.

Sources

Books

Adopt-a-Stream, Steve Yates (Seattle, WA, University of Washington Press, 1988).

A Pattern Language, Christopher Alexander et al. (New York, Oxford University Press, 1977).

Blueprint for a Green Planet, John Seymour and Herbert Girardet (New York, Prentice Hall Press, 1987).

Greywater Use in the Landscape, Robert Kourik (Metamorphic Press, 1988). This booklet is available for $6 postpaid (plus $.36 tax for California residents) from Edible Publications, P.O. Box 1841, Santa Rosa, CA 95402.

Nontoxic, Natural and Earthwise, Debra Lynn Dadd (Los Angeles, Jeremy P. Tarcher, Inc., 1990).

Water and Sexuality, Michel Odent (London, Arkana, 1990).

Well Body, Well Earth: The Sierra Club Environmental Health Sourcebook, Mike Samuels and Hal Zina Bennett (San Francisco, Sierra Club Books, 1983). Distributed by Random House, New York.

Newsletter

Detergent Fact Sheet is available from the Ecology Center, 2530 San Pablo Avenue, Berkeley, CA 94702 — send SASE.

Organizations

Clean Water Action Project, 317 Pennsylvania Avenue SE, Washington, DC 20003. (202) 547-1196. "The only major environmental group working to organize rural Americans." Concerned with a wide range of water quality issues—write to find out what is happening in your area.

9
HEALTH

The best measure we have for designing our future is human health. It is here that we feel the greatest urgency to solve problems of environmental pollution, and it is here that the consequences of our actions are most dramatically demonstrated.
—Mike Samuels and Hal Zina Bennett,
Well Body, Well Earth

Introduction

Our health provides a guide to the state of the environment we live in, and health is an essential prerequisite to change because, as Michel Odent writes in *Primal Health*, "Only healthy people can be conscious of the long-term consequences of their actions and decisions; only healthy people can tackle the real priorities."

Carol Venolia, architect and author of *Healing Environments*, writes, "I believe that the planet cannot be healed by people who are not healing themselves. It starts with us. The self-determination you gain by increasing your awareness of your surroundings and enlivening them can eventually play out into global healing."

Looking at our health is a way of deciding what specific things we want to change about the way we live, and many of the other chapters in *Home Ecology* discuss particular aspects of this. Deciding that we want to improve our health changes our priorities—about radiation dangers, air pollution, and the pesticides in modern agriculture.

We cannot improve our health until we improve the health of the earth we live on and the society we live in. Health is influenced by the way we care for each other, for babies, and for the dying. The hopelessness of long-term unemployment and the helplessness of an abused child become part of the general crisis in our relationships with other people and with the natural world.

Dying seals in the North Sea, acid rain damage to Canadian forests and lakes, and the algae blooms which kill fish in the ocean are evidence of the way we affect the health of the planet, since human activity is causing these disasters. We have been preying on our environment—biting the hand that feeds us.

Ecological Perspectives

Human beings have evolved over millennia to live in a certain physical and social environment. The rapid technological changes of the past century have put our bodies in a vulnerable position because physically we are no different from early hunter-gatherers, whose way of life was vastly different from our own.

Our bodies need uncontaminated food, clean water and sweet air, seasons of light and dark, a supportive and stable social environment. When we ignore these simple requirements our health will suffer because our minds and bodies are being put under impossible strain.

Allergies and food sensitivities are on the increase, heart

disease and cancer are the so-called diseases of civilization, and most of us tolerate minor complaints like athlete's foot or a stiff back which keep us from living fully and vibrantly.

Unfortunately, the assumption is that if something—say, petrochemical products or chlorine in drinking water—doesn't make us overtly ill, it must be okay. This ignores the subtle effects that traces of toxic chemicals can have on us, and says that powerful manufacturers and profits are more important than people. The health of the natural world suffers too.

What Is Health?

If you go for a physical examination and get a clean bill of health, you may still have bad breath, flat feet, and suffer from indigestion. Health has come to mean merely the absence of an obviously debilitating disease—although when we read about health and fitness we have other things in mind: good diet, exercise, and so on.

Think of words which would describe the attributes of someone who is really healthy. Vitality, vigor, energy, enthusiasm, radiance, equanimity, confidence, adaptability, and humor are some which come to mind. Health is fitness—fitness for the things we want to do, for growth and development and pleasure.

The success of the medical profession is judged in terms of the number of people treated for illness; doctors do not win praise *for the people they do not need to treat.* But the health which you and I want to enjoy is something other than the absence of obvious illness.

Modern Attitudes

Although there is a great deal of interest in health these days, you may feel that real vitality is the prerogative of a few lithe, young creatures in fluorescent-colored training clothes. Do you get pleasure out of complaining about your aches and pains, about how you are working long hours, smoking too much, not getting enough exercise? Some people don't use a bicycle because they are afraid they'll look awkward or silly, or because they worry about what the neighbors—or the children—will think.

Our lives are cushioned, cocooned, and sheltered in a way which our ancestors would not have been able to imagine. We have become alienated from our bodies, as Dervla Murphy reflects: "The machine-age has dangerously deprived Western man of whole areas of experience that until recently were common to the entire human race. Too many of us are now cut off from the basic sensual gratifications of resting after violent exercise, finding relief from extremes of heat or cold, eating when ravenously hungry and drinking when the ache of thirst makes water seem the most precious of God's creations" (*In Ethopia with a Mule*).

The availability of medical attention and the overwhelming demands of modern life mean that many people abdicate all responsibility for their own health, and indeed become career patients. They want access to medication and high-tech medical care in emergencies, and ignore the other indignities that come with chronic ill health—the breathlessness after climbing a few flights of stairs, for example, which plagues people who don't get much exercise.

Some three-quarters of our illnesses are caused by the way we live. Circumstances like poverty and homelessness adversely affect health, but so do many things over which we have complete control, like what we eat and how much exercise we get. In *The Road to Wigan Pier*, George Orwell commented that the poor wanted jam on bread and sweet tea instead of healthier fare, because this food was one of their few pleasures. Social change is sometimes necessary before people can make healthy choices.

An entirely different approach, taken by most alternative practitioners, is that illness is a positive thing because it tells us something is wrong. Fatigue is a sign that your body, and maybe your mind, needs a rest. Indigestion is a request for a change of diet. A chronically stiff neck might tell you that you are tense, or that you're spending too much time hunched over your desk. Clinical ecologists (see below) point out that disease—eczema, for example—is not the primary event; they look to the cause, perhaps a sensitivity to milk, and try to treat that.

The connection between the mind and body shouldn't be underestimated. Continual colds may mean that you aren't eating well and your immune system isn't up to scratch as a result, but they may also be a way of avoiding a job you don't like, a way of asking for sympathy and support from those around you. Headaches and back pain are frequently related to stress or emotional problems.

Illness has become something to conquer (advertisements for aspirin talk about "hitting back at pain") with an instant remedy, so that it doesn't interfere with our busy lives. We treat the body as a machine, which needs an occasional oiling and maybe a replacement part now and then, instead of as a complex and self-sustaining system. Getting well naturally, on the other hand, demands action from us.

Drugs

The pharmaceutical industry and the medical profession have disturbingly close links. Magazines aimed at doctors have pages of advertisements for pharmaceutical products, and all drug companies have salespeople who try to convince doctors to use their brands. Direct advertising is, however, only a small part of the promotion process for prescription drugs. The pharmaceutical industry spends millions each year promoting its products, via advertising, personal visits, free samples, and luxurious conferences.

Millions of dollars are spent on drugs every year in the United States. Some doctors claim that patients demand a prescription and they sometimes write one on the assumption that taking something—anything—will make the patient feel better. There have been fascinating studies done on the effects of placebos, where patients are given plain sugar tablets but told that they are drugs. The placebos often have the same success rate as the drug. Patients, on the other hand, often feel frustrated when the doctor pulls over the prescription pad as soon as they begin to describe their symptoms.

Drugs are powerful chemicals, and have side effects which are often not taken into account. For graphic and terrifying descriptions of the way medical students are taught to deal with patients when prescribing drugs, get a copy of Dr. Robert Mendelsohn's *Confessions of a Medical Heretic*. Doctors should, of course, inform patients about possible side effects when they prescribe a drug, but some doctors feel that this alarms patients unnecessarily and interferes with the trust a patient should feel for his or her doctor. Patients should become more involved in treatment, spend more time discussing alternatives, and quite possibly reduce the amount of drugs they take.

Environment

Unhealthy Living

Although it is often difficult to connect specific aspects of the way we live with a particular health problem, there are many aspects of modern life which affect our state of health.

The amount of time we spend indoors under artificial lighting, in sealed buildings; uncomfortable seating; a long and stressful commute to your job; electrical wiring and appliances; soulless architecture and traffic noise—all affect the way we feel.

Social factors such as crowding, noise, and "tough culture" are important too. A tough culture, as explained by Mike Samuels and Hal Zina Bennett in *Well Body, Well Earth,* is one where the supportive dimensions of the social environment have broken down, where you are on the defensive as soon as you step outside your door.

People let their dogs mess there. Car windows are smashed and neighbors share stories about the latest mugging ("in broad daylight, my dear—just over there!"). These things are part of everyday life for many of us, and until we recognize this street pressure we may suffer without the slightest idea of why.

Clinical Ecology

Foods, food additives, chemicals, radiation, and other pollutants can cause disease, allergies, depression, fatigue, and plain old feeling below par. Environmental medicine (also called clinical ecology) is a medical speciality which concentrates on finding solutions to these increasingly common problems.

An allergy is an overreaction of the immune system to some element in the environment and may be fixed early in life, but improving the environment you live in can make it less of a problem, and strengthening the immune system is another way you can help yourself. Finding causes and removing them are the work of the clinical ecologist.

Noise

Whether you live in the center of a large city or well outside the city limits, the volume of sound in your environment will have increased substantially over the past 70 years or so. In the country busy roads and highways, farm equipment, and airplanes are probably the main sources of noise, while in town our ears receive an onslaught from traffic, street repairs, and construction sites, trains, sirens, loud music, and more airplanes.

Steve Halpern, a sound researcher and musician, has pointed out (*Sound Health*) that the siren volume used by police and fire vehicles in urban areas has risen to 122 decibels, louder than a jet engine. Before World War I, a brass bell was sufficient to clear the road.

As a result, we do not hear as well as our ancestors. Loud sounds destroy sensory hair cells in the inner ear, and these do not regenerate. The process of hearing loss is gradual and cumulative, and we have come to expect it as a normal part of aging. Carol Venolia, however, cites studies which compared the hearing of western city dwellers with that of Africans from remote areas. One study found that West Africans in their 70s had considerably better hearing than Londoners in their 20s (*Healing Environments*).

Sound, for our ancestors, provided useful information about the environment. Loud noises—the crack of thunder or falling rocks—were signals which helped them to deal with the world. Most of the noise (definition: unwanted or undesirable sound) we face tells us nothing meaningful. Besides that, we rarely hear pleasant sounds in the city.

Noise has profound effects on both body and mind, and is a surprisingly important source of environmental stress. Our bodies instinctively treat loud sounds as warning signals—our hearts beat faster, breathing speeds up, and muscles tense. This reaction can lead to a wide range of health problems—from high blood pressure and headaches to ulcers, cardiovascular disease, and disturbed sleep. Noise interferes with concentration, makes us raise our voices—or turn the television up increasing the overall noise level.

People who live near airports or busy interstates suffer from even louder "normal" environments than inner city dwellers. European studies have shown that people living near an airport visit the doctor two to three times more often than average, and suffer increased rates of high blood pressure, heart disease, and psychological problems.

Of course, many of us claim to be able to tune out distracting or irritating noises, but this places a strain on our systems which can lead to long-term problems. Although with time one might be able to sleep through almost any amount of noise, sleep patterns are disturbed and this affects the way we feel during the day. David Rousseau has noted (*Your Home, Your Health and Well Being*): "The most insidious effect of chronic noise exposure is that we are able to eventually accept and adapt to very dangerous conditions."

The question is, what can you do about it? Traffic noise is an important aspect of road schemes for the people affected by them, but is not taken into account by planning authorities, whose only criteria can be physical safety. Consciousness of excessive noise as a form of pollution is an essential long-term strategy.

There are four main ways of dealing with unwanted noise: avoidance, building and landscaping, dampening, and pleasing sound.

AVOIDANCE

Let noise be an important consideration when you choose a place to live. Visit your prospective home at different times of day, and during the week as well as weekends. Cars are an omnipresent source of modern noise pollution, and you will want to know whether heavy trucks use your new street during the night.

BUILDING AND LANDSCAPING

Vegetation—hedges or rows of trees—and fencing can do a great deal to muffle traffic noise, and buildings can incorporate such things as sealed double-pane glass, shutters, and solid doors, walls, and floors. Closets and cupboards built between rooms provide excellent soundproofing. Energy-saving insulation cuts down on noise, as well as heat loss.

DAMPENING

Soft furnishings are a help: carpets, rugs, and wallhangings are all effective. Choose quiet appliances, eliminate unnecessary and noisy ones, and place rubber mats or pads underneath fridges, typewriters, and other sources of domestic noise. Separate quiet and noisy rooms as much as possible. Heavy furniture, like an old-fashioned wooden wardrobe, placed against shared walls is a good way to reduce noise. Turn down music (insist on the use of headphones if necessary) and wear protective ear covering when working with loud equipment, even an electrical drill, if you are at it all afternoon. In shared houses negotiate a noise agreement—times of day and maximum levels on the volume control.

PLEASING SOUND
Sometimes your best defense is to use something pleasant to cut out undesirable noises. Music, falling water (even an aquarium pump can make a pleasant background sound), wind in trees, chimes, birdsong are all possibilities. Try to become conscious of how sound and noise influence you, and think about practical ways of increasing or highlighting desirable sounds.

Immunity

Health, or even the absence of disease, does not depend on an absence of germs. Germs are simply types of bacteria, viruses, fungi, and protozoa, which are with us all the time and some of which we need. Bacteria in our digestive tract help to digest food, and organisms on our skin protect us from potentially harmful bacteria. A strong immune system is what will keep you well, not a sterile environment.

French obstetrician and writer Michel Odent (*Primal Health*) suggests that health is a capacity for adaptation, and that without both bacteria and stress we become incapable of adapting to new stimuli and new challenges—physically and mentally. Resistance to disease is a natural phenomenon, not a result of vaccination although vaccination is aimed at encouraging the body's natural defenses. This is easy to see if we just think of the common cold. I'll bet you know someone who suffers from colds and flu nearly all the time, while another friend is smug over not having missed a day's work for years.

"Good health," says Carol Venolia, "means having the flexibility and the inner resources to respond to both assaults and opportunities" (*Healing Environments*). Diet, exercise, mental attitude, happiness at home and work are all involved in

whether or not we get ill. Think about the times you have been sick recently, and whether this has coincided with special pressure at work, or coming back from vacation, or a time when you'd been living on hamburgers and diet cola. The last couple of years I've fallen ill at Christmas, which tells me something about preparing for the holidays next time they come around.

The plight of seals has important lessons for human beings. Like us, seals are at the top of a food chain, and industrial pollutants like PCBs concentrate in their body fat. The poisons are released when they are under particular stress, when breeding and giving birth for example, depressing their immune systems making them vulnerable to a deadly virus. Analysis showed 5,000 different man-made toxic chemicals in the fat of dead seals!

Some of the research into AIDS—Acquired Immune Deficiency Syndrome—is coming up with interesting information about the role of the immune system in human health and disease. Instead of concentrating on developing drugs, we can concentrate on strengthening our natural resistance. Enormous sums have been spent trying to find a cure for cancer, while methods of treatment that concentrate on restoring the body's natural defences receive relatively little attention.

Cancer is a prime example of the neglect of basic preventative care, even though it is commonly agreed that some three-quarters of all cancer is caused by food, smoke, and chemicals. Substances which have been shown to cause cancer in laboratory animals can be detoxified by enzymes in healthy human cells. By cleaning up our environment, in the home and outside, and by concentrating on building up our health, we could eliminate the majority of cancers without any more research, without any need to find a cure.

Even animals get heart disease in stressful situations, and although every life is bound to have its share of difficulties and grief, the way we deal with painful situations has an important impact on our immune systems, and on whether or not we get ill. How do you cope with disappointment or loss? A desire to improve our health requires some thought about the social support network we have available—and about how willing we are to offer support to friends in need. A feeling of powerlessness leads to a weakening of the immune system, the body's ability to cope with threats to health. When we individually feel that there is nothing we can do to help ourselves, a physical crisis can ensue.

Odent has coined a term for the body's basic capacity for adapting to the environment—he calls it "primal health." He thinks that each person has a particular *terrain*, a fundamental temperament and ability to cope with disease, which is determined to a large extent by our experiences during the "primal period": in the womb, during birth and the early months of breastfeeding. Learned helplessness—when a baby is left to cry, for example—depresses the immune system, and, claims Odent, to some extent determines that child's capacity for health for the rest of its life.

Self-care

Home ecology puts the home at the center of health and healing. After all, "health is not merely a genetic characteristic; it is also a nurtural characteristic and, as such, is inevitably handed on from parent to child. So, a healthy family is more likely than an unhealthy one to create an intimate environment favorable to the acquisition of health, and in that sense the odds are in favor of an inherited 'tradition' of health" (*The Peckham Experiment*).

This doesn't apply only to families. People who live together are bound to be affected by each other. Notice how you feel with different friends: some may make you excited and enthusiastic about life, while others leave you feeling deflated and inadequate.

The other chapters in *Home Ecology* will help you to make your home a healthier environment. Don't forget that a healthy environment is more than the sum of its parts—carefully filtered water and good ventilation are not enough. Think about what makes your home alive, stimulating, and pleasurable. A really comfortable private place to sit down and read, to paint or frame pictures, may do more for your health than a new heating system.

Eating well is easier if you have the right foods on hand and get rid of unhealthy temptations. A shelf of cookbooks in the kitchen makes it a lot easier to opt for an easy homecooked meal on evenings when inspiration fails.

Move toxic cleaning and do-it-yourself products into a garage or storeroom if possible, and get rid of cans of insecticides through your local hazardous waste collection center.

Go through the bathroom cabinet; return old drugs to the doctor. Separate nonprescription drugs you'd be better off without: laxatives, antacids (often high in aluminum), diuretics, and aspirin. If you don't feel happy about getting rid of these all at once, you might put them in a box and see whether you can do without them for a month.

An estimated nine out of 10 headaches are caused by tension, anxiety, and other emotional states, and over-the-counter pain relievers have little or no effect on them, except in that you may start to feel better simply because you feel that you have done something by taking an aspirin. Try a cup of hot sage or peppermint tea, a nap or a short walk. Ask someone to rub your neck, or do some stretching exercises. Or sit down and sort out why you feel worried, and decide on some constructive step you can take to resolve the problem.

Health Assessment

A professional health assessment can be useful, but even more important is your own assessment. Arrange an hour or so to yourself, and settle down comfortably with a piece of paper for some quiet reflection. Remember that health should be your normal state. What you want to consider is the barriers to health in your life.

Ask yourself these questions (it may help to close your eyes and mentally examine yourself from head to toe): What is the condition of your hair, your eyes, your skin? How is your hearing? Are you overweight or underweight? What about aches and pains, creaky joints? Don't restrict yourself to big worries which you would take to a doctor. What about athlete's foot or mouth ulcers, or even general stiffness? Don't assume that these things are the inevitable result of being human, or of growing old, and don't forget to look at good signs too.

Make a list as you go along. Do you feel tired all the time, or get depressed easily and for no particular reason? Do you have trouble sleeping? Feelings of anger or aggression? Allergies or hayfever? Nervous mannerisms?

Consider your job, the place you live, your relationships, your way of life. How satisfied are you? Can you laugh at yourself?

At the end of this you may have noted down two or three items—or you may have filled several pages. Of course you can't solve all these problems at once, and you may need professional help for some of them. The key is to decide on one or two you really would like to sort out. Write those two things on a separate sheet of paper and start thinking about what you can do about them. Put the other list away for future reference.

If you are being treated by a doctor, find out as much as you can about the problem and about any medication you are taking. Make a list of questions and take it with you when you go to see the doctor, especially if you find him or her intimidating. Change doctors if yours is reluctant to answer questions, and don't assume you are getting the full facts. Medical treatment is usually undertaken on the basis of a best guess about what is wrong, but doctors still prefer to have you put complete trust in them and their diagnoses. Making an informed choice about the type of treatment you get is your right, and responsibility.

If you are taking a course of prescription drugs and do not feel satisfied with the information you get from your doctor, go to a reference library and consult the *Physician's Desk Reference* (*PDR*), which lists all drugs used in the United States, with indications for use, contra-indications, and potential side effects. This will help you evaluate over-the-counter remedies too.

Consulting an alternative practitioner can be an essential source of information about a chronic or serious problem.

Stress Management

Virtually everyone who reads this is likely to be suffering from at least one stress-related symptom. Stress seems an inescapable part of modern life. A lot of minor stresses can add up to a large total stress burden, and be just as hard on you as a serious catastrophe.

Yet, as we have seen, stress is not necessarily a bad thing. Much depends on how we respond to it—in fact, on our capacity for responding. The reason modern stresses seem to have an adverse effect may be that they arise from things outside our control—radioactive emissions from a nuclear power plant or dumping of toxic chemicals into our water supply—or which we don't know how to change or respond to.

Standard stress management tests focus on life changes— the idea is that any change puts us under stress and that too many within a short period may well do us in. But Don Ardell sees this as negative and unrealistic, asking "Who's to say that divorce is a 73-point event? . . . Not getting a divorce could be a 73-point event, day after day after day! It just depends on who is divorcing you, or vice versa" (*High Level Wellness*).

Everyday hassles and irritations—a partner who never telephones when likely to be late, the way the television volume goes up during commercial breaks, your neighbor's choice of music—may affect you far more than losing a job or going to jail (events which, after all, happen infrequently in most of our lives).

If you are stuck in a traffic jam, you can beat your head on the steering wheel, heckle other drivers, and send your blood pressure soaring, or you can resign yourself to being late. Use the time to hunt for classical stations on the radio, or make faces at the children in the car next to you. Better yet, think about finding a job closer to home, plan to start bicycling, or take the bus next time.

Taking action depends on increasing our awareness of what goes on around us. Many of us find that we "become exhausted from living out of sync with ourselves, and we can no longer tell how our environment is affecting us. We tell ourselves that any adverse effects are either inconsequential or unavoidable and that we must be doing okay because we're getting by somehow. This shut-down state produces apathy and alienation, increasing our susceptibility to disease" (Carol Venolia, *Healing Environments*). Alertness, the sort of environmental awareness that was instinctive and crucial for our ancestors, helps to restore both our health and our capacity for making positive changes in the world around us.

Exercise

I once read a suggestion that we should have joggers run on machines which would turn some of the energy they expend into electricity. Think how ridiculous an aerobics class must seem to someone who gets all the exercise she needs hauling water from a well three miles away and growing the food for her family. We have to allocate special time for exercise because we lead sedentary lives. A simple switch from driving to walking or cycling can provide a reasonable amount of exercise, probably enough to substantially lower your chances of dropping dead of a heart attack at 55.

Instead of passive forms of recreation, why not think of hiking, cross-country skiing, swimming, or cycling? Walking, in a nearby park or on the seashore, refreshes the mind as well as the body, and provides city dwellers with much needed contact with the earth. Remember that driving through the countryside does not count as outdoor recreation. Find an outdoor sport or activity you enjoy, so that you get light and fresh air along with the exercise.

Apart from positive physical effects, regular exercise is one of the best ways of improving your emotional health. Researchers have found that exercise, even walking, can have profound effects on people who are seriously depressed. A number of trials have had remarkable successes with people suffering from paranoid schizophrenia, alcoholism, and drug abuse. A 15-minute walk every day has proved to be more effective at combatting stress than taking tranquilizers, probably because exercise raises levels of a hormone called norepinephrine and improves the blood supply to the brain.

Exercise not only improves the way you look. It makes everyday burdens seem less heavy, and leads to inner changes: more energy, increased resistance to disease, better disposition, sounder sleep, better sex, less susceptibility to injuries, and easier menstrual cycles.

Diet and Supplements

A mostly organic diet, high in fresh foods and low in meat and dairy products, is a healthy one—ecology and health go hand in hand (see Chapter 2). Some nutritionists say that we get all the nutrients we need from a well balanced diet, and that the only thing that gets healthy as a result of our taking vitamin tablets is the pocketbooks of the manufacturers and health food shops. Admittedly there is plenty of hype in the health food industry, but vitamin and mineral supplements may compensate for some of the poor quality food we eat, and can help our bodies cope with pollutants.

SUPPLEMENTS CHECKLIST

❏   First, eat a healthy diet. Pills aren't going to make up for a lack of fresh, nutritious food.

❏   Try food supplements: bioflavinoids from the white pith of citrus fruit, pectin—found in apples, yogurt, brewer's yeast, lecithin, and beetroot.

❏   Vitamin C is a detoxifier and helps the body to eliminate lead.

❏   Vitamin E is a natural antioxidant and offers some protection against the effects of carbon monoxide, pesticides, and solvents.

❏   Seaweeds prevent the body from absorbing radioactive materials and protect us from other environmental pollutants too.

❏   Use garlic, wheatgerm, liver (only if organically reared), and seaweeds as ingredients in your cooking instead of taking them in tablets or capsules.

❏   Take products in simple forms whenever possible (codliver oil rather than tablets—if you can bear it—and nutritional yeast stirred into water or juice instead of swallowing dozens of tablets). Tablets are expensive and contain excipients and binders.

❑ Look for sympathetic packaging. In general, this means glass and paper rather than plastic. Buying in bulk will save money and cut packaging.

Taking Charge

The idea of self-care—that is, taking charge of your own health and actually taking care of yourself instead of depending on professionals—was popularized by Tom Ferguson when he founded *Medical Self-Care* magazine in the 1970s. I'm not entirely happy with the way medical self-care mimics the medical profession (you wield the otoscope or speculum instead of your doctor), but it is certainly a step in the right direction, and the *Medical Self-Care Catalog* (see Sources) has some handy items.

A perspective on health which I find congenial—profoundly ecological and highly amusing—is that of Robert Mendelsohn. He calls himself a medical heretic, considers annual physical examinations a health risk, and insists that hospitals are dangerous places for sick people.

Health Care

Traditional Medicine

Although specialized operating facilities are necessary for a small percentage of patients, innovative doctors and other health practitioners have been talking and writing for many years about the need for decentralized, community-centered health services.

Money does not buy good health; in fact, the more doctors and the more numerous the remedies, the more we seem to become ill. Social critic Ivan Illich points out: "The fact that the doctor population is higher where certain diseases have become rare has little to do with the doctors' ability to control or eliminate them. It simply means that doctors . . . tend to gather where the climate is healthy, where the water is clean, and where people are employed and can pay for their services" (*Limits to Medicine*).

It goes without saying that the larger a hospital is, the less personal it can be, and the less accessible the staff is. A friend commented on the indignity of being examined by doctors he had never seen before, who did not even bother to introduce themselves. In *Healing Environments* Carol Venolia says: "Most hospitals are good examples of how not to create healing environments. They seem to say, 'The power here resides with the institution; the important people are the doctors; you represent an illness, and we have tests, drugs, and machinery to control it'" (and you). This must be discouraging and disheartening for people who spend extended periods in a hospital. A study showed that patients who were able to look outside at a tree while convalescing got well faster than patients stuck in a room with nothing but bare walls to look at. The personal quality of the care they get is going to be equally helpful.

When you visit a doctor with a minor ailment, a sports injury for example, you are almost certain to be told to take it easy, lay off the exercise, and take painkillers. As long as we can walk, talk, and—most importantly—go to work, a doctor has little interest in dealing with the cause of the problem. How many women feel really free to ask about small worries when they find out they are pregnant? Sadly, most doctors are far too busy to get to know patients, and find prescribing drugs easier, and faster, than trying to understand a human being. If a man comes in with a bad back, pain relief and bed rest are standard treatment. The fact that he is unemployed and having problems with his teenage children isn't taken into account, and this lack of caring may actually make the suffering worse.

Our attitudes toward doctors are at fault too, because many of us want an instant cure—we don't want to make any changes in our lives but simply want some help in the process of compensation for ill health. Illich talks about the physician's role being to exonerate the sick from moral accountability. If this is true, only we can change it by taking responsibility for our own health.

Dentistry

Dental philosophy and dental care are changing. Instead of treating decay as a cancer to be eradicated as quickly and thoroughly as possible (even when this meant drilling out surrounding areas of sound tooth), some dentists are choosing to leave teeth alone. Teeth are not dead; they can remineralize and heal themselves. If left untouched, small patches of decay will sometimes disappear, especially with improvements in diet and brushing.

Most dentists have not yet converted to this benign approach. Students get insufficient training in preventative care, nutrition, and concepts of whole patient treatment. Nonetheless, the trend is a welcome one.

One of the most important areas of debate is about metal amalgam fillings. Dental amalgam contains up to 50 percent highly toxic mercury, and some dentists think that slow release of this recognized poison is responsible for long-term debilitation of the immune system. If you have a mouthful of fillings you will know how they gradually wear away, and sometimes even fall out. Mercury also vaporizes. It is not enough to say that metal fillings have been used for a long time, so they must be safe; lead was used in pipes for over a thousand years!

Metal fillings can be replaced with white bonded material, which seems to be inert, looks nice, and has other advantages. Because it bonds, or sticks, directly to the tooth there is no need to drill away sound tooth in order to place a filling, and your dentist will not need to use X-rays to check for hidden decay under existing fillings because no room is left for the growth of secondary decay.

Natural Family Planning

Birth control is a knotty issue, which no one has satisfactorily resolved. The Pill has been associated with a wide range of health problems; IUDs have been the subject of dozens of court cases and massive settlements. Other forms of contraception are inconvenient, messy, and require the use of chemical spermicides, with their attendant health risks.

A completely safe alternative is called Natural Family Planning (NFP), or the Billings Method. The woman charts her ovulation cycle by keeping a record of her temperature, cervical shape, and vaginal mucus, that change very regularly throughout the menstrual cycle. Opponents claim that there are too many other factors that will affect temperature, but if you get to know your body, you will be well aware if there is any exceptional change affecting you, and most women find that they can recognize their own patterns with great accuracy after several months' practice.

The method requires some diligence and concentration, especially in the first year or so, but when one considers that most women have to think about birth control for some 30 years of their lives, this method could be less trouble in the long run than other forms of contraception. Its success rate is roughly comparable to that of using a diaphragm with spermicide. Another thing to keep in mind is that wild animals and birds can choke on condoms so dispose of them in the trash. They should not be flushed down the toilet.

Alternative Medicine

Once you start to understand the complexity of our bodies and the myriad influences upon them, the all too common dismissal of any form of treatment that does not depend on medication starts to look positively stupid.

Vaccination against smallpox was used before it was fully understood, because it clearly worked. Acupuncture, too, clearly works, even though a generally agreed scientific explanation has not been established.

Instead of these forms of treatment being useless or fraudulent, the problem is our means of testing, our whole acceptance of the idea that nothing is true until it is proven in a particular way. Subtler means of dealing with problems in the human body and mind are likely to need subtler means of testing.

The scientific method is difficult to use on human beings (and it is impossible to replicate the complex demands and pressures of our lives when doing tests on laboratory rats) because this sort of analysis requires an untreated, generally equivalent control group, and a way of isolating a particular treatment. With drug testing this is easy: one group gets the drug and the other does not. Establishing whether complementary techniques work is far more difficult.

Broad comparisons are intriguing: middle-aged Cretan men eat just as much fat as the average American, yet heart disease, our primary cause of death in this age group, is virtually unknown. Researchers are trying to explain this. It's interesting to look at the way medical advice about the role of cholesterol in heart disease has changed over the past fifteen years.

SIDS—Sudden Infant Death Syndrome—is essentially unheard of outside the industrialized West. Michel Odent has observed that in other countries children sleep with their parents, and spend almost all their time being carried close to an adult.

These phenomena are not scientific evidence of specific cause and effect, yet they offer us useful information.

When loaves of French bread are baked in Seattle or St. Louis from ingredients that are, according to chemical tests, exactly the same as the ones used in Paris—even when the ovens have been imported at great expense—the end result is different. Cheese making shows similar variations. No one knows exactly why, although we can think of possible explanations (the air is different, the water harder or softer, yeasts behave differently, the bakers are less skillful), but no one denies that the bread or cheese tastes different.

Similarly, the way each person responds to his or her environment—physical and social—is different. Holistic medicine aims to treat the whole person, and not just a symptom. Many holistic practitioners do not like to think in terms of disease. Instead, they describe a particular set of symptoms as a common pattern of coping responses. The actual cause, which is what they want to deal with, may be different for each person—every treatment needs to be individually tailored.

Of course, this sort of analysis takes more time than a typical office visit to your doctor. A first visit to an alternative practitioner is likely to take an hour or so because of the need to discuss your health history and way of life.

You may want to consult a homeopath or some other alternative practitioner. The real problem is just how to find a good one. Finding a doctor you feel contented with can be difficult, let alone tracking down a suitable acupuncturist. Most of us depend on recommendations from friends, or simply look in the Yellow Pages. The variety of techniques makes it difficult to decide which specialist is going to be able to help with your particular problem, too. Should you see a Rolfer, a medical herbalist, or an acupuncturist?

In some alternative fields, there is no legal restriction on who is qualified to practice. There are, however, bodies which accredit schools and award particular qualifications, and you would be well advised to consult one of these before choosing a practitioner.

Going to a group practice, if there is one in your area, is a good idea, because you can easily be passed to someone else if the person you first consult feels that this is appropriate. A good alternative therapist will be aware of other disciplines and happy to make referrals—beware of anyone who seems to think that their own speciality is the only way.

Look for a practitioner who makes you feel comfortable, who is enthusiastic and encouraging, and who clearly takes an individual approach to your health problem. Willingness to explain the treatment and to enlist your support is important, as is confidence in the body's ability to heal itself. Treatment frequently consists of removing impediments to that natural healing, rather than a direct treatment of symptoms.

Aging and Death

Michel Odent closed the first International Conference on Home Birth in London by saying that we also have to understand the importance of home death.

It's easy to make fun of American attitudes to death, the Hollywood piped-music crematoria and cemeteries for cats and dogs, but we have come to accept a medicalized death in a hospital as the usual, and even desirable, thing.

Dying is a part of living, and the way people end their lives should be part of all of our lives—marked by dignity and within a community of friends and family. Tragically, this is not the case for many people, who end their lives alone in a hospital bed, strapped to monitors, with none of their own things to look at and cherish, with no familiar face to offer comfort and to communicate with.

Our care of the elderly says a great deal about attitudes towards aging and death. Carol Venolia explains how we could change this: "Old age can be a time of flourishing and fulfillment in a social and physical environment that acknowledges the uniqueness of the later years of life. For most, it is a time of increased personal maturity and decreased responsibilities—a fertile combination. If we don't relegate the elderly to deadly institutions, and if we consider the full span of life when we create our homes, public buildings, and outdoor spaces, the potential vitality of the elderly can be available to enrich everyone's life" *(Healing Environments)*.

This is not an abstract question, but part of the future faced by each of us. Has death become institutionalized because we want to give the dying every possible chance, or because we do not want to have to come to terms with our own future deaths? Our dependence on medicine means that we expect it to solve every problem, including death.

The hospice movement, however, is a sign of better understanding about the needs of the dying. Pain relief and nursing care are often all that someone needs in the concluding days, along with a homelike atmosphere, the care and attention of friends or family, and appropriate spiritual succor.

Sources

Books

Confessions of a Medical Heretic, Robert Mendelsohn (Chicago, Contemporary Books, 1979).

Healing Environments: Your Guide to Indoor Well-Being, Carol Venolia (Berkeley, Celestial Arts–Ten Speed Press, 1988).

High Level Wellness, Donald B. Ardell (Berkeley, Ten Speed Press, 1986). The gung-ho fundamentalist tone of the book gets rather irritating, but Ardell's approach to health is sound.

How to Have a Healthy Baby . . . In Spite of Your Doctor, Robert Mendelsohn (New York, Ballantine, 1987).

In Ethiopia with a Mule, Dervla Murphy (John Murray, 50 Albemarle Street, London W1X 4BD, 1968).

Limits to Medicine, Ivan Illich (Marion Boyars Publishers, 24 Lacy Road, London SW15 1NL, 1976).

The Peckham Experiment, Innes H. Pearse and Lucy H. Crocker (Wolfeboro, NH, Longwood Publishing Group, 1985).

Physician's Desk Reference, edited by Ed Barnhart (Oradell, NJ, Medical Economics Books, 1989).

Primal Health, Michel Odent (Century Hutchinson Publishing, 62-65 Chandos Place, London, WC2N 4NW, 1986).

The Road to Wigan Pier, George Orwell (San Diego, CA, Harcourt Brace Jovanovich, 1972).

Sound Health: Music and Sounds That Make Us Whole, Steven Halpern and Savary Louis (New York, Harper & Row, 1985).

The Well Adult Book, Mike Samuels and Nancy Samuels (New

York, Summit Books, 1988).

The Well Baby Book, Mike Samuels and Nancy Samuels (New York, Summit Books, 1979).

Your Home, Your Health and Well Being, David Rousseau (Berkeley, Ten Speed Press, 1988). Contains useful information about chemical sensitivities.

Well Body, Well Earth: The Sierra Club Environmental Health Sourcebook, Mike Samuels and Hal Zina Bennett (San Francisco, Sierra Club Books, 1983). Distributed by Random House, New York. A comprehensive book with lots of Native American lore.

Magazine
Medical Self-Care, P.O. Box 1000, Point Reyes, CA 94956. Free catalog, also: P.O. Box 999, Point Reyes, CA 94956.

Organizations
Society for Clinical Ecology, 2005 Franklin Street, Suite 409, Denver, CO 80205. (303) 831-7335.

American Holistic Medical Association, 2727 Fairview Avenue East, Seattle, WA 98102. (206) 322-6842.

10
THE NONTOXIC HOME

It is becoming increasingly clear that our health is integrally related to the toxicity of our environment, but while television news and daily newspapers run stories about chemical spills, toxic waste, and industrial pollution, little attention is given to positive, immediate actions we as individuals can take right now.
—Debra Lynn Dadd, *The Nontoxic Home*

INTRODUCTION
    Ecological Connection—Chemical Sensitivity—Children and Pregnant Women—Alternatives—Petrochemicals—Fragrances
CLEANING
    The Environment-friendly Cleaning Cupboard
PESTS
    Flies—Ants—Cockroaches—Moths—Insect Repellants
CLOTHES CARE
    Washing Products—Whiteners—Fabric Conditioners—Ironing—Drycleaning—Stain Removal
TOILETRIES
    Bath Products—Body Powder—Antiperspirants and Deodorants—Toothpaste and Mouthwash—Shampoo—Hairspray—Hair Coloring—Nail Polish—Cosmetics
HOME BUILDING AND MAINTENANCE
    Building Materials—Decorating
MISCELLANEOUS
    Plastics—*Plastics Checklist*—Paper Products—Fabrics and Furnishings—Office Supplies—Car Maintenance
PROPOSITION 65
SAFETY
SOURCES

Introduction

Since World War II there has been a vast increase in the number of chemical substances in common use. A 1978 estimate was 63,000, and the number is rising by at least 1,000 per year. The majority of them have not been adequately tested for risk to either human health or the environment. Products we use every day and even the building materials used for our homes contain chemicals which are known to be carcinogenic (cancer-causing), mutagenic (mutation-causing), and teratogenic (defect-causing —that is, leading to birth defects).

We cannot underestimate the consequences of this. Toxic chemicals from industry, disposed of or accidentally released into the environment, pose a constantly increasing threat. A number of scientists, including a Committee on Science and Public Policy of the National Academy of Sciences (1970), have pointed out that the genetic hazards from chemicals are probably of even greater importance than those from ionizing radiation, barring nuclear war.

Chemicals cause cancer, miscarriages, and birth defects, and in the longer term affect the human gene pool. They also have subtle, low-level effects which we may not be aware of or be capable of analyzing. The problem of chemical sensitivity is an inevitable consequence of the array of products with which each of us comes into contact, from food additives and colorings to chlorine bleach and enzyme detergents.

This chapter can be no more than a brief overview of an increasingly complex subject. I've chosen to concentrate on the practicalities of choosing nontoxic alternatives, rather than explaining the potential hazards of every product because there are detailed sources of this information such as *Clean and Green* by Annie Berthold-Bon.

Ecological Connection

What does drycleaning have to do with home ecology? Cleaning and do-it-yourself products affect our home environment, and things that are hazardous for us are almost always hazardous to the outside environment. The detergents, bleach, and cleaners we pour down the drain find their way into lakes and rivers, where they have a devastating effect on water plants and animal life, and some eventually end up back in our food or in the water we drink.

Toxic waste is a growing problem in the industrialized world, and domestic trash too has its share of toxic contaminants. Think how casually we throw away used batteries, an old box of mothballs, or a couple of cans of dried up paint. Some towns have special toxic waste collection points, but many of us have no choice about how to discard these items.

Byproducts of chemical production are, at present levels, impossible to deal with safely. According to Professor Barry Commoner, 99 percent of the petrochemical industry's toxic wastes are now put into the environment, half of them into underground wells and the rest on the surface. He points out that incinerating the present annual output of toxic waste would cost three times the total profit of the petrochemical industry ("High-risk high tech: Who decides how it is used?" Cambridge, MA, Science for People, March/April 1987, reprinted in *Utne Reader,* March/April 1988).

In *The Turning Point,* Fritjof Capra says: "In the long run the problems generated by chemical waste will become manageable only if we can minimize the production of hazardous substances, which will involve radical changes in our attitudes as producers and consumers." The main thing we can do, individually, is to stop using as many toxic products as possible, and to encourage the producers of environmentally sound ones.

Chemical Sensitivity

Although our bodies are able to deal with a certain quantity of environmental poisons, each person's chemical tolerance point is different. Once it has been passed, severe and debilitating illness can result. Removing a proportion of the environmental toxins may enable coping mechanisms to function again, but certain people become permanently sensitive to things that they were previously able to tolerate.

This is an area of research that has received considerable attention in the United States over the past 10 years from toxicologists, clinical ecologists, and consumer groups. Possible symptoms include asthma and eczema, depression, chronic fatigue, skin rashes, and migraine headaches.

Debra Lynn Dadd worked as a classical musician until 1980,

when she was diagnosed as having a severe breakdown of her immune system, caused by stress and heavy chemical exposure. She had no occupational exposure; all the chemicals that made her ill were things she used at home.

Sensitive individuals find that pesticide residues on fresh fruits and vegetables, traces of detergent and solvents in and on many products, and today's battery of food additives make them ill. Reactions to petrochemical products are common.

It is very difficult to test the effects of individual chemicals on human beings. The so-called "chemical cocktail"—the wide variety of chemicals we are exposed to in our food, air, water, building materials, and domestic products—may well have serious consequences. There is no way to test the effects of every possible combination of chemicals.

Judging safe levels is equally difficult, and recommendations are frequently lowered as scientists discover more about the way particular chemicals affect people. For example, a high rate of miscarriage and infertility among hospital operating room staff, resulting from exposure to anesthetics, has led to improvements in hospital ventilation.

Children and Pregnant Women

Children take in more air and more food for their body weight than do adults, and are more vulnerable to environmental toxins, just as they are to ionizing radiation.

Allergies, including asthma and eczema, seem to be more and more common, and children's reactions to chemicals can include hyperactivity and even psychiatric disorders. Dr. Jean Monro of the Lister Clinic has been successfully treating chemically sensitive children and recently, with Dr. Peter Mansfield, co-authored a useful guide for parents, *Chemical Children* (see Sources).

Pregnant women and their unborn babies are also particularly vulnerable to toxins. Whatever they consume or come into contact with will affect, to some degree, their baby. If you are pregnant, make a special effort to avoid contact with strong household chemicals, particularly aerosols. Watch out with cosmetics as well. Chemical hair colorings and hair sprays, and of course smoking, are thought to be the greatest dangers to the fetus.

Alternatives

Take a look at the variety of cleaners you have in the house right now. How many do you actually use? Spray polishes and carpet fresheners are enticingly packaged and expensively promoted, and advertisements about laundry detergents are inescapable.

I suspect that one reason we are so prone to trying new products is that few of us devote substantial amounts of time to housecleaning, and we're eager to try anything that might make the job easier and faster. We buy the promise rather than the product, and end up with a cupboard full of luridly colored plastic bottles, each used once or twice and then superseded by the next bright aerosol to catch our eye.

Rather than buy more, why not keep a supply of basic cleaning products which will harm neither you nor the environment? Virtually all cleaning chores can be efficiently tackled with nothing more than soap, vinegar, and bicarbonate of soda (I know this sounds extreme, but please read on). You can also buy several safe commercial cleaners.

Switching to nontoxic toiletries is even simpler because there are more commercial products available. It is also possible to make your own nontoxic alternatives, and I've included a number of simple formulas.

Look behind the druggist's counter: you'll probably see a range of old-fashioned products which are a delightful change from complicated modern concoctions and work just as well. These include surgical and camphor spirits, almond oil, tincture of benzoin, rosewater, and glycerine.

Don't think that anything that calls itself natural will be. "Natural" wild-mountain-honey-and-herb shampoo may contain exactly the same ingredients as any other detergent shampoo, with the addition of a little honey and a different fragrance. Full product labeling is an important step towards offering consumers an informed choice.

Finding substitutes for potentially hazardous building and decorating materials is more difficult, but there are several sources of information and safe products.

Petrochemicals

Many people are sensitive to petroleum-based chemicals—one estimate suggests that a third to half of the population may have some reaction to them. Toxic waste from the petrochemical industry is a leading source of world pollution, and Barry Commoner comments: "You need to regard the products of the petrochemical industry as evolutionary misfits and therefore very likely to be incompatible with the chemistry of living things. The failure to understand this basic fact has caused the whole problem in chemical pollution. We keep being surprised that chemicals that were perfectly nice and simple to make turn out to have very serious biological consequences" ("High-risk high tech").

It isn't easy to avoid petrochemicals in everyday life, as they include plastics, synthetic fabrics, newspaper ink, and a nearly infinite array of other common items. You can, however, cut out at least some of the petroleum products you use on your body.

Petroleum jelly and mineral oil are obvious things to look out for; many cosmetics, lotions, and creams contain them. In the body, absorbed through the skin, they take up oil-soluble vitamins A and D. Ordinary baby oil is simply scented mineral oil, and many years ago the nutritionist Adelle Davis advised parents against using it. A plain vegetable oil works beautifully—olive oil is traditional in many countries.

The same goes for adults. Try using an unrefined vegetable oil for removing makeup. If you don't want to smell like a salad, choose a mild oil and add a few drops of your favorite essential oil.

Fragrances

The most common cause of allergic reactions to cosmetics and beauty products is their fragrance. Natural essential oils are derived from plants, and many people who cannot tolerate artificial scents find that they have no problems with natural fragrances.

Unscented products allow you to choose how you are going to smell, instead of having your deodorant, shampoo, and face cream all competing. With a small range of essential oils, you can concoct your own distinctive scents, as well as experiment with their subtle psychological and physical effects.

Cleaning

Household products are designed to clean, to disinfect, and to deodorize. To achieve these aims we use vast quantities of detergent, bleach, air fresheners, and other dangerous products.

None of us wants to go back to great-granny's day, of scrubbing clothes on a washboard or scouring floors with ashes. But nontoxic cleaning is easy, with fewer supplies to think about. Nontoxic products seem to take far less rinsing, and one doesn't have to worry about traces of noxious substances left behind.

As Peg Bracken wisely pointed out in her *I Hate to Housekeep Book*, that if something is worth doing, it's worth doing badly. Don't wait till you have a can (a CFC aerosol spray, at that) of the latest wallpaper spot cleaner when a quick wipe with a soapy dishcloth would have done the trick. And if you apply a wax polish to clean tiles, they will be easy to wipe down. Scrubbing with bicarbonate of soda on a sponge is effective on water spots, as is a 50/50 vinegar and water mixture.

Cleaning expert Don Aslett has many useful tips about saving time and energy in *Is There Life After Housework?*—although the cleaning supplies he recommends are not ecologically sound. He says that we use too many cleaning products and far too much of them. The first and best cleaner is water, and his rule of thumb is "eliminate—saturate—absorb." Rather than grinding away at the cake batter that has dried on a bowl, fill it with water and leave it alone for ten minutes while you mix a drink, or feed the cat, or close your eyes and reflect on higher things. Then wash. This principle works on clothes (soak overnight) and floors (wet the floor and leave it for half an hour—you'll be amazed at the amount of dirt which comes up), as well as on dishes.

Another useful hint from Aslett, for all of us who want to avoid both chemical cleaning products and cleaning in the first place, is to use good doormats at every door. Carpets last longer if they are kept clean—it's the abrasiveness of dirt, rather than traffic, that does most of the damage. Aslett says this will save the average household 200 cleaning hours a year. In addition, mats will cut down on the pollutants, including lead and canine parasites, you bring into the house. But don't shake mats onto the garden or you'll end up eating the lead in next year's lettuces.

Burning scrap timber which has traces of paint on it—even modern paints contain some lead—and using the ashes as a source of potash for your potatoes is something else to avoid.

Taking your shoes off when you come in works the same magic. The Japanese have always done this, and you can buy inexpensive straw slippers to keep by the door, for guests as well as yourselves.

The Environment-Friendly Cleaning Cupboard

Take those shiny, colorful aerosols, and powerful, potentially dangerous cleaners off your shopping list. Instead, here is a list of basic supplies which should get you through every domestic task.

Look out for containers that can be reused to package your basic cleaning supplies conveniently. Shakers are useful for bicarbonate of soda and borax, and spray bottles are good for a window cleaning mixture.

SOAP

A constant refrain in books on housekeeping and saving money is the soap jar. This is where all those slivers of hand soap go when you start a fresh bar. Pour on a little boiling water and you'll get a soft jelly which can be used for washing dishes or pantyhose, or diluted as a spray for the aphids attacking your hibiscus. Another way to use soap scraps is to keep them in a metal tea ball or strainer, which you swish in your dishwater.

Household soap or plain soap flakes will do the trick as well, perhaps with the addition of a little washing soda.

DISH SOAP

You may not need this, if you become a soap jar aficionado. But biodegradable dish soap is effective, and truly easy on hands unlike the advertised brands, which cut the natural oils on your skin as efficiently as they cut grease on dishes. In a hard water area, add a little water softener to the wash basin—you'll need less soap.

LAUNDRY SOAP

A number of biodegradable detergents are available from wholefood stores and by mail order. In my experience, you will need to add a water softener to get clothes clean in hard water.

People used to air clothes overnight and get another day's wear out of them—you'll know yourself whether this will work! Brushing with a good natural bristle clothes brush is a butler's trick for reviving garments. Machine washing and tumble drying make clothes wear out more quickly.

BICARBONATE OF SODA (BAKING SODA)

This is almost infinitely useful around the house. Buy a box from the drugstore rather than the tiny ones you get for baking. I've seen large bags of bicarbonate of soda at a Chinese supermarket. It is a water softener, can be used as a scouring powder on sinks and bathtubs—effective, and very easy to rinse away—as a coating on ovens to make them easier to clean next time, an excellent polish for chrome, and a neutral cleaner when dissolved in water.

Bicarbonate of soda also makes a good plaque-fighting toothpowder, and can be used in solution as a garden fungicide for mildew on roses and other plants (half a teaspoon per pint of water, applied every seven days).

TABLE SALT

Salt is a mild disinfectant, and makes an abrasive but benign scouring powder. Keep drains clear with a weekly handful of salt and kettleful of boiling water.

CLEAR DISTILLED VINEGAR

Mix vinegar 50/50 with water in a spray bottle for cleaning windows and mirrors. Polish with clean, lintfree cotton or linen rags, or newspaper. This works beautifully, but if you've been using commercial glass cleaners you may find that it smudges the first time because there is a waxy build-up from your old spray. If this happens, wipe the windows down with a little alcohol or soda to remove the film. Use vinegar and water to descale your pots or remove stains from a teapot. Mixed with salt or baking soda, it will polish brass and copper.

The ring in your toilet comes from hard water, just the same as the limescale in the tea kettle, and can be removed with an acid like vinegar, left to stand.

WASHING SODA

Sodium carbonate or washing soda is a water softener, and cuts grease. Used sparingly, this makes a good heavy duty cleaner for walls and floors, and a few tablespoons added to your regular biodegradable detergent will help with really dirty clothes.

Polish small silver pieces by simmering for 10–15 minutes in a saucepan containing hot water, a piece of aluminum foil, and a tablespoon of washing soda.

BORAX

This can be bought at the supermarket, and is recommended as an all-purpose alternative to bleaches and disinfectants. Use borax to soak diapers, whiten clothes, soften water, and increase the effectiveness of plain soap. It is also good at keeping down mold and preventing odors. (I have, however, talked to people who are concerned about the use of borax because it can be poisonous. Like pesticides, which are a particularly hazardous type of chemical because they are designed to destroy forms of life, any product which kills bacteria should be used with discretion.)

The brown bottles of hydrogen peroxide you buy at the drugstore can be used as a bleach for delicate clothes. The ideal alternative for clothes would seem to be an oxygen bleach, which breaks down into water and oxygen. Non-chlorine bleaches are generally sodium perobate or borax, with artificial fragrances.

A water and borax solution can be used to wipe down the

bathroom if you like to use a disinfectant, perhaps with a few drops of pine oil.

WATER SOFTENER

The major commercial water softener is simply scented sodium hexametaphosphate. Scented products are often implicated in allergic reactions, so buy a softener with no added fragrance. Large chemical supply houses might even sell you sodium hexametaphosphate, which Debra Lynn Dadd highly recommends. It is, however, a phosphate, and should be used discreetly.

A softener will improve washing results and enable you to cut down on the amount of detergent you use. Before you switch to a biodegradable detergent, run your clothes through a wash cycle with a double dose of water softener to remove detergent residue. A softener can also be used as a bath salt, with the addition of a scented oil or fresh herbs.

TRISODIUM PHOSPHATE (TSP)

TSP is a powerful and moderately toxic cleaner sometimes available from paint shops, since this is the mixture you buy to clean walls before painting. Try to buy it straight rather than mixed with detergents and fragrance It is a phosphate and therefore has a harmful effect on water supplies, but chemically sensitive people find it useful as it gives off no fumes. Use it only when absolutely necessary and wear rubber gloves.

A completely nontoxic heavy duty cleaner is available through the Vermont Country Store: a simple pumice bar which works on all durable surfaces, including tiles.

FURNITURE POLISH

Don't use cream polish because of its emulsifiers and never use aerosol polishes, especially those containing silicone. Aerosols give instant shine but do not fill in scratches, they make the furniture surface slippery, and continued use leads to a milky finish because of the solvents they contain, which can only be removed by stripping and refinishing the piece of furniture.

Use furniture wax once, or at most twice, a year. In between, just dust or rub with a soft cloth—not a feather duster. A slightly dampened cloth will remove sticky marks, and a little vinegar in the water will cut old polish film.

Make your own beeswax polish by grating beeswax (from the drugstore—or your own beehive) into a jar and covering it with natural turpentine. Shake occasionally until the beeswax has dissolved.

A revitalizing liquid polish can be made by combining two parts boiled linseed oil and one part turpentine. Buy both at the hardware store (don't try boiling your own linseed oil). Applied sparingly and rubbed in well, this is suggested as an alternative to refinishing a piece of furniture.

FLOOR POLISH

A hard, traditional carnauba (palm) wax is appropriate for fine wood floors. The West German firm Livos (see Sources) is a good source of information about caring for wood floors, and sells wax polish.

Many people get by perfectly well without waxing or polishing their floors at all. Linoleum will survive nicely with an occasional mopping with soapy water.

CLEANING CLOTHS AND SCOURERS

Some people are keen on those round knitted nylon scourers, which last virtually forever. A metal scourer can stand in for a lot of scouring powder. Use plain steel wool rather than steel wool pads impregnated with chemicals—you can tear off the small piece that is all you really need.

DISHWASHING

This is worth dwelling on because if you cook at home and don't have a dishwasher, you'll spend more time at the kitchen sink than at any other household task. Everyone has his or her own favorite method, which may look unhygienic to a fussy roommate. My mother continually complained about the way we did the dishes, but I have a *laissez-faire* attitude, glad for any domestic cooperation.

Most powders for automatic dishwashers are high in phosphates, contributing to eutrophication. Try a low- or no-phosphate brand. (A friend who tried them was unhappy with the results—if this happens to you, let the company know. Firms that are developing nontoxic products need and want customer feedback.) Dishwashing liquids, however, do not contain phosphates, and an oft-quoted green advertising scam has been to label them "phosphate-free," when every brand on the shelf is phosphate-free, too. There are liquids made with vegetable oils instead of petrochemicals. Ordinary liquids also contain colorings and fragrance which can irritate sensitive skin, in addition to a drying agent which can increase the body's absorption of hazardous pesticides. This substance remains on the dishes even after rinsing.

Some people like to wash under hot running water, with no detergent at all. This works pretty well, but consumes a lot of energy and water. As an alternative, here's my method for getting dishes clean with a minimum expenditure of time, heat, and soap or detergent:

❑ You'll need a small pan or bowl, a biodegradable dishwashing liquid and a brush or scrubber.
❑ Soak or rinse any really dirty dishes or pans in cold water first.
❑ Put the bowl in your sink, squirt a little dishwashing liquid into it and fill with very hot water. Wash glassware, then cutlery, plates, and pots and pans last of all, by dipping your brush or scrubber into the hot soapy water. Set the washed but unrinsed dishes aside.
❑ Rinse the whole lot at once in cold running water. Allow them to dry in the dishrack.

Each dish gets hot soapy treatment, but you need only a small bowl of washing water. For lots of dishes, just do this in batches. And make sure you enlist help—washing up needs to be shared!

AIR "FRESHENERS"
Don't equate the smell of bleach or other harsh cleaners with freshness. Try these ideas:

❑ Allow plenty of ventilation. Opening windows at least once a day is the best way to clear stale or offensive odors, as well as any toxic fumes which might build up. An extractor fan can help in the kitchen and bathroom.
❑ Keep things dry and reasonably warm. Clothes should be aired thoroughly. Borax inhibits the growth of mildew and

mold, so you can sprinkle it around or wipe surfaces with a borax solution.

❏ Empty your trash frequently and sprinkle a little borax or bicarbonate of soda in the bottom of the bin. Once you start composting, your garbage can stays dry and is very unlikely to smell.

❏ Compost buckets should be emptied every couple of days, and probably every day in the summer. A cover keeps flies away.

There are a number of ideas for natural air fresheners in Chapter 7. Quite a few people seem to regard commercial air fresheners as part of good hygiene around the house but they work by masking unpleasant odors, coating your nasal passages with an oily film, or numbing your sense of smell with a nerve-deadening agent. As Debra Lynn Dadd points out, most air fresheners do nothing to freshen the air—they only add more pollutants.

Pests

Insecticides are poisonous and should be avoided both because of their environmental effects and effects on our health. First, remove whatever is attracting the pests. Food should be stored in airtight containers like glass jars, and you'll need to take special care with cleaning. Wash up dishes immediately after eating, don't leave crumbs in bed, and empty wastebaskets frequently. Dirty disposable diapers attract pests, another reason for avoiding them.

Then try the following ideas. There are dozens more in Debra Lynn Dadd's books and in other easily available books of household hints (see also Pesticides in Chapter 7).

Flies

Flies do not like the smell of orange and lemon peels, cloves, or mint. You can also use a flyswatter. Buy nontoxic fly strips from the grocery store or make your own from brown paper and a sugar syrup (see Chapter 7 for instructions). And remember to be kind to spiders!

Ants

Sprinkle dried mint, chili powder, or borax wherever they are coming in—of course, your first step should be to block the hole, if possible. Plant mint outside; ants don't like the smell. Or learn to love them; they are a fascinating introduction to colonial life.

Cockroaches

Unfortunately, cockroaches would probably survive a nuclear bomb, but you can try baking them out—heating the house as hot as it will get for a couple of hours. Easier, and probably safer, is to leave out a mixture of flour, cocoa, and borax, or bicarbonate of soda and powdered sugar, or flour and plaster of paris (out of the reach of children, of course). All of these should lead to a quick death for the noxious creatures. Another method is to make a fall trap by putting a little sugar in the bottom of a glass jar, with a bit of wood for a ramp. Roaches climb in but cannot get out.

Moths

Mothballs are made of paradichlorobenzene, a volatile chemical which is a respiratory irritant and can cause depression, seizures, and long-term damage to kidneys and liver. Although the packet may warn you to avoid prolonged breathing of the vapor, the way mothballs are used, distributed among your clothing, makes prolonged exposure unavoidable.

The most important thing is to ensure that woollens are cleaned before being stored. Pressing with a steam iron or tumbling in a dryer will also kill any moth eggs. Cedar wood, lavender, and camphor are natural, traditional moth repellants. Buy cedar blocks, hangers, and storage boxes from L. L. Bean or The Vermont Country Store (see catalogs among Sources, Chapter 3 and this chapter).

Insect Repellants

Rather than apply commercial repellants which contain Deet (diethyl toluamide), a strong irritant which can eat through plastic and dissolve paint, rub your skin with vinegar on a cottonwool ball, and allow it to dry. The smell disappears as it dries, but vinegar makes you taste nasty. Or oil of citronella or pennyroyal can be diluted in a little vegetable oil and rubbed on. Eating lots of garlic is also said to repel insects.

You can get an effective herbal repellant called Bugg Off from Wyoming Wildcrafters, P. O. Box 874, Wilson, WY 83014— free products list.

Clothes Care

Washing Products

Modern detergents contain a variety of additives including optical brighteners, enzymes, and fragrances. All of these have environmental and health effects. Instead, there are biodegradable, enzyme-free products available.

Before you switch to a detergent that does not contain optical brighteners, Debra Lynn Dadd suggests running your clothes through a wash cycle with a double dose of water softener. Otherwise they can turn slightly yellow because of detergent film. On the other hand, they may simply be returning to their natural color.

To make your own detergent, combine 1 cup soap flakes and 1/2 cup baking soda. In soft water areas you can use a higher proportion of soap flakes, and in hard water areas you'll need more baking soda. I don't expect many people to go this far, but add the information in the interest of thoroughness. You might want to try it some rainy day when you have time on your hands.

If you're hooked on spot spray, try rubbing clothes with a damp bar of household soap. In her *Cheaper and Better,* Nancy Birnes (see Sources) recommends the following mixture as a homemade spot spray: 1/2 cup ammonia, 1/2 cup white vinegar, 1/4 cup baking soda, 2 tablespoons liquid soap and 10 pints of water.

Better yet, to avoid the ammonia in this mixture, try presoaking in plain water or in soapy wash water. Use the prewash cycle or just switch the machine off after it has filled and leave it for a couple of hours or overnight. Then wash as usual.

Whiteners

Find alternatives to bleach, because it is a dangerous product which should not be used routinely. Water softeners are useful alternatives. Add a couple of tablespoons of sodium hexametaphosphate, sodium sesquicarbonate, or washing soda (sodium carbonate) to particularly grimy loads of washing. With very delicate fabrics, presoak for 10 to 30 minutes in a mixture of 1 part hydrogen peroxide to 7 parts water.

Hanging on a line in the sunshine is good for whitening clothes, and an old method was to spread them on green vegetation—a lawn, for example—the oxygen produced by the plants is said to have a whitening effect.

Boiling sounds prehistoric to anyone who wasn't raised in an era when dishcloths were boiled daily. But as long as you have a large soup pot, it is easy enough and certainly effective. I'm not suggesting that we go back to routinely boiling clothes, but as an occasional treat for white cottons, why not? Allow to cool, drain off most of the water, and spin in your washing machine or spin dryer. (Remember that this will only work with 100 percent cotton or linen—not polyester blends.)

Fabric Conditioners

Conditioners were designed for use with synthetic fabrics, to prevent static cling. If you are using natural fiber fabrics, this shouldn't be a problem. In a hard water area conditioners do seem to make handwashed woollens softer, but a little white vinegar (soak a few dried herbs in it if you want a pleasant fragrance) should do the trick. Running a warm iron over a dry sweater also softens it.

Or mix 1 part bicarbonate of soda, 1 part white or herbal vinegar and 2 parts water. Use it as you would a commercial fabric softener.

People often use softeners to make clothes smell "fresh." Hanging them outside does a far better job, and you don't have to worry about possible allergic reactions. Artificial fragrances do not freshen anything. If you cannot dry outside, how about herbal bags in your drawers and closets?

Ironing

Rather than using spray starch in an aerosol can, with its inherent dangers, why not try one or more of the following ideas:

❑ You can still buy old-fashioned starch, which you mix up with cold water, then add boiling water and stir to a smooth paste. Clothes are dipped and wrung out before ironing.

This is obviously more complicated than using an aerosol spray. But just how many of your clothes really need to be starched? It's fun to give linen napkins and lace collars an occasional stiff starching, but 100 percent cotton and linen have a naturally crisp finish after ironing. It is synthetic fabrics that tend to need perking up with starch.

❏ Mix starch powder (or even ordinary cornstarch) with water in a sprayer. Add a little cologne or a few drops of an essential oil if you want it scented. A rounded tablespoon of starch to a pint of water will give an average hold. Shake before spraying and wipe the nozzle with a damp cloth when you finish—but don't keep it for long or you will have some amazing mold.

❏ Try taking your freshly laundered garments to a drycleaning establishment for pressing only, with their special high-temperature equipment. Many cleaners will do this; call around.

Drycleaning

"Dry" cleaning is done by using a solvent instead of water to wash clothes. The industry has a history of fatal worker illness as a result of the chemicals used. Carbon tetrachloride was used until it was found to cause cancer. The most common solvents at the moment are two organochlorines, trichlorotrifluoroethane and perchloroethylene. They, too, are toxic, and the former is a chlorofluorohydrocarbon, one of the CFCs which are causing the deterioration of the ozone layer. Short-term, acute exposure can cause giddiness, nausea, and unconsciousness. Chronic exposure is even worse because the compounds accumulate in body tissue and lead to organ damage and cancer risk.

Although drycleaning chemicals evaporate after a short time, the environmental consequences of manufacturing, transporting, and disposing of them mean that we should avoid drycleaning as much as possible. We should also consider whether we want to pay for other people to spend their days working with such hazardous chemicals.

Drycleaning machines are common at laundromats, and are considerably cheaper than professional drycleaning. These machines generally use the stronger perchloroethylene, and people have been known to pass out after driving off with still-damp drycleaned clothes in the car. It is essential, should you use one of these machines, that you do not overload it and that the clothes are completely dry when the cycle is finished. If they are not, close the door and call the manager for help.

According to an article in *Mademoiselle* (September 1981), William Seitz, executive director of the Neighborhood Cleaners Association, a national trade association of drycleaners, says "the best possible advice is to be a smart consumer and not to buy clothes that are difficult or even hazardous to clean." Better yet, avoid drycleaning entirely, since drycleaning is hazardous. Most garments can be handwashed. "Dryclean only" labels sometimes mean that the manufacturer does not want to be held responsible for careless washing by the customer.

Wash cotton garments in the machine, and silk and wool by hand (silk in cold water and wool in cool or lukewarm). Use a mild soap, or soft soap made with soap scraps. Add a little vinegar to the rinse water to cut soap film. Sweaters should be squeezed out in a towel then dried flat, and silks should be allowed to drip dry, then ironed while still slightly damp.

If you do have clothes drycleaned—and it's hard to imagine coping with business suits any other way, although steaming may be an alternative—ensure that they are thoroughly aired, outdoors or in an unoccupied room, before being put away.

Stain Removal

Drycleaning fluid, like drycleaning, should be avoided as much as possible. Complicated advice on dealing with stains is lost on most of us modern housekeepers, but a simple range of products should enable you to deal with most domestic crises.

The most important thing to remember is to start with *cold* water, particularly on protein-based spots like blood, egg, or gravy. Hot water will cook and set the stain, and you'll probably never get it out.

❏ The standard trick of pouring salt on a wine stain is usually effective, and is also worth trying on fruit and vegetable stains.
❏ Plain soda water or a bottle of whatever fizzy water you drink, works on many stains.
❏ A borax solution—1 part borax to 8 parts water—is worth

keeping around (out of the reach of children) for treating a wide range of stains. Debra Lynn Dadd suggests it for blood, chocolate, coffee and tea, mildew, mud, and urine. Sponge it on and let it dry, before washing with soap and cold water.

❑ Plain old boiling water is good for fruit and tea stains— preferably poured on taut fabric from a great height. Center the spot over a bowl and stretch it tight with an elastic band, put it in the bathtub, and start pouring.

❑ Rub grass stains with glycerine (from the drugstore) before washing—this works well on football uniforms and is worth trying on cosmetic stains. You may need to follow this with washing soda to remove any oily element in the stain.

❑ Eucalyptus oil will deal with nasties like tar and oil and grass stains. Get it at the drugstore. Rub it in well, then wash as usual. An effective tar remover is lard (or any solid fat), thoroughly rubbed in and then washed out—use some washing soda to cut the grease.

❑ Soak perspiration stains in water with a good dollop of white vinegar or a handful of bicarbonate of soda—try both and see which works for you. This apparently depends on your particular body chemistry.

❑ Try lemon juice and salt on rust stains, then lay them in the sunshine for a couple of days. People used to bleach clothes in this way as they dried over bushes or on the clothesline. It both whitens and deodorizes, and line drying saves energy. Lemon, salt, and sunshine are worth trying on even the most impossible of stains; friends of mine used them for ink marks on a white silk shirt, with great success, and sunshine bleaching is essential for cloth diapers.

Toiletries

Choose a plain, mild soap for general use, with no deodorant and no fragrance, or buy good quality, naturally scented soaps. This sort of soap is expensive, but luxurious. If you store it with your shirts or underwear for a couple of months, the bars will last longer, having dried out, and in the meantime your clothes will smell wonderful.

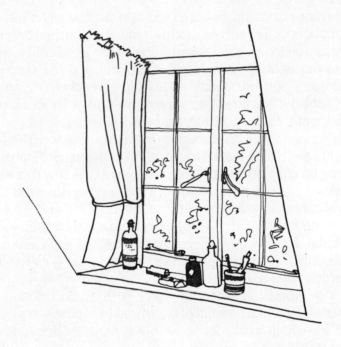

Bath Products

Although I am not especially sensitive, bath salts from the supermarket or drugstore make me itch. You can easily make your own bath mixture.

Here are a few ideas: a couple of handfuls of sea salt, bicarbonate of soda, or Epsom salts for a mineral bath; oatmeal and powdered milk in a muslin bag for a soothing bath; vegetable oil beaten with an egg and some milk for a creamy rich bath (store this mixture in the refrigerator). Add your preferred scent to any of these. Or try a therapeutic bath with dried seaweed.

Body Powder

Talc can be contaminated with asbestos fiber, and some people are allergic to the fragrances used. Ordinary cornstarch is soft and absorbent. There are commercial powders made from a variety of natural ingredients (I've seen one containing silk powder). Check *Nontoxic, Natural and Earthwise* for recommendations, or look in your natural foods store.

Antiperspirants and Deodorants

Antiperspirants frequently contain as their active ingredient aluminum chlorhydrate, which blocks your pores and prevents perspiration, and can contain other heavy metals. Deodorants use bactericide and fragrance, but do not actually stop perspiration. Both can irritate delicate skin, and antiperspirants can cause severe and painful rashes. Blocking sweat glands is a bad idea anyway, and concern over the biological effects of aluminum suggest that aluminum salts should not be applied to the skin on a regular basis.

As long as you wash frequently enough with soap and water these strong chemicals should not be necessary, and there are very effective alternatives—giving up your antiperspirant is not the antisocial step you might imagine. Try one or more of the following:

❑ That old standby, bicarbonate of soda, can be patted on with a piece of cotton. Apply after your bath or shower, while skin is still slightly damp. Even heavy perspirers find this effective, and the packaging couldn't be simpler.

❑ Some people can get away with just a little essential oil— rose or sandalwood or whatever you like—mixed with a little vegetable oil or body lotion and rubbed under the arms after bathing.

❑ Nontoxic commercial products by Weleda (lemon juice base) and Tom's of Maine (with coriander as its active ingredient) do the job and are very pleasant to use.

Toothpaste and Mouthwash

Excellent natural varieties, available at wholefood shops, will not contain ammonia, ethanol, artificial flavors and colors, formaldehyde, mineral oil, saccharin, sugar, or carcinogenic PVP plastic, as commercial brands may. You can also brush your teeth with bicarbonate of soda, perhaps mixed with a few drops of peppermint oil. This has been shown to help prevent the buildup of plaque.

You may or may not want your child to have fluoride. If you do, rather than haphazard intake from toothpaste, why not give fluoride drops or tablets? Some children make a habit of eating toothpaste, which is not a good idea.

Mouthwashes contain some of the same germ killers which go into bathroom disinfectants, and a persistent problem with bad breath is likely to be a sign of other health or dental problems. Good oral hygiene—frequent brushing and using dental floss—and a healthy diet low in sugary food will do more for your teeth and breath than any number of cleaning products.

Shampoo

Shampoos contain a variety of additives that cause problems for some people and add to the chemical burden we live with. Products you use to fight dandruff may in fact aggravate the problem.

Anti-dandruff shampoos contain toxic chemicals, primarily selenium sulfide, which can, if swallowed, cause the degeneration of internal organs. Not a nice thing to use on your body regularly. Another dangerous chemical is recorcinol, which is easily absorbed through the skin. Many people who think they have dandruff do not, but once you start using an anti-dandruff shampoo, it can be very difficult to stop.

If you have a dandruff problem, the first things to look at are your diet and general health. Thorough brushing and regular scalp massage are preferable to chemical shampoos. Dandruff is sometimes stress-related, another possibility to consider.

Debra Lynn Dadd recommends a method which she promises will clear up dandruff forever: instead of shampooing, massage handfuls of bicarbonate of soda into your hair and scalp, then rinse thoroughly. Do not use anything else. Your hair may look like a haystack at first, but apparently the treatment works after a couple of weeks—dandruff gone and hair in good condition. You then alternate the soda treatment with a natural shampoo.

Hairspray

Hairsprays contain toxic polyvinylpyrrolidone (PVP) plastic resin and propellant gases. When these are finely dispersed, as they are in an aerosol, they can cause a lung disease called thesaurosis—which is, fortunately, reversible. They don't do much for your skin and eyes either. Instead, try using a safe commercial gel, or make your own:

LEMON HAIRSPRAY

This gives good hold, shine, and body—and it smells nice. Try it. Slice or chop two lemons and put them in a saucepan with two teacups of water. Simmer until the lemons have become very soft. Cool and strain through a piece of cheesecloth or fine sieve. Put the mixture in a spray bottle and store it in the fridge, or add a tablespoon of vodka to preserve it at room temperature. Dilute it with water to suit your hair. If it seems sticky, add a little more water.

Other ideas include a mixture of honey and water—experiment with proportions; a gel made from ordinary gelatin powder (try 1 teaspoon gelatin to 1/2 pint water); or vegetarian alginic gel, available from wholefood shops.

Hair Coloring

Laboratory tests have shown hair dyes to be mutagens and suspected human carcinogens. These chemicals can easily penetrate the scalp, and an independent consumer research laboratory advises against their use by pregnant women or women of childbearing age. This is a good example of casually used products that have potentially damaging effects. Fortunately there are a variety of safe plant-based products around.

You can also try homemade mixtures, ranging from lemon juice and chamomile for blond hair to black coffee or walnut hulls to cover grey in dark hair.

If you must use chemical dyes, try to avoid contact with your scalp—hair painting and foil-wrap highlighting can be done in a salon.

Nail Polish

Acetone solvent not only has a strong and pervasive odor, but also can cause skin rashes, dry out nails, and dissolve plastics. Nail polishes are based on formaldehyde resin and any beauty book will tell you that nails need to be left unpolished from time to time to allow them to breathe.

Nail buffing kits will give you an attractive natural shine with no chemicals to worry about. If you use polish, ensure that the room you are in is well ventilated—better yet, sit outside until the nails are thoroughly dry.

Nail hardeners are also made from formaldehyde. A general improvement in diet will do more for your nails and your health.

Cosmetics

More and more cosmetic houses are becoming aware of skin sensitivities, and are cutting out irritating ingredients, particularly scents. Some ingredients in lipsticks have been shown to cause cancer in animals (PVP plastic, saccharin, mineral oil, and artificial colors).

Choose unscented products and avoid artificial fragrances and colors. Many are available in natural food stores. You'll want to avoid cosmetics and toiletries that have been tested on animals. Many companies are now responding to consumer concern about this, most notably the Body Shop.

Overpackaging is a problem with most cosmetics. The amount you buy is small, the price large, and the elegant plastic compact makes the exchange seem less unreasonable. A few firms sell refills, but on the whole there is little you can do except buy the largest size possible. Write to the head office of your favorite firm about this.

Home Building and Maintenance

Building materials

Asbestos is a well publicized danger, but asphalt, plastics, and even particle board also pose a threat to human health.

You have little choice about the materials of which your house is built, but when making any additions you could consult one of the books listed below. New homes are likely to have large amounts of plastic and pressed woods (bound with urea-formaldehyde resin) which it would be both difficult and expensive to replace. This is another incentive for improving old housing stock whenever possible.

Formaldehyde is particularly hazardous because it seems to act as a trigger for acute chemical sensitivity. After exposure to high levels of formaldehyde—after installation of new particle board cupboards, for example—quite a number of people have become chemical cripples, unable to tolerate even small quantities of the many other man-made chemicals that surround us.

In general, sticking with natural and biodegradable materials is the safest course of action (though of course some natural materials are hazardous too: lead and asbestos for example).

Decorating

Paints, varnishes, and the various solvents we use to mix them and to clean up afterwards can be dangerous, and also present disposal problems.

Good ventilation is the first thing to consider when using any product containing solvents. Plenty of fresh air will dry paint more effectively than heating the room.

Special paint techniques have become popular, and there is now growing interest in making one's own paints as they have more varied finishes and subtle colors than commercial paints. Ingredients include sizing, whiting, and artists' pigments.

A fascinating range of West German natural and nontoxic decorating products is available by mail order. Check the *Earthwise Consumer* (see Sources, Chapter 3).

Miscellaneous

Plastics

In Chapter 3 we looked at the ecological problem posed by our excessive use of plastics. Plastics also pose a problem for human health. Many are suspected human carcinogens.

PVC (polyvinyl chloride) plastic is extremely common, used for everything from tablecloths to shoe soles, credit cards to squeezy toys. It contains vinyl chloride, which is recognized as causing cancer, birth defects, skin diseases, and liver dysfunction as well as many other health problems. It is relatively unstable, especially if it contains added plasticizers, and small quantities of vinyl chloride monomer (a gas) are given off. NASA has banned the use of PVC in its space capsules because it outgassed and condensed in optical equipment.

The list of proven and suspected health effects of different sorts of plastic is a long one. Although none of us can avoid plastics entirely, we can reduce the amounts in our immediate home environment. Stephanie Winston, author of *The Organized Executive,* says: "I've made a fairly serious effort to get along with a minimum of plastics and synthetics. This is not so much for philosophical reasons as that I feel better when there's not too much synthetic stuff floating around."

PLASTICS CHECKLIST

❑ Choose alternatives to plastic whenever possible.
❑ Let new plastic items (such as a shower curtain) air outside or in an unused room until any noticeable smell has disappeared.
❑ Avoid food coming into direct contact with plastics, particularly soft plastics. Buy food packed in glass, paper, or natural cellophane in preference to plastic.
❑ Do not drink hot drinks from polystyrene cups.
❑ Use plasticizer-free food wrapping.

Paper Products

Although a few people react to the dyes and fragrances in commercial toilet paper, all of us need to be aware that all bleached paper—white toilet paper, kitchen towels, facial tissues, coffee filters, and so on—has been found to contain traces of the highly toxic chemical dioxin. This is the result of standard pulping and bleaching operations, and because the chemicals are also released in large quantities into lakes and rivers, paper mills are one of the most polluting of industries (see Chapter 3).

Fabrics and Furnishings

Attention has been focused on urea-formaldehyde cavity insulation as a source of formaldehyde in the home, but the resins used to bind plywood, chipboard, and furniture are also significant sources of this vapor. A 1979 study at the Lawrence Berkeley National Laboratory found that the concentration of formaldehyde vapor in the air tripled once furniture was installed in an otherwise empty house (*New Scientist,* December 5, 1985).

Clothing and furnishing fabrics receive a variety of chemical treatments. Even natural fabrics can be loaded with dyes and chemical residues. Permanent press fabrics are treated with formaldehyde resin (a well-known allergen), as well as with other chemicals. Choose natural fibers—cotton, wool, linen, and silk—in preference to synthetics, and beware of any special fabric treatments. It's a good idea to wash new clothes before you wear them.

Futons provide excellent bedding for sensitive individuals, and latex foam is a possible choice for pillows and cushions.

According to Peter Mansfield and Jean Monro (*Chemical Children*), cheap expanded polyester furniture stuffing can release irritant vapors for a considerable time. They suggest that you choose feathers or horsehair, and say that if you are allergic to these, you can probably be desensitized. The slow accumulation of volatile chemicals interferes with detoxification mechanisms and can lead to other health problems.

Wool carpets are sometimes treated with mothproofing and soil repellants. If anyone in your household is chemically sensitive, new rugs or carpets should be steam cleaned with plain water immediately after installation.

Office Supplies

Watch out for office products that contain toxic solvents. In general, you can tell by sniffing: try to stick to items that are odor-free.

Car Maintenance

If you are the sort of mechanic who takes the carburetor to bits and cleans it in a bowl of gasoline, please take care about breathing the fumes, which contain toxic benzene. A few service stations offer engine steamcleaning equipment, which not only saves many hours of labor but does a terrific job.

A world shortage of ethylene glycol has led to a drastic increase in the price of conventional antifreeze. As a result, antifreeze based on the nontoxic propylene glycol is now cheaper than the normal type. The nontoxic product was previously more expensive, and was used only where it could come into contact with food or water.

Proposition 65

In 1986 the voters of California approved a nontoxics initiative which came into force early in 1988. A $6 million campaign against Proposition 65 was sponsored by vulnerable business interests, and they were able to get the original list of notifiable chemicals reduced to a mere 29. Nonetheless, this initiative represents an important victory for the environmental lobby.

It is now illegal for businesses knowingly to dump chemicals that cause cancer, sterility, or birth defects, and individual citizens can more easily sue violators. The listed chemicals will eventually include the approximately 200 known carcinogens identified by the National Toxicology Program.

Unfortunately, warning labels are not required on all products containing known toxins; instead, consumers have to telephone a free hotline to ask about particular items—not very useful when you are out shopping. But warning signs will be posted in shops, restaurants, and workplaces, reading something like this: "Chemicals known to the State of California to cause cancer, birth defects, or other reproductive harm may be present in foods or beverages sold or served here." Or "Caution: You will be exposed to carcinogenic substances."

As more people become aware of the danger chemicals pose to our health and to our environment, legislation like this will become the rule rather than the exception. The idea is not to spoil our fun but instead to increase consumer awareness of the chemical dangers around us, and to enable us to protect ourselves and our children. In addition, there will be a considerable incentive for businesses to clean up their products.

Safety

We all use hazardous products on occasion. Take a close look at warning labels. Here is one from a can of aerosol auto adhesive: "Contains: methylene chloride, hydrocarbon propellant. Highly flammable. Harmful by inhalation. *Possible risk of irreversible effects* [my italics] from vapors or spray. May cause eye irritation." This product could even give off carbonyl chloride, an infamous war gas, if burnt. Frankly, after reading the label I wouldn't dream of using the stuff.

Here are some precautions to take:

❏ Buy only what you need.
❏ Read warning labels and follow directions. The information on labels is often sparse. Err on the side of caution.
❏ Don't use more than the directions call for, and you might even start with a bit less.
❏ Close containers tightly.
❏ Work outside if possible, and try not to breathe fumes— take ventilation seriously. Or wear a thick sweater and keep the windows open.
❏ Do not mix chemicals.
❏ Wear protective clothing and a mask if necessary, and protect your hands with rubber gloves.
❏ Avoid wearing soft contact lenses while working with any solvent.
❏ Clean up carefully, both yourself and your work area.
❏ Store products in the original containers; don't leave any in an unlabeled jam jar, for example.
❏ Try to use up what you've bought. Dispose of any leftovers through a hazardous waste program, should your town have one, or carefully sealed and wrapped in the garbage can—not down the drain!
❏ Keep dangerous chemicals well out of children's reach.

Sources

Books

Cheaper and Better: Homemade Alternatives to Storebought Goods, Nancy Birnes (New York, Harper & Row, 1988).

Chemical Children: How to Protect Your Family from Harmful Pollutants, Peter Mansfield and Jean Monro (New York, David & Charles, 1988). Distributed by Sterling Publishing Co.

Clean and Green: The Complete Guide to Nontoxic and Environmentally Safe Household Cleaning, Annie Berthold-Bon (Woodstock, NY, Ceres Press, 1990). A collection of some 600 recipes for easy-to-make cleaning products, along with a guide to commercial cleaners.

Everyday Chemicals: A Windstar/Earth Pulse Handbook, Beth Richman and Susan Hassol (Snowmass, CO, Windstar Foundation, 1989).

I Hate to Housekeep Book, Peg Bracken (London, Arlington Books, 1963).

Is There Life After Housework? Don Aslett (Cincinnati, OH, Writer's Digest Books, 1985).

The Nontoxic Home: Protecting Yourself and Your Family from Everyday Toxics and Health Hazards, Debra Lynn Dadd (New York, Jeremy Tarcher, 1986). Distributed by St. Martin's Press.

Your Home, Your Health and Well Being, David Rousseau et al. (Berkeley, Ten Speed Press, 1988).

Catalogs

Allens Cruelty Free Naturally, P.O. Box 514, Farmington, MI 48332. (313) 453-5410.

The Body Shop, 1341 7th St., Berkeley, CA 94710. (415) 524-0360.

The Ecology Box, 425 East Washington #200, Ann Arbor, MI 48104. (800) 735-1371.

L.L. Bean, Casco St., Freeport, ME 04033. (800) 221-4221

Livos Plantchemistry, 614 Agua Fria St., Sante Fe, NM 87501. (505) 988-9111.

Organizations

National Anti-vivisection Society, 100 East Ohio Street, Chicago, IL 60611. (312) 787-4486. Publish *Personal Care With Principle*, a guide to personal care and household cleaning products.

PETA (People for the Ethical Treatment of Animals), Box 42516, Washington, DC 20015. List of companies that manufacture cruelty-free products.

11
RADIATION

Not that I wish in any way to belittle the evils of conventional air and water pollution; but we must recognize "dimensional differences" when we encounter them: radioactive pollution is an evil of an incomparably greater "dimension" than anything mankind has known before. One might even ask: what is the point of insisting on clean air, if the air is laden with radioactive particles? And even if the air could be protected, what is the point of it, if soil and water are being poisoned?
—E. F. Schumacher, *Small Is Beautiful*

Introduction

After the Chernobyl disaster in 1986, people living in Europe, myself included, were suddenly conscious of the peculiarly frightening nature of radiation. We wondered whether it was safe to go outdoors or to drink the innocent-looking milk from the bottles delivered to our doorstep, and whether we could trust the government experts who sallied forth on every news bulletin to reassure us that all was well. There are many nuclear power stations much closer to home, but Chernobyl made it abundantly clear that distance provides no safeguard.

Welsh, Cumbrian, and Scottish sheep farmers suffered from both loss of income and fears for their own families' health. Two years after the accident many sheep were not being passed as fit for human consumption and it is estimated that several thousand Britons will eventually get cancer as a result of the radiation released from Chernobyl. As with almost all deaths resulting from radioactive contamination of the environment, these victims will be anonymous.

Why is radiation so unnerving? Like cancer, which it can cause, it seems mysterious and uncontrollable. Literary critic Susan Sontag has suggested that the solution to the demoralizing effect of cancer is to de-mythologize it. Just as most of us are trying to familiarize ourselves with computers, we need to gain some understanding of the technical aspects of environmental issues: what radiation is, where it comes from, and what its effects are. Only then can we make choices about the increasing levels of radiation in our environment and about military and industrial uses of radioactive material.

We are, however, at a disadvantage in an increasingly technological world. I used to think that the scientific community wanted to frighten us, but finally realized that most of the time scientists are attempting to reassure us that things are not dangerous. We need to keep in mind that most scientific research is paid for by government and industry. Debate over the hole in the ozone layer has shown how disastrous scientific principles can be when applied to environmental problems. Scientists err on the side of caution, waiting until there is conclusive evidence of damage. By that time, it may be too late to save an ecosystem or an animal species.

Instead, we need to apply precautionary principles—when damage is seen and there is a suspected link with human activity, that activity should be on trial. It should have to be proved safe before being used again.

Many modern dangers are difficult for the ordinary person to understand. Thomas Kuhn, Harvard scientist and philosopher, has pointed out that one of the characteristics of modern scientific research is that it is no longer "embodied in books addressed, such as Franklin's *Experiments . . . on Electricity* or Darwin's *Origin of the Species*, to anyone who might be interested. . . . Instead, [it] will appear as brief articles addressed only to professional colleagues." (*The Structure of Scientific Revolutions*, University of Chicago Press, 1970). Turning this situation around is one of the biggest challenges facing us in the late 20th century.

Psychologist Paul Slovic has attempted to measure public perception of a wide variety of risks in "The Axis of Fear" (*Harper's*, May 1988). Three of the five greatest perceived risks were connected with radiation: radioactive waste, nuclear reactor accidents, and nuclear weapons fallout. Also in the top five was DNA technology (genetic engineering), and in that field, too, the issue of who controls science and the scientists is increasingly important.

We cannot sense—see, touch, or feel—low level radiation, as we can sense some other modern hazards. If your family starts to itch when they put on clothes washed in an enzyme detergent, you switch to not using it without needing any technical information at all—whereas you might eventually die from a cancer caused by radiation you were never aware of having been exposed to.

Determining the effects of various sorts of radiation is highly contentious. For every figure that one expert presents, another is thrown down to counter it. Statistics can tell us whether the rate of a particular disease in a given area is higher than average, but gives no clue as to causes. Besides this, results can be dramatically altered by simple adjustments in the boundary lines for a statistical survey.

The question of whom we can trust for information about radiation is a difficult one. Many residents around Three Mile Island (TMI) in Pennsylvania complained of a metallic taste in their mouths after the accident there in 1979. TMI authorities contend that this is impossible because the symptom only occurs when millions of curies of radioactive isotopes of iodine are present, and emissions had been no more than 14 curies. Just how much radiation escaped is rather difficult to determine because the Metropolitan Edison Company (Met Ed), owner-operator of TMI, insists that records of airborne emissions for the first two days after the accident are missing.

Nonetheless, thousands of residents have suffered as a result of the accident, and some 2,000 are suing Met Ed. Many have had malignant tumors removed, and have suffered still-births, spontaneous abortions, heart failure, stroke, or hypothyroidism. Cancers are rife, somewhat sooner than would be expected after a nuclear accident, and some researchers suspect that previous routine ventings from the plant may have set the stage for even more devastating medical damage delivered by the Unit Two disaster. Dr. George Tokuhata, Chief of the Pennsylvania Epidemiology Division, is quoted as saying: "In the long run, it seems, people are the most reliable dosimeters" ("The Disaster at Three Mile Island Is Not Over," Harvey Wasserman, *Harrowsmith*, Charlotte, VT, May/June 1987) .

Ionizing Radiation

Radiation is a form of energy and is emitted as streams of particles or in waves of vibrating electromagnetic energy. When the particles or vibrating energy strike matter, they set up corresponding vibrations which can be strong enough to disintegrate or permanently alter the matter. What makes radiation so important is that it does not simply kill individual cells, but can alter DNA molecules and change the way cells reproduce.

Ionizing radiation consists of alpha or beta particles, gamma rays, X-rays, and part of the ultraviolet light spectrum. Radiation hazards and radiation discharges result from the decay of unstable atoms, some occurring naturally and some artificially produced in, for example, a nuclear reactor.

When cells are affected by ionizing radiation, they generally die or fail to reproduce (radiation is of course also used to kill cancerous cells), and a healthy body can destroy sick cells. Some damaged cells may, however, reproduce abnormally, resulting in cancerous growth, and the damage can cause miscarriage or be transmitted as a genetic mutation.

Health Effects

We are all exposed to artificial radiation, at home and at work, because there are many sources of ionizing radiation in our environment. As you read through the rest of this chapter, try to get an idea of the sources of exposure in your life and consider ways to reduce the total. For example, people exposed to radiation in the course of their work should try to reduce occupational exposure while taking special care to cut down on exposure from other sources.

In general, we only think of severe genetic defects and cancer deaths as the consequences of increased radiation in our environment, and the odds against these affecting any particular person are perhaps greater than those against dying in an automobile accident. Rosalie Bertell explains in her excellent book *No Immediate Danger* that risk/benefit decision-making balances health effects for you and me against "economic and social benefit"—often for a particular industry or for national defense. These decisions require value judgements that ignore long-term collective damage and often take no account of public opinion. In fact, the public has so little information to go on that most of us would be unable to make a reasoned decision.

Bertell claims that the "early occurrence of heart disease, diabetes mellitus, arthritis, asthma or severe allergies" are part of the "subtle widespread degradation of public health" which is never mentioned in official information about health risks from radiation.

Radiation is more hazardous to children than to adults, and most hazardous of all to unborn children, because body cells are dividing so rapidly—and because there is ultimately longer for cancer to develop. Although women are thought to be up to 2.5 times more vulnerable to radiation than men, genetic disorders can be passed on from either parent. Mild mutations can show themselves as allergies, asthma, hypertension, slight muscular or bone defects which, says Rosalie Bertell, leave the individual slightly less able to cope with ordinary stresses and hazards in the environment. These genetic mistakes are passed on from one generation to the next, made worse by increases in other hazardous elements of our modern environment, such as toxic chemicals.

The effects of cumulative, low-level radiation are hard to judge because it may be 40 years or more before we see the full effects of today's dose of radiation, and it is impossible to separate it clearly from other environmental influences on our health over that period of time. But do you want to be used as a guinea pig?

Safety Levels

Any industry that has acknowledged environmental consequences and poses a risk to human health will talk of "acceptable levels" and "acceptable risk." Unfortunately, researchers do not agree about acceptable risks. Estimating risk is difficult, and controversial. The authors of *Well Body, Well Earth* use three major sources of data on radiation, each of which estimates the number of excess cancers caused by one rad of radiation. Because each study uses different criteria and takes different variables into account, comparable estimates range from 100 to 3,771 per million. To some extent, each one is a value judgment.

Dervla Murphy makes the apt point that "this civil war is being fought almost entirely with statistics, a weapon distrusted by every sensible person. And, since no non-expert can assess the reputations of scientists, we must instead assess their motives." She observes that in almost every case anti-nuclear scientists "started out happily associated with the nuclear industry, then were turned against it by what statistics seemed to reveal. Most of them have sacrificed secure careers to their principles" (*Race to the Finish? The Nuclear Stakes*).

There are no cumulative records on public radiation exposure from nuclear testing and the nuclear industry, which makes it virtually impossible to get a clear picture of the consequences of our defense and energy choices over the past 40 or 50 years. Nonetheless, worker studies show that standards have been set for toxic substances for which there are no safe levels—there is no safe level of exposure to ionizing radiation (an obvious fact, apparently, to anyone involved in the controversy, but I always thought that a little radiation was just fine).

Risk estimates are based on cancer deaths, although this is not entirely satisfactory. Any cancer—even if completely cur able—would have important effects on your life in terms of stress, finance, relationships, and career.

The permissible radiation doses for both the public and workers were set in 1957 by the International Commission on Radiological Protection (ICRP), an organization that has strong links with nuclear industry—and which, by the way, has never appointed a female member. The standards were based on then current research into the effects of the atomic bombs dropped on Japan in 1945, and although recent research has shown that these effects were greatly underestimated, the levels have not been changed, in spite of international pressure on the ICRP.

Sources Of Ionizing Radiation

The nuclear industry is potentially the most dangerous source of artificial radiation, but a variety of other sources also pose a danger to our health. You may not be able to shut down a nearby nuclear power plant, but you can cut your exposure to radiation by making changes in the way you live. Increased awareness of the dangers of domestic radiation will lead to a more determined attitude the next time you buy a house or go to the dentist—as well as the next time you vote.

Background Radiation and Radon

Light, radium, radon, uranium, and potassium-40 in the earth are natural sources of ionizing radiation. Living at high elevation or traveling in an airplane exposes people to radiation from cosmic rays. These have always been part of the environment human beings have lived in, but the term "background" radiation is not quite as straightforward as we are led to believe. It includes naturally-occurring radiation, but also covers fallout from nuclear weapons testing over the past half-century, and artificial radiation from fission products after they have been in the environment for a year. This is an extraordinary state of affairs—do we consider extremely persistent and dangerous chemicals like PCBs part of the natural composition of sea water simply because they have been there for some time? Background radiation levels have steadily risen over the past 50 years, giving a deceptive turn to any statistics on radiation from the nuclear industry.

The form in which natural radiation affects us at home is as radon, a colorless and odorless gas given off by the radioactive decay of elements in the earth. The degree to which radon is a hazard depends a great deal on where you live and on what your home is built of. In well-insulated, poorly ventilated buildings, radiation has been known to reach a level that is twice the legal limit set for nuclear power workers, and one report suggests that 20 percent of U.S. homes are affected by radon.

Government agencies seem happier to talk about the dangers of radon than about other radiation hazards, because it can be treated as separate from the nuclear industry. However, some of the radioactive products that produce radon have been removed from their relatively harmless natural state—by being blasted out of the ground with dynamite or leached with acids, and pulverized into very small particles (*No Immediate Danger*, Bertell) in order to provide material for nuclear power stations or atomic weapons, and are hardly what most of us would call "natural" radiation.

According to one estimate, there are about six billion tons of accumulated uranium mine and mill tailings throughout the world—which meant that a new term had to be found, "technologically enhanced natural radiation" (TENR)—which is now the major source of "individual internal radiation exposure in the USA . . . [and] ranks a close third, after medical and radio-pharmaceutical exposures, as a source of general population dose" (*No Immediate Danger*, Bertell).

Radon is the usual cause of lung cancer in nonsmokers and a 1988 public health warning compared the radon levels in many homes to smoking a half pack of cigarettes a day. (Polonium-210, an alpha emitter like radon and its daughter products, is also found in tobacco smoke.) Glass, ceramics, bricks, cement, natural gas, phosphate fertilizers, gypsum board, and even deep well water can release small quantities of radon, depending on where they come from. As radon problems increase, more care will have to be taken with the materials used in building, as well as with where we build and how homes are ventilated and insulated.

RADON CHECKLIST

The most important step is to prevent radon from entering the house through the floor. General rules for homes with high radon levels are:

❑ Floors and walls should be sealed with caulking and cement.
❑ Good ventilation is crucial, especially on the ground floor.
❑ Basements can be separately ventilated with a small exhaust fan and stairs can be sealed with a weatherstripped door.
❑ Radon testing devices can be obtained at your local hardware store.

Medical Radiation

Medical diagnosis by X-ray is the largest source of artificial radiation that affects humans. On average we receive higher organ doses from medical procedures (which include X-rays, radiation treatment, and radioactive drugs) than from any other source except rare industrial accidents.

In spite of these facts, many people have no idea that they could be adversely affected by X-ray treatment. Only pregnant women are advised to avoid unnecessary X-rays (in the past, these were used for routine monitoring during pregnancy). If it is unsafe to X-ray fetuses, what about X-raying the ovaries, which contain the eggs which will produce future offspring? And if we don't know, shouldn't we be erring on the side of caution?

Of course the benefits of X-rays frequently outweigh the risks involved. If your leg has been shattered in an accident, you are unlikely to quibble about the X-rays needed to make a decision about how to set it. The important point about this, however, is that even when an X-ray is essential, the doses given by different equipment, in different hospitals, can vary by as much as a factor of 100.

Dental X-rays are another source of radiation exposure. Some recommendations are for routine dental X-rays no more often than every 5 to 10 years. A full mouth X-ray can be the equivalent of 18 partial shots, and is something to be particularly wary of.

My conscientious dentist wanted to take routine X-rays after two years, although I have not had a new filling in 15 years, because there is a slight risk that decay could start under a metal amalgam filling, where he would be unable to see it. You may decide, as I did, that decay is the lesser of two risks—with white bonded fillings, which do not contain mercury, this problem should not arise.

X-RAY CHECKLIST

❏ Avoid precautionary and routine medical and dental X-rays.

❏ Discuss alternative diagnosis methods with your practitioner. If a doctor suggests high radiation X-rays, insist on discussing the situation to your complete satisfaction before going ahead. Be a pain—it's your DNA.

❏ Women in childbearing years should have X-rays only in the 10 days following menstruation. This is the so-called "ten-day rule," officially abandoned but still recommended by some experts. I'd rather play it safe.

❏ No X-rays during pregnancy or while trying to conceive, unless absolutely unavoidable.

❏ No X-rays for children unless in a genuine medical emergency.

❏ Insist that X-ray films are transferred with you if you are referred to another doctor.

❏ Tell your doctor that you want to limit X-rays to a minimum, and ask for an explanation and dose estimate before agreeing to any X-ray treatment.

❏ Do not agree to "defensive" X-rays (a growing problem because of doctors' fears of litigation).

❏ Ask the radiologist what dose you are getting, and do not accept "very low" as an answer! Keep a record of the number of X-rays you have received.

❏ Ensure that you are wearing a protective lead shield over your body, especially over sex organs, any time you are X-rayed, even at the dentist.

❏ If possible, choose a radiologist or hospital with efficient, modern equipment, which can achieve the same results with far lower X-ray doses.

Consumer Products

The nuclear industry provides a cheap source of Americium-241, an ionizing radiation source that is used in smoke detectors. What could look more innocuous than that white plastic disc on the ceiling? They are sold without any sort of warning on the package or on the detector, but there is an increase in radiation around them for several inches. One wonders about possible effects on store staff who spend days and weeks working next to a stack of smoke detectors displayed at gonad height.

Optical smoke detectors work for smoldering fires, but the common ionization chamber model is required for the flash fires which have become a hazard with the advent of highly combustible foam materials in furniture. The ionizing material is not well protected, and a child could pry the detector apart.

While the amount of radiation given off by a luminous watch dial or a set of false teeth is generally small, the cumulative amount is substantial because there are so many potential sources. As Mike Samuels and Hal Zina Bennett write: "We must look not at the amount of radiation emitted by single consumer products, each one of which is safe by itself, but at those amounts multiplied by the number of similar products being produced.... If the lifetime of a radioactive element is 20 or 30 years, the accumulation of such items could present a significant health hazard" (*Well Body, Well Earth*).

WHAT TO DO

❑ If you use a smoke detector, treat it with caution. Don't leave it lying around where a child could get hold of it, and don't carry it in a pocket.
❑ Take old smoke detectors to a hazardous waste collection point.
❑ You may want to avoid fluorescent materials, luminous dials and so on—or at least keep them at a distance from your body and well away from children.

The Nuclear Industry

The nuclear threat makes other environmental problems look inconsequential by comparison, and has had an insidious effect on many people's attitudes toward the environment over the past few decades. Although it seemed that global destruction might be imminent, it was difficult to get people worked up about a few polluted lakes. Why shouldn't we, in the words of Isaiah, "eat and drink, for to morrow we shall die"?

The events of 1989, however, lessened the threat of nuclear war, and the environment is one of the beneficiaries of a new optimism about the future. Reducing present stocks of weapons may take some time, and we still need to take note of the ways in which nuclear fuel and weaponry endanger human beings: through mining and manufacture, reactor operation, fuel reprocessing, plutonium storage and waste, and fallout from nuclear testing. Indigenous populations, in particular, have suffered from uranium mining in the United States, Canada, Australia, and Africa, and from weapons testing, particularly in the South Pacific.

The problem and eventual cost of nuclear waste storage should not be underestimated. There is a misleading linguistic ploy being used, contrasting deep sea "disposal" with other forms of "storage." The fact is that the sole option with nuclear waste *is* storage, and only the location and methods vary. It is incredible that nuclear power has been allowed to expand for decades, while the experts tried halfheartedly to figure out a way of dealing with the inevitable and highly dangerous waste products. In *Small Is Beautiful*, E. F. Schumacher quotes a British government report, *Pollution: Nuisance or Nemesis?* (HMSO, 1972): "We are consciously and deliberately accumulating a toxic substance on the offchance that it may be possible to get rid of it at a later date. We are committing future generations to tackle a problem which we do not know how to handle."

Although we have been told for years that nuclear power is our only hope for the future, public resistance has been growing, and economic pressures—including the largely unknown, but potentially astronomic, costs of decommissioning power stations—are making it look less and less likely to expand. The industry's continuing insistence that all is well—in spite of the evidence—is beginning to look thoroughly naive.

Getting to grips with the issues involved is not easy, but I've found that I feel less rather than more anxious as a result of more knowledge—not because the facts are reassuring, but because the subject no longer seems so alien.

If you have always thought of yourself as a pragmatist who supports nuclear energy because it is the only way forward (seeing anti-nukes as woolly hatted and woolly minded folk who wouldn't know a neutron from a narwhal), please look at *Race to the Finish? The Nuclear Stakes* by Dervla Murphy, or *Small Is Beautiful* by E. F. Schumacher (see Sources).

Food Irradiation

Early research into food irradiation took place as part of the Atoms for Peace program, and the technique was developed by the U.S. Army, not by the food industry; the preferred isotopes that are used to irradiate food are products of nuclear reactors. Irradiation has been aptly described as a technology looking for a use.

Although irradiation is billed as good for the consumer, it patently is not. The beneficiaries would be the irradiation industry itself, the nuclear industry, and certain parts of the food industry. Irradiation would make it possible for manufacturers to sell lower quality food which would last longer in commercial storage or on the supermarket shelf, and still appear fresh and wholesome. Contaminated and spoiled food can be sterilized, and some forms of contamination can even be disguised through the use of irradiation.

Rather than eliminating the need for additives in food, irradiation would require a new range of additives to deal with the effects of irradiation. For example, polyphosphates would be necessary to reduce the bleeding of meats and antioxidants to offset the rancid flavors that can develop after irradiation.

One industry claim has been that the technique would cut down on food poisoning, but as Tony Webb and Tim Lang point out in their *Food Irradiation: The Facts*, if chicken is irradiated to kill dangerous salmonella bacteria—an increasingly common cause of food poisoning, thought to be connected with unhealthy and unsanitary conditions in which battery chickens are raised—the technique would also kill organisms that are natural competitors of botulinum (a bacterium that causes a lethal form of food poisoning), as well as the organisms that would naturally cause the putrid odor that signal that something is not safe to eat, but would not destroy the deadly botulinus toxin!

Irradiated food is not itself radioactive, but employees in irradiation plants are exposed to the same health risks as other radiation workers. We need to ask whether we would want to buy products that carry this cost in risk to human health. Irradiation plants add to radioactive emissions into the environment and to the radioactive waste transported on U.S. roads.

WHAT TO DO

❏ The industry has come up with some amusing irradiation symbols, incorporating stylized leaves and flowers to suggest freshness and innocence. Don't be misled—read the label and don't buy food that has been irradiated.

❏ Tell your supermarket manager that you don't want irradiated foods and would prefer that the store not stock these.

Non-ionizing Radiation

Unlike nuclear or ionizing radiation, which consists of either particles or waves and which can knock the electrons off other atoms (causing molecules to become ionized), non-ionizing radiation consists only of energy waves and acts on matter by transferring energy, usually in the form of heat.

We are surrounded by electrical appliances which have potentially serious effects on our well-being. Think of the electrical equipment in your home, the power cables above our heads or running underground along our streets, as well as the television and radio broadcasting networks which have become an essential part of our lives. Until recently it has generally been claimed that non-ionizing radiation is completely benign and could not possibly affect or harm human beings unless it actually heated tissue, but this is now disputed by many researchers. Paul Brodeur's *Currents of Death* (see Sources) has exposed the complacency with which this hazard has been handled.

Microwaves, TV, and Radar

Although most of us have a vague notion that leaking microwave ovens are a risky business and that we shouldn't sit too near the TV, the real dangers of these forms of radiation are largely uncertain. Paul Brodeur's earlier book, *The Zapping of America*, detailed the ways in which military and industrial interests have prevented biologists from fully researching the effects of microwaves and radar, in the West at least. The military depends on unrestricted use of microwave radar for surveillance, and the whole system depends on the assumption that there are no biological effects.

The Soviet authorities bombarded the U.S. Embassy in Moscow with microwave radiation from the late 1950s until 1980, and although the embassy staff were assured that this posed no risk to their health, employees were found to have white blood cell counts that were 40 percent higher than normal. Two of the four ambassadors during the period of the "Moscow Signal" have since died of cancer, and a third developed a rare blood disease.

The U.S. government said nothing to the Russians about the beaming until the matter was made public in the late 1970s, but in 1959 they established a group of scientists whose job it was to monitor the signal, try to figure out what the Soviets were doing, and to study the effects on embassy staff. Only in 1976, after media exposure of the problem, did they install metal mesh screens on the windows of the embassy, reducing the radiation, they claimed, from 18 microwatts to 1 microwatt per square centimeter. Brodeur points out the irony of taking this measure to protect a couple of hundred American citizens from radiation levels that were well below what millions of others were being exposed to back home.

Civilian and military radar technicians; microwave workers; TV, radio, and other communications personnel are exposed to microwave radiation. So are the rest of us, from TV and radio broadcasting stations and radar systems. FM towers pose a particular hazard because the radiation they emit is pulsed.

Microwave radiation seems to cause a variety of nonthermal effects. Tests with animals have shown an almost immediate decline in work performance and decision-making capacity, along with chronic stress problems, inefficiency, and central nervous system disturbance. Headaches and nausea are among reactions observed in people, and microwave radiation is suspected of causing cancer and genetic damage. In one case, the children of men who worked as radar technicians at a military base in Alabama had an exceptionally high rate of birth defects.

Video Display Terminals

There has been a considerable amount of publicity about the dangers of video display terminals (VDTs). These are computer monitors or screens, and workers who spend a lot of time in front of them have been found to suffer from a variety of ailments ranging from headaches, eye strain, fatigue, anxiety, and depression to repetitive strain injury. Even more serious is the suspected connection with reproductive problems.

Attention was first drawn to this when a group of women working on VDTs at a newspaper office had an usually high rate of miscarriage. Other studies have confirmed that there is a higher rate of miscarriage among VDT workers, as well as a higher rate of birth defects. The extent of the risk, and the exact reasons for it, are unclear. Most VDTs do not emit more than very low levels of ionizing radiation, which is what most of us think of when we hear the word "radiation." They do give out varying amounts of VLF (Very Low Frequency) and ELF (Extremely Low Frequency) electromagnetic waves, and these are suspected of causing the problems.

Many of us work in front of VDTs, not only data entry clerks and secretaries, but bank tellers, writers, and physicists. Lower paid workers, however, are more likely to spend unbroken time working directly on the screen, and have less freedom to move about and take rest breaks. Their output is sometimes directly monitored by the computer, which increases stress and makes it even more unlikely that they will take sufficient breaks from the screen.

It has been estimated that half of all U.S. workers are now using electronic terminal equipment. Computers, however, like other tools, need to be used within the constraints of human and environmental health and safety. The first U.S. legislation on this regulates the use of VDT screens in private companies. Employees in Suffolk County, Long Island, who use VDTs for more than 26 hours a week must have a 15-minute break every three hours, and employers must pay 80 percent of the cost of annual eye examinations. All new workstations have to have mobile keyboards and antiglare screens, and offices with VDTs must have diffused overhead lighting.

These regulations are, in fact, minimal, and far more stringent safety measures will eventually need to be taken. Some activists suggest that no employee should spend more than four hours or half the working day at a terminal, that they should take regular breaks, and that computers should be properly shielded.

What other choices are there? Radiation problems are eliminated if you can use either a liquid crystal display (LCD) or gas plasma screen. If a VDT is needed, perhaps for graphics, insist on low radiation units. Protective clothing is not recommended. The "silver lining" slip, made from silverplated nylon, is said to protect the user from electric fields, but researchers suspect that it is the low frequency magnetic fields which cause the problems.

VDTs can be fitted with antiglare screens, which may help prevent eye strain but do nothing about the radiation. Studies have found that fine conductive mesh screens can virtually eliminate ELF and VLF emissions. The machine casing is even more important, and a screen over the monitor will do little good if most of the radiation is escaping through a plastic machine case. Tony Webb, British radiation expert, says that the low frequency fields are often strongest to the side and rear of the unit. A grounded conductive cage around all the components emitting radiation should be a standard requirement for all VDTs. Jeanne Stellman and Mary Sue Henifin, in *Office Work Can*

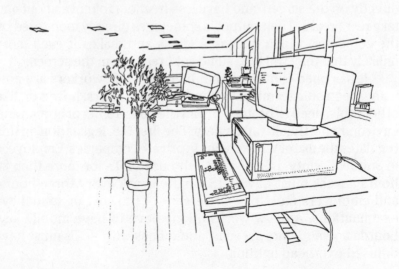

Be Dangerous to Your Health, point out that custom modification of an individual VDT is expensive, but that the protection would be considerably cheaper if it were done as a standard feature on the assembly line.

This shielding would also eliminate the problem of static. Many computer users know to their chagrin how static can wipe out a day's work in a flash. It is also unpleasant, and can result in invisible paper dust in the air bombarding the VDT worker in the face, contributing to eye and skin problems. Some attachable screens cut out static, and it helps to avoid synthetic materials in your computer room. Choose or ask for wool carpeting. Humidity is another way to lessen static—keep plenty of plants in the room, and a spray bottle of water handy. Keep the central heating as low as possible to avoid drying out the air. Many people find that ionizers improve the atmosphere too.

VDT CHECKLIST

❑ Prevent eye and muscle strain by careful positioning of both monitor and keyboard. Raising or lowering your seat can help.

❑ Adjust room lighting and screen brightness till it suits you. Working in dim light is often less taxing than in a brightly lit room. Use full-spectrum lighting.

❑ If possible, position your VDT so that you do not have to sit in front of it while doing other work or while the computer is doing a lengthy piece of storage or correction that does not need your guidance. This could mean two desks, or placing the VDT on an adjacent table.

❑ Turn it off when not in use, or turn off the monitor.

❑ Take frequent breaks, of at least 10 minutes. Simply looking away from the screen is not enough.

❑ Convince your boss or company to buy mesh conductive screens as a start. When new equipment is purchased, adequate shielding should be a prime consideration, and look at liquid crystal displays, or plasma screens.

Like many women, I am concerned about the amount of time I spend in front of a VDT because of its association with reproductive problems. Although a word processor makes the job of writing a book infinitely easier, when I was pregnant I pulled out my old manual typewriter. I used it to draft text, so I was able to spend less time at the terminal. There seems no doubt that women who are pregnant or planning to become pregnant should be extremely cautious about using VDTs, and should have the right to transfer to other work. Male reproduction may well be affected, so men should take these cautions to heart too.

Electromagnetic Radiation

The effects of low-level electromagnetic radiation have been of concern to a number of biologists for many years, but only recently have they attracted much public attention.

Although the most worrying effects have been noted under high-voltage power lines, all of us are surrounded by this form of artificial radiation in our homes, from the main current, electrical wiring, and appliances—everything from hairdryers to irons. One study showed a 40 percent increase in the suicide rate among people living under power lines, and low levels of electromagnetic radiation seem to cause depression and mood changes. Health effects include childhood leukemia, higher rates of miscarriage, and increased allergies. Several recent U.S. studies have shown higher cancer rates in people exposed to strong electromagnetic fields, and a study in New Zealand found an excess of leukemia among electronic equipment assemblers and radio and television repairmen.

Electromagnetic radiation is not all bad. The earth has its own magnetic fields, which govern such things as animals' migration patterns. Human tissue has electric and electromagnetic properties and these fields are sometimes used to promote the healing of broken bones and wounds. But during the 20th century, intense and chaotic electromagnetic phenomena—some call it electromagnetic pollution—have become common throughout much of the world. Electromagnetic fields and Extremely Low Frequency electromagnetic waves exist all the time; an electrical installation is "live," even while it is turned off.

Russian research suggests that the difference between living and nonliving matter is electricity. Western medicine is based on a biochemical understanding of the body and its systems, ignoring the likelihood that electrical influences are equally important in growth, healing, and metabolism. Yet it seems likely that electromagnetic fields in the human body offer some explanation for the Japanese idea of *ki* (vital energy which radiates from the *hara,* or center of the body), auras, and perhaps even some psychic phenomena. It is thought that acupuncture's proven effectiveness may be dependent on a subtle understanding of these forces.

Electromagnetic radiation in our homes may well prove to be a significant hazard, one that is difficult to reduce, given our dependence on electricity and electrical appliances. A new engine that may revolutionize domestic energy use by generating both heat and electricity might be a way of decreasing general levels of electromagnetic radiation because there would be considerably less need for power lines.

ELECTROMAGNETIC RADIATION CHECKLIST

❏ Limit or reduce the number of electrical appliances in your home, and use hand appliances whenever possible. This saves energy *and* reduces your exposure to electromagnetic radiation.

❏ Cut down on time in front of the television (good for you in more ways than one), make sure you sit at least six feet away from the screen when you are watching, and put the set against an outside wall of your home.

❏ Use a hot water bottle to warm your bed instead of an electric blanket. There is some evidence of a decrease in fertility in couples who sleep with electric blankets. German building biologists recommend replacing metal-framed beds with wooden ones and choosing mattresses without metal springs. Fleece underblankets, like those used for babies but much larger, are another option.

❏ You may want switch the power breakers off at night, but you'll have to run a spur for the refrigerator and any other equipment that has to stay on all the time—and you'd have to feel your way to the bathroom.

❏ Block the fields which emanate from electrical wiring by using shielded cables or conduits.

Stopping the Threat

Rosalie Bertell evokes a poignant image in explaining how we have allowed radiation to become part of our environment in spite of its life-threatening nature.

During the early years of the Third Reich, the Nazis forced Jewish people into the Warsaw ghetto by telling them that this was the only way police could protect them from public prejudice. Under these circumstances, simple survival absorbed most people's time and attention, and resistance was weak because they were ill-fed and suffering from disease.

Bertell goes on:

> "Everyone, whether wall-builders, Nazi police, Jewish manufacturers, corporate financiers or community leaders, played a role in the death system. Although their actions ultimately bred death, they also bought a few more days of life, however uncomfortable, for each individual in the ghetto. The vast majority of people quietly resigned themselves to cooperate, and to pretend things were 'normal'. . . . Anyone who tried to sound an alarm was met with disbelief" (*No Immediate Danger*).

We too are faced with serious threats to our health and to our future, individually and corporately. But like the people in the ghetto, most of us have preferred to pretend that things are really not so bad. Now is the time to face the dangers of radiation. We can take a number of immediate steps to protect ourselves, proceed by learning more about the problems, and put pressure on government and industry to change tack. This is an area in which we cannot act alone, but in which we can certainly act together.

Sources

Books
Currents of Death, Paul Brodeur (New York, Simon & Schuster, 1989).

Food Irradiation: The Facts, Tony Webb and Tim Lang (New York, Inner Traditions, 1987). Distributed by Harper & Row.

No Immediate Danger, Rosalie Bertell (Summertown, TN, Book Publishing Company, 1986).

Office Work Can Be Dangerous to Your Health, Jeanne Stellman and Mary Sue Henifin (New York, Pantheon, 1983).

Race to the Finish? The Nuclear Stakes, Dervla Murphy (John Murray, 50 Albemarle Street, London W1X 4BD, 1981). Order from Books for a Change.

Radiation and Human Health, John W. Gofman (San Francisco, Sierra Club, 1981).

Small Is Beautiful: Economics as if People Mattered, E.F. Schumacher (New York, Harper & Row, 1975).

Structure of the Scientific Revolution, Thomas Kuhn (Chicago, University of Chicago Press, 1970).

Well Body, Well Earth: The Sierra Club Environmental Health Sourcebook, Mike Samuels and Hal Zina Bennett (San Francisco, Sierra Club Books, 1983). Distributed by Random House, New York.

The Zapping of America, Paul Brodeur (New York, Norton, 1977). Out-of-Print.

Newsletter

Microwave News, edited by Dr. Louis Slesin, P.O. Box 1799, Grand Central Station, NY 10163.

Organizations

Food Irradiation Project, New York Public Interest Research Group, 9 Murray Street, New York, NY 10007. (212) 349-6460.

Nuclear Information Resource Service. Antinuclear umbrella organization for groups and individuals concerned about nuclear power issues. 1424 16th Street NW #601, Washington, DC 20036. (202) 328-0002.

12
LIGHT

Few things have so much effect on the feeling inside a room as the sun shining into it. If you want to be sure that your house, or building, and the rooms inside it are wonderful, comfortable places, give this pattern its due. Treat it seriously; cling to it tenaciously; insist upon it.

—Christopher Alexander et al.,
A Pattern Language

Introduction

People who live in northern countries have a reputation for stoicism, while people in sunny climes are generally considered more relaxed and easygoing. But we compound the natural disadvantages of dull skies and dark winters by spending more and more of our time indoors, under artificial lighting. It is estimated that we receive at least one-quarter less natural light than did our grandparents.

Human beings are phototropic—that is, they naturally gravitate toward light. This is easy to see in practice. When you take a packed lunch to the park near your office, do you choose a sunny bench or a dark corner? We need sunlight and this need affects how we feel, how we spend our time, and even where we live.

Think of your favorite rooms. What are the characteristics of these special places? One of them is likely to be diffuse natural light. I shall always remember the long, light bedroom I stayed in as a child in upstate New York, where there was a sunny window seat to curl up in and read. You may have similar memories.

You've probably heard of biorhythms, which biologists suggest may depend on the play between day and night, light and dark. This seems obvious—after all, we wake up in the morning and go to sleep after dark. But the advent of convenient and cheap artificial lighting has changed our habits, and until recently it has been assumed that human evolution takes us beyond any dependence on the natural hormonal rhythms and cycles that affect animals.

A few people suffer intense depression during dark winter months. This condition is called Seasonal Affective Disorder (SAD), and the characteristic symptoms are severe winter depression, unrelated to other events in one's life, accompanied by cravings for carbohydrates, weight gain, and excessive sleeping—just like a hibernating bear! The syndrome lifts at the arrival of spring.

The generally accepted explanation is that light suppresses the production of a hormone called melatonin, which otherwise causes the depression. French obstetrician Michel Odent has suggested that our individual adaptation to darkness may depend on cycles of light and darkness during the period immediately following birth. Some babies are kept in artificially lit nurseries 24 hours a day.

Although some people suffer from SAD so severely that they need specialist treatment, most of us are familiar with winter blues. It seems reasonable to assume that we too can use a little help during the darkest months of the year, whether from full-spectrum lighting indoors or a special effort to spend extra time outside. Christmas celebrations sensibly fall at the winter solstice, when days are shortest. But when that excitement has passed I find myself sleeping more and waiting eagerly for the first primrose and daffodils, and longer daylight hours.

Light should be our primary source of vitamin D, but we generally need supplements or foods fortified with vitamin D because it is not formed in our bodies but reabsorbed from the skin's oils. Soap and frequent bathing wash most of what we get directly from the sun straight down the drain. Lack of vitamin D can lead to poor calcium absorption, and in turn to osteoporosis in elderly people, a condition not entirely rectified by vitamin pills.

The dangers of too much sunlight and the aging effects of excessive tanning are much in the news. Moderation is crucial. Modern living tends to isolate us from direct sunlight: we spend such a lot of time behind glass that we don't get the full benefit of the light. In the future, light deficiency is likely to be an accepted explanation for a variety of illnesses, as well as a contributor to general malaise.

The Ozone Layer

The most alarming environmental aspect of light is the danger posed by destruction of the ozone layer, which acts as a buffer between us and highly dangerous ultraviolet radiation from the sun.

The hole in the ozone layer over the Antarctic should come as no surprise. Environmentalists have been predicting breakdown of the ozone layer for some 15 years. The tragedy is that whatever we do has come much later than it might have, and too late to prevent considerable ecological damage and many cases of cancer.

Ozone (O_3) is a volatile gas forming an essential protective layer around the earth. But ozone is vulnerable to a number of gases that are manufactured and released by humankind, particularly those containing chlorine. Chlorofluorocarbons, or CFCs, are a group of chemicals mainly used as the propellant in aerosol cans (deodorants, hairsprays, furniture polish, insecticide, etc.), as well as in the blowing of polystyrene packaging and in refrigerants—the liquids that circulate in refrigerators and freezers to carry heat away.

According to Friends of the Earth, we can expect to see a sharp rise in the number of skin cancers, as well as an increase in eye diseases like cataracts; damage to agricultural crops (will they have to be sprayed with sunscreen?); and a worsening of smog pollution.

Even if all CFC production were stopped now—and sadly, it won't be, though the manufacturers are responding to public pressure to a substantial degree—there are already hundreds of thousands of tons of CFCs hanging over our heads, and the effects of a damaged ozone layer will be with us for at least their lifetime, which is more than 100 years. This is a problem we are all going to have to live with, although we can see to it that our great-grandchildren don't inherit it from us.

The danger of excessive sunlight is nothing new, but we have all the more reason to take warnings about sunbathing seriously. It is good for us, in moderation. We all know how good our skin looks with a bit of color in it—remembering, however, that the holiday effect is also due to lack of stress and to fresh air and sea.

Of course we all know people who seem to turn brown overnight, but if you have fair, sun-sensitive skin, you won't get a chocolate-colored tan no matter how much sun you get and you are at much greater risk of skin cancer than your swarthy friends.

Why not aim to be fashionably pale? Spend time outside, but not in direct sunlight; sip cool drinks on the patio under an umbrella, or some variation that fits in with your bluejeans and three children.

But if you can't resist the temptation to tan, at least moderate your goal to a pleasant golden shade, and give your skin plenty of time to achieve it. This is a luxury no one will be able to afford if we continue to destroy the ozone layer.

Every drugstore now stocks a wide range of sunscreen creams, numbered on a scale from 1 to 45. The lower numbers are for darker skin or faster tanning, and 45 is a complete block. Put sunscreen on before you go out, and reapply it frequently if you are swimming or sweating.

Health and beauty writer Leslie Kenton says sunbathing for health should be done with no oils or creams. Think of it as a bath, wear as little as possible, and keep it brief.

Sun beds have been heavily promoted as safer than tanning outside, but much of the information consumers receive is misleading. Shorter UV-B rays have received bad publicity because they cause superficial reddening and burning, while longer UV-A rays have been advertised as "safe" tanning rays because they develop melanin particles in the skin and create a tan without burning.

Sad to say, these UV-A rays are probably far more damaging in the long run than UV-B burning rays, because they cause premature and irreversible aging of the skin, just as the sun does.

PROTECTING OURSELVES CHECKLIST

❑ First and foremost, do not contribute to the problem. Stop using aerosols that contain CFCs. Better yet, switch from aerosols to pump sprays, as they are less hazardous and polluting.

❑ Wear a moisturizer with sunscreen in it all the time. This will become more important as time passes—and as you get older! Men are as vulnerable as women, but are unlikely to convert en masse to the virtues of moisturizers. Before long, however, we may all be forced to use sunscreens in order to avoid skin cancer.

❑ Sunbathe cautiously, if at all, particularly if you have fair skin. Stay away from sun beds.

❑ Watch out for skin growths, which could be cancerous. These can almost always be treated successfully.

❑ Write to your congressman about CFC legislation and contribute to Friends of the Earth, who have been campaigning to save the ozone layer for many years.

Light and Health

Sunlight has exciting effects on our metabolic rate and hormones—which partly explains why we feel so wonderful on the beach. Before trying to improve your indoor lighting, think about how to get more direct sunlight.

❑ Spend as much time as you can outside. This will take special effort during the winter: try walking to work, or at least part of the way (catch a bus 15 minutes down the road or get off early), or go for a walk during your lunch hour.

❏ Choose outdoor activities in preference to indoor ones: tennis instead of squash, running rather than a rowing machine. Walk or cycle instead of driving.

❏ Keep track of how much time you spend in natural light each day, and how you feel as a result. An absolute minimum is 15 minutes in summer and 30 minutes in winter, when the sun is less intense, but try to get much more than that. John Ott (*Light, Radiation, and You*) suggests six hours a day; this does not have to be direct sunlight and you do not have to be outdoors to get it. The older you are, the more sunlight you need.

❏ Try to work close to a window, preferably with it open.

❏ Make the nearest part of your yard (or the sunniest, if you have deep shade immediately next to the building) an outdoor living area by equipping it with a table, comfortable chairs and adequate protection from direct summer sun. Informal and permanent seats, even if only a low brick wall, make a yard far more hospitable anyway. Even if you live in an apartment, it may be possible to turn the area near a window, or near one of those narrow balconies that are common in modern blocks, into a sunny spot to work and eat.

❏ Clean windows will let more light in—a good window cleaner is worth his or her weight in gold. (Lightbulbs also need to be cleaned, with a slightly damp cloth. Make sure the bulb is cold. Lampshades gradually darken with dust, so dust them occasionally.)

❏ Check the light levels around your home. A camera with a light sensor in the viewfinder is a surprising tool—a room can be considerably duller than you think. We tend to use minimal lighting, but this increases eye strain and doesn't provide enough background lighting. One woman who suffered SAD used to turn on every light in the house when she came in. Does this sound like you, or someone you know?

❏ Experiment with different types of artificial lighting. Debra Lynn Dadd, known for her work on nontoxic household products, says that after trying full-spectrum bulbs she went back to ordinary warm-white bulbs from the super-market because that's what she feels best with.

❏ Do your eyes a favor by emphasizing any views you have available: one of the problems with urban living is that we seldom have to look at anything further away than a retreating bus. Or go for walks in the country on weekends, where you can use your eyes. Try counting sheep on a distant hillside!

Fluorescent Lights

Many people who have lived or worked under fluorescent lighting are instinctively aware of how uncomfortable it is, though we don't know quite why. Last year I was at a university for a series of lectures on ecology. Waiting in line for lunch I overheard a woman complaining about the green conferences she'd been to. "I wish they wouldn't always have them at these places, under these lights, where there's no air. I always have a headache by the end of the day."

Fluorescent lighting is standard in offices, banks, and stores. It is cheaper to run than incandescent lighting, needing only one quarter the energy in continuous use. Recent studies, however, show that improving the quality of light reduces absenteeism, and cuts down on headaches, eye strain, and fatigue. Even though we are not consciously aware of the 100-times-a-second flicker of fluorescent lights (except with a dud bulb, and we all know how irritating that is), at a subconscious level it is extremely stressful. New types of fluorescent lights are being developed that flicker much faster than the old ones—at 30,000 times a minute—and are supposedly much easier on both eye and brain.

At home, you can fit full-spectrum bulbs in fluorescent fixtures, but at the office the best option is mixed lighting sources, with adjustable lights at each work station. You may be able to use an incandescent desk lamp and turn off the overhead fluorescent lights. If not—and many workers have no choice about the continuous overhead fluorescent lighting—you might mention the new type of bulb to the relevant person.

Full-spectrum Lights

There is agreement about at least one of the problems of artificial lighting. The spectrum of light produced by artificial sources is different from natural daylight. Daylight has a more even spread of light across the colored wave bands, with a higher proportion of blue and green.

Makeup artists know how much of a difference the color of light makes. My mother used to have a makeup mirror with three different light settings. It was great fun to play with: our faces looked fine set on Daylight, ghastly on Office, and ghostly on Evening.

When I asked a lighting consultant which type of light he preferred he said promptly, "Halogen. It makes things look wonderful. You should see jewelry under it." What about people's faces? "Oh," he sighed, "Faces. Well, faces are difficult. Candle-light is good."

You know the problem of buying a tie to go with a particular suit and finding that it is a different color when you get it home? You are advised to check the color in daylight, but in a big department store this is virtually impossible. It surprises me that makeup counters aren't lit with more care, although I was told that they are always happy for customers to put something on and go outside to look at it.

Home Design

The key to saving energy and increasing well-being is to maximize our use of natural sunlight—solar energy, as a matter of fact.

Modern buildings are designed on the principle that artificial lighting is just as good as, perhaps better than, natural daylight. But it must be said that even architects of the past don't seem to have given a great deal of consideration to the provision of light. Houses on opposite sides of a street, which have completely different sun exposures, are laid out in exactly the same way, with living rooms at the front and bedrooms at the back. Kitchens always used to be in the basement, because no one cared if servants were confined below ground.

What surprises me is that people with an entire house often choose to use the basement as the kitchen/family room, and leave the bright rooms upstairs empty during the day.

Alistair Best suggests that: "If by placing the kitchen in the basement the family finds that most of the household duties have to be carried on under artificial light, then in my view serious consideration should be given to positioning the kitchen elsewhere. . . . Indeed, it seems to me logical that if the kitchen is acknowledged to be the most important room in the house, it should also occupy space at the house's center of gravity" (in *Putting Back the Style*, see Sources).

Orientation

In *A Pattern Language*, British-born architect Christopher Alexander of the Center for Environmental Structure in Berkeley, California, and his co-authors set out a number of design principles which can be used by anyone in arranging rooms and lighting. They suggest arranging rooms by the availability and timing of daylight. A southerly exposure is desirable, for house and garden. Because we live in the northern hemisphere, the sun is always in the southern part of the sky. Rooms you use in the morning should face east, rooms which are used in the afternoon and evening should face west.

Artists are the only ones who seem to like a northern exposure, because they need consistency of lighting, and don't want direct sunlight with its resultant glare. Perhaps you can rent out an unused north-facing room as a studio, or take up painting!

If you are interested in rethinking the layout of the rooms in your home, it is far easier to make changes when you have just moved in, or at least before you have custom-made bookshelves installed in the den.

ORIENTATION CHECKLIST

❏ Figure out where north is—if you have my kind of sense of direction, a map is probably the easiest way, or use a compass.

❏ Make a light chart of the rooms in your house or apartment. When is sunlight available? Use 1 for bright; 2 for moderately light; 3 for dull.

❏ Draw up a similar chart for room use. Your kitchen is probably used most in the late afternoon and early evening, but it's also nice to have a bright kitchen in the morning. Bedrooms need light in the morning, and living rooms in the evening. Playrooms and rooms used as a home office probably need as much light as possible throughout the day.

❏ Consider some room switching. Light is by no means the only consideration in deciding how to use rooms, but it is an important criterion, and one almost always neglected. The key thing is to get the rooms that are used most in the right position. Kitchens and playrooms should be given special priority. Formal living and dining rooms are often used only in the evening, and can sometimes be switched to a less light-valuable part of the house.

❏ Look outside, at anything that gets in the way of the light that reaches you. There isn't much to be done about the house across the street or a railway station, but trees and shrubs can be pruned, or even moved. If the problem is acute, remove them and plant replacements somewhere else.

❏ Dark rooms, facing north or into a blank brick wall, or with no windows at all, should be used least. Special treatment can help: careful lighting, and lots of mirrors to break up the wall surface and reflect light.

❏ If you should be buying or building a new house, a long east-west axis has been shown to minimize energy consumption by keeping the heat in during the winter and out during the summer. For details, consult *A Pattern Language*, pages 616–67.

❏ If you have a room in which you could bake fish on a July afternoon, take this into account when deciding on layout. But it is much easier to block some of the light than it is to maximize light during dark months. Curtains and blinds can be used (an outside blind is most effective), and eaves and deciduous trees can be used to block hot summer sun, while allowing low winter sun to enter the house. Another appealing long-term solution is to grow climbing plants around the windows. Choose varieties that lose their leaves in winter so they don't block light and warmth when it is in short supply. For the short term, try morning glories and other annual climbers.

WINDOW CHECKLIST

❏ To maximize available light, drapes, when open, should pull back so that they don't mask any of the window, which may mean you need a longer track or rail. Of course if the drapes are already there you'll have to try something else. Simple tiebacks can make a difference. Also make sure that blinds are easy to pull all the way up, out of the way. Curtains and blinds should be easy to draw.

❑ Shutters are efficient insulators and pull well off windows during the day.

❑ Windows should open wide. Window glass blocks the beneficial rays from sunlight, but with windows that open you can fling them open on nice days and have fresh air and sunshine inside. Casement windows and floor-to-ceiling French windows are the right idea. Some variation on these is easy to achieve in a new house, but if you have sash windows, just make sure they open easily.

❑ Window seats and low sills with a chair and table set nearby make pleasant areas where you'll probably spend a lot of time—so will your cats!

❑ With whatever type of window you have, do be sure to install appropriate locks. I imagine that burglar alarms are a great disincentive to opening windows, because you have to ensure that they are all closed again properly to reset the alarm when you go out. Take this up with the alarm company if you are having a system installed.

❑ Try to have privacy and security without losing your light. And you want to be able to see outside. Filtered light is a good thing and you can sometimes achieve privacy with plants climbing around a window from tubs or windowboxes.

❑ You can get extra light into some dark rooms by placing cheap, fixed windows in interior walls, and by using glazed doors between rooms where privacy is not important (they can have curtains to pull if necessary—extra insulation too).

❑ Use mirrors freely, not only where you want to be able to see yourself but as if they were pictures to hang on the wall. This can be very inexpensive and very pretty. I like old mirrors, the kind you can find in junk stores for a couple of dollars. The glass is beveled, and there is something about the silvering, dark spots, and slight irregularities in the glass which makes the light they reflect prettier than the light new mirror glass produces. Mirrors can be framed, too; old frames can be picked up cheaply—try house clearance places in seedy areas, or auctions for grander items. Have old mirrors cut by a specialist firm. Try a long mirror between windows.

❑ A friend of mine has a small-paned window salvaged from a demolition site hanging on her hall wall. It has delicate lace curtains tied back with ribbons, and behind the glass is a print of a country landscape—this is an innocent trompe l'oeil which gives a feeling of spaciousness even though one knows it isn't real. This could be really useful in a room without a window. I mean to do it in my windowless bathroom, one of these days. You could put a mirror behind it instead, or even light it.

Sources

Books

Entering the World: The De-medicalization of Childbirth, Michel Odent (New York, New American Library, 1984).

Light, Radiation, and You, John Ott (New York, Devin-Adair, 1990).

A Pattern Language: Towns, Buildings, Construction, Christopher Alexander et al. (New York, Oxford University Press, 1977).

Putting Back the Style, Alexandra Artley (Evans Brothers, 2A Portman Mansions, Chiltern Street, London W1M 1LE, 1982).

13
GARDENING

It is one thing to sit around talking about how the balance of nature is being upset and how black the future looks . . .; it is quite another to ask ourselves what we are doing about our own plot of ground, whether it is a little four by four foot square, or an acre, or a whole farm or forest. This is where we should be expressing some ecology in a practical fashion, where we should be doing some original landscape architecture which combines art with preservation and conservation, which produces a growing beauty, and which inspires other "artists" to do the same.

—Edith Schaeffer,
The Hidden Art of Homemaking

INTRODUCTION
GETTING STARTED
　　Bulbs—Garbage Gardening—Green Thumbs
GARDEN ECOLOGY
　　Green Gardening Checklist—Organic Gardening—
　　"Organic?"—Pest Control—Feeding the Soil—
　　Water Conservation—Paraphernalia
FOOD FOR THE TABLE
　　Soil Testing—Raised Beds—Community Gardens
　　—Seed Savers
THE DOMESTIC GARDEN
　　Flowers—Trees—The Organic Lawn—*Lawn
　　Checklist*—Paving
OUTDOOR LIVING
WILDLIFE
　　Wildlife Gardening Checklist
CULTIVATING A GREEN THUMB
　　Gradual Gardening Checklist
SOURCES

Introduction

I once met a fellow from southern California who admired the plants in my office. He told me that he had dozens in his apartment, perhaps I'd like to see them some time—"and what is this beautiful creature called?" he asked, as he stroked my philodendron. I never found out if his thumbs were really green. But some people do seem to have a knack with plants, while others struggle to keep even a valiant ivy alive.

Every office has potted plants scattered about, but unless they are tended by a landscaping company (the kind who can be called out in an emergency—"the dieffenbachia is wilting!") these are usually a sad and scruffy lot.

They probably came from a chainstore, and the plastic care tags are still stuck in the soil. Every couple of weeks, when they look particularly feeble, someone throws the dregs of a cup of coffee on them. Unfeeling souls stub out cigarettes in their soil. The secretary whose boss likes plants but who can't stand them herself may resort to poisoning them with nail polish remover.

Modern offices are hardly ideal environments for plants, or people, for that matter. The air is dry and there is little or no natural light. Small wonder most plants do not thrive.

Getting Started

I want, nonetheless, to make a case for keeping those plants and even adding to your little menagerie. Herbaceous plants, like trees, really do improve our environment. They increase the oxygen content of the air, act as a humidifier, and can filter dangerous contaminants from the air. Studies by NASA scientists have found that common house plants, including spider plants, golden pothos, philodendron, and aloe vera, remove carbon monoxide and formaldehyde vapors.

If you think you have a black thumb, rather than sticking with boring easy-care plants, why not try growing something that you really like—because it's pretty or odd-looking or smells nice or is edible. Even if you have a few casualties, nursing a plant you like is going to teach you more than desultorily tending the office yucca.

Bulbs

A fun way to start gardening is by growing bulbs, which will bloom indoors during the winter, or even for Christmas if you plant at the right time.

They can be planted in bulb fiber, but grow better in either commercial potting compost or garden soil. After they have flowered, find a spot for them in the garden. Hyacinths, huge heavy stalks of blossom the first year, will gradually get smaller until eventually they look like large bluebells. You'll need to buy new bulbs each year for indoor potting.

Some bulbs on sale in the United States have come from the wild and you will want to avoid these because of the environmental impact the trade has on the countries they come from—one example is wild cyclamen dug from Turkish hillsides. Because the bulbs are generally packed in Holland there is no definite way to identify them. If you are buying cyclamen or snowdrops, watch out for misshapen and irregularly sized tubers, signs that they are likely to have come from the wild. Reputable seed companies will be able to tell you where their bulbs come from.

Garbage Gardening

Another way to start gardening without too much commitment is to buy a bag of potting compost, or use some sifted garden soil, and fill a couple of pots. Put them in a sunny spot, out of drafts, and start collecting seeds. Orange and lemon pips grow nicely, and will turn into attractive little trees. They stay dark green and healthy even in a dark corner, and although you won't get fruit, the leaves are good for garnishing food. Grape seed grows into pretty vines, apple seeds will grow into little apple trees, and you can try everything from mangoes to walnuts to avocados.

A kid's trick with carrots—parsnips and rutabagas will work too, but they don't have such delicate foliage—is to pack the stubby tops (leave 3/4 inch of the root) in a shallow layer of aquarium gravel, add water to the top of the gravel, and wait. Fine silky leaves will begin to sprout, and look very pretty on a windowsill. Pineapple tops will grow by this method too. What an undemanding and intriguing form of recycling.

Green Thumbs

A friend used to say that she grew vegetables for her stomach and flowers for her soul, while architect Christopher Alexander believes that growing vegetables is a fundamental part of human life. How can we appreciate the food we eat, and take proper care in buying and preparing it, if it always comes off supermarket shelves? He suggests that this must lead to feelings of insecurity in city dwellers. Producing at least a little of one's own food provides an immediate connection with natural life cycles.

Growing things is good for you—fresh air, sunshine, and exercise; and homegrown food is good for you—delicious, nutritious, and uncontaminated by artificial chemicals. Even if you stick to growing nonedible shrubs and flowers, they disguise unattractive features, can offer privacy, shelter, and food for wildlife, and generally beautify our surroundings.

City dwellers don't have much space, tall buildings shade what little ground they have, and getting hold of manure is virtually impossible, but it is city dwellers who have the most to gain from even a tiny garden. A well cultivated window sill may be as much room as you have and may take as much time as you can spare.

Before you start a gardening project, assess your circumstances. How much ground do you have? Is it sunny or shady? Wet or dry? Are there other spaces where you can grow things— walls, patios, or steps? Indoors, is there enough light to grow plants? (Don't give up—growlights will transform even a sunless city apartment.) If you have a greenhouse or a balcony your choices expand considerably.

Just as important, how much time do you have? Who will share the work? If you are away a lot, is there someone to take over watering? And how much money do you want to spend? If you have a largish garden and don't seem to manage to keep up with it, consider hiring a local student to help with the heavy work. A well kept garden will entice you to use it more often, and muscle often costs less than expensive fertilizers and plants that die because they've gone into the wrong spot or are never watered.

A large garden could also profitably be shared with someone who wants space for a vegetable garden—you could exchange a patch for a share of the produce, or for some help in the rest of the garden.

Finally, how much do you know about gardening? Most of us haven't grown up helping our parents to maintain a garden or grow vegetables. But green thumbs can be cultivated, and depend on a combination of knowledge, instinct, keen observation, and love.

When I read that when you move to a new house it's best to leave the garden alone for a full year and just watch and see what comes up, I was horrified. A year seemed like forever. But the good gardener will cultivate patience along with the impatiens, and becomes attuned to rhythms and signals which other people miss. For this reason many people suffering from stress find gardening a particularly satisfying pastime.

You learn to grow things by getting your hands dirty, but there are scores of books, and several good organizations, to guide you.

Garden Ecology

GREEN GARDENING CHECKLIST

- ❏ Organic growing techniques (no chemicals)
- ❏ Native plants
- ❏ Permanent plantings
- ❏ Self-sowing annuals
- ❏ Food plants
- ❏ Household scraps for compost
- ❏ Spaced paving rather than concrete
- ❏ Wildlife sanctuary
- ❏ Natural materials instead of plastics

Organic Gardening

Chemical fertilizers, herbicides, and insecticides have no place in an ecologically sound garden. If you are a chemical gardener, however, this exclusion will probably make you nervous—you can't imagine life without triple NPK and rose spray. But a look through this section or, better yet, at one of the books recommended at the end of the chapter should convince you that organic gardening isn't complicated or peculiar. It's simply the way people always grew things until the last 40 years or so, with various improvements based on recent research.

High-input chemical gardening is polluting, energy-intensive, and bad for the soil. Some people say that although homemade garden compost is all right, you can't get good yields or healthy crops without using chemicals. This is blatantly false, as organic growers are demonstrating around the globe. One of the paradoxes of chemical agriculture is that the more artificial fertilizer you use, the more insecticides you need. Too much nitrogen makes for soft, leggy growth, which is more vulnerable to insect damage.

A substantial benefit of chemical-free growing is that you will no longer have dozens of poisons in your garden shed. It strikes me that the large number of poisonous products we live with are a source of unidentified stress in modern life. And you can make fewer mistakes in organic gardening: it is almost impossible to overdose plants with liquid seaweed, for example, and you can mix it in a juice pitcher if you want to. If you have garden chemicals to dispose of, do *not* put them down the drain. They should be taken to a special toxic waste collection point— call the EPA Hotline at (800) 424-9346 for details.

"Organic?"

When gardening books talk about "organic" fertilizers they may mean animal- or plant-based products rather than chemical powders and solutions. Examples are processed manure and garden peat.

Most of these will not be organic in the sense of being organically grown. Horse manure from the local stable, for instance, will contain residues of chemicals from the horses' feed and worming products. There is some debate about whether organic farms, which depend on good supplies of manure, should use manure from intensively reared animals.

Pest Control

Keeping insects under control without dangerous chemicals is not the hurdle you might think. Healthy plants are more disease-resistant, and organic gardeners make use of techniques like companion planting (chives around the rose bushes) and of natural predators like ladybugs. There are organic sprays and powders available to help you deal with any serious problems. Plain old baking soda, diluted in water, is an effective treatment for mildew. A few well-known plant-derived pesticides —derris and pyrethrum, for example, are suitable for organic gardens.

Slugs and snails are probably the worst problem for the organic gardener and there are many techniques for dealing with them, ranging from saucers of beer to night hunts with a flashlight and a bucket of soapy water. On a gastronomic note, you could eat the enormous snails that are devastating your peas, but only if you clean-feed them on cornmeal for several days first.

Chemical slug pellets are a well-known danger to birds because they eat the dead slugs, but this form of pest control has other disadvantages. A 1986 study at the Long Ashton Research Station in England suggests that methiocarb, a commonly used slug killer, leads to higher aphid populations because it kills natural aphid predators.

Weeds are controlled by close planting, mulches, and hand weeding. You can use newspapers or old carpets to smother tough perennial weeds. If weeds have not yet seeded, they can be dug up and allowed to dry for a few days to ensure that they don't come to life again, and then added to the compost. Burning is a waste of nutrients and humus, and only necessary for diseased plant material and weed seeds.

Swedish tests have found that stinging nettles make a rich liquid fertilizer which has a better effect on plants than a chemical solution with the same concentration of nutrients. If you have nettles available, don gloves and pack your nettles into a bucket, fill it with water, and cover it. Stir it every couple of days and after two weeks you can strain off a potent (and smelly) liquid feed for all your plants. Nettle water can be made with fresh or dried nettles, and can be used as a spray to control aphids.

Feeding the Soil

Compost is to the organic gardener what the soup pot is to the cook—a way of using up leftovers to create something new. It is a home recycling system, a way of cutting down your domestic garbage—compostable kitchen scraps make up 30 percent of the material going into landfill sites. Any organic gardening book will give you the basics of the New Zealand box and double bins, and *Garbage*, a practical environmental magazine, will keep you informed about composting methods (see Robert Kourik's article in the November/December 1989 issue).

The simplest approach is to mark an area about four feet square, loosen up the soil with a fork, and make a layer of twigs to keep the bottom aerated, then add organic matter as it comes along. Sides can be built of scrap timber, if you like, and in wet weather the compost bin should be covered with a piece of old carpet.

You can use kitchen scraps, grass clippings, leaves, manure, animal litter—anything made of natural materials. W. G. Shewell Cooper, founder of the Good Gardeners' Association in England, threw his old tweed jackets onto the compost pile. Egg shells won't rot, but they are a valuable source of nutrients. Throw them into the compost pile if it suits you, or let them dry, crumble them and sprinkle them on the soil around lime-loving plants.

Compost needs to be activated with something high in nitrogen. Fresh manure, seaweed, and nettles work well, but a cheap and readily available activator is urine. This is perfectly safe, by the way. Urine is not a source of bacterial contamination. Manure can be used to activate a compost heap or simply dug into the soil after it is well rotted; fresh manure will burn plants.

Worm compost is sold commercially, but you can make your own in a plastic garbage can. This technique is perfectly suited to small gardens as it takes up no actual garden space. Kitchen waste is added as it accumulates, and the worms turn it into rich compost. There is an excellent book on the subject called *Worms Eat My Garbage* (see Sources).

Leaves are a valuable source of organic matter. Think of the soft dark leafmold one finds under trees in a forest. Making your own leafmold is a better choice than using peat, because it is richer in minerals, available locally, and because the mining of bog peat has undesirable ecological consequences. If you can get hold of large quantities of leaves, simply pile them where they can't blow away and leave them till they break down. Or bag the dry leaves in heavy plastic bags and stick them out of the way for a year or two. If you do this each autumn, after the initial wait you will have a steady supply.

Seaweed is available in granular or liquid form, and is a potent fertilizer. Gather your own if you get the chance—put a bucketful of seaweed in the trunk when you come back from the beach.

A simple way to add nutrients to the soil, smother weeds, and cut down on watering is to use a mulch. This is a thick layer (you should not be able to see the soil) of some organic material like straw, leafmold, or homemade garden compost. A newspaper mulch is a good way to eradicate perennial weeds.

Water Conservation

Anyone who has lived through a drought knows about using dishwater to keep the roses alive. Because reducing water use is becoming increasingly important, you might want to install a "graywater system" which allows you to use the 60 to 65 percent of relatively clean indoor waste water to water your yard. At the moment this is legal only in Santa Barbara County, but I have no doubt that it will become common as sources of water become increasingly precious. If you are handy with a wrench, you may want to join the many frustrated gardeners in drought areas who have converted their home plumbing systems (see *Greywater Use in the Landscape*).

Another way to reduce your water use drastically is a landscaping technique called *xeriscape*, its name coming from the Greek word meaning dry. This gives you a drought resistant and low-maintenance landscape and is good for wildlife. Your local nursery should be able to help.

Paraphernalia

The average nursery is full of plastic gardening string and netting, and plants often come in plastic pots or polystyrene trays. But the green gardener sticks with natural, biodegradable materials and is on the lookout for recycling opportunities.

Avoid collecting plastic pots, save money, and get stronger seedlings with far greater variety by growing them yourself in recycled containers. Yogurt cups and plastic packing trays can be used for this, and you can cut the bottoms off plastic mineral water bottles. Net bags that held oranges or potatoes can be opened to provide supports for climbing plants, and newspapers can be used to make a homemade version of peat pots. Wrap six or eight sheets around a bottle to form a cylinder and fasten them with a little paste. When it's dry, cut the cylinder into suitable lengths, place the rings of newspaper in a large garden tray, and fill them with potting soil. The rings can eventually be transplanted, without disturbing the roots.

While black polythene is often used as a mulch, it has several disadvantages. It flaps in the wind, tears at inconvenient moments and regularly clutters up the garbage can because, as a plastic, it does not break down. Organic mulches are preferable; they give off carbon dioxide as they decompose, which is extremely beneficial for your plants.

Choose a biodegradable gardening string, or use strips of cotton cloth to tie up your tomatoes. These are good because they do not cut into soft stems. Both plants and ties can go straight onto the compost pile.

Food for the Table

Soil Testing

Before you start growing edible plants, you may want to have your soil tested. Some town and city soil is badly contaminated with lead from car exhausts, and other heavy metal contamination is possible. Your county agricultural extension agent will be able to advise about this.

The home test kits available at nurseries will tell you about pH, nitrogen, phosphate, and potash levels, but organic gardeners recognize that a wide range of trace minerals are important to plants and to human health. This is one reason organically grown food is tastier and more nutritious than food grown with chemical fertilizers.

Raised Beds

Also known as the French Intensive Method, raised bed gardening is ideal for small space vegetable growing. First developed in market gardens around Paris in the 19th century, the method has been adopted and refined over the past 25 years in California and around the world.

Divide the garden into narrow beds which can be worked

without walking on them (3 to 5 feet wide, depending on how long your arms are, with 12- to 18-inch paths in between them), and plant very closely on well composted soil. Yields can be up to four times better than with conventional techniques.

According to John Jeavons of Ecology Action and author of the essential *Grow More Vegetables*, it is possible to grow enough vegetables for one person's annual consumption on 100 square feet of ground (that's 10 feet x 10 feet, the size of a small bedroom). If you eat a lot of vegetables you might need a bit more room. Double that area and you can also grow a year's supply of soft fruit. And, he says, after the initial hard work, only 5 to 10 minutes a day will maintain that 100 square feet.

Sound enticing? Novice gardeners, on neglected city soil, can't expect those yields, but Jeavons recommends that you start with a small plot anyway. In a magazine interview he once suggested starting with only a three-foot-square patch—far better than tackling more than you can handle. Jeavons says it takes 10 years in the garden to produce a fully experienced food grower!

Ecology Action (see Sources) runs projects in developing countries, applying intensive but soil-enriching, undemanding and unmechanized techniques to the problem of world hunger, and you can become a supporting member.

Community Gardens

I was once involved in an organic gardening project started on several acres behind the Palo Alto city library. It was rototilled and divided into groups of raised beds. Each section was allocated to several families who were to work it jointly. In spring we started enthusiastically, but the degree of commitment among members varied, and some people lived within walking distance while others didn't. A member with small children came often because it was a pleasant outing.

There are lots of people who like the idea of growing their own vegetables, but my impression is that they are often stopped by two factors: they take on too much, too soon, and they don't know enough about what they are doing. Community gardening can be an excellent way to grow your own food, but keep the following points in mind:

- The closer the garden is to your home, the more often you will visit it.
- If you haven't gardened much before, try to start with a small plot, no more than 10 feet square if possible.
- Share a plot with a friend. You can cover each other over holidays, and provide moral support during bad weather.
- Make an effort to meet the other gardeners. They can tell you about the soil, sources of manure, and so on.
- Look at what is growing well in other plots for clues as to promising crops.
- Remember that some community gardening will not be organically run, and you may have to tolerate some chemical spin-off from other plots.

Seed Savers

A simple way to help the environment when you garden is to buy your seeds from small firms, and to grow heirloom plants. Ecology Action/Bountiful Gardens offers an excellent range, and I've listed a couple of other favorites at the end of the chapter.

Many of the larger seed companies are owned by the very same chemical companies that are responsible for promoting and maintaining destructive agricultural methods, and they profit at the expense of smaller, family-run seed companies. The hybrid seeds that are sold to commercial growers require large inputs of chemical fertilizers and pesticides. And there is serious concern about genetic variety being lost as seed houses disappear because of buyouts by larger companies.

The Domestic Garden

A traditional garden is a rewarding habitat for both people and animals, rich in color and scent, full of permanent plantings and underplantings. You may have nothing but a small patio, a tiny portion of shared garden, a balcony, or a rooftop. These all present exciting challenges! You have the great advantage that everyone will rave about the transformation, no matter what you do, and there's the special pleasure of creating something from nothing.

When you put in trees and shrubs, consider varieties that

will offer crops as a bonus. Fruit trees, grape vines, and quince bushes—which have lovely pink and white flowers, and sulphur-colored fruit excellent in pies and jam—are favorites.

Tuck herbs into your flowerbeds, and keep some parsley, mint, and other favorite herbs near the kitchen. Protective plants for the flower garden are clumps of chives, which are especially pretty in bloom, French marigolds, and calendulas—these deter insects from other plants.

Flowers

Faced with a bare garden, the first thing one does is head for the garden center to buy trays of pansies and petunias. Then you pull them out and plant something else the next season. This is what I call the municipal gardens approach, which is wasteful and time-consuming.

Plant old-fashioned scented flowers, which are enjoying something of a revival. Modern hybrid roses appeal to some, but the glorious fragrances of old roses will be a delight to everyone who comes into your garden. Like vegetables, flowers have been bred for size and appearance in recent years, and more subtle charms have been neglected. But even the big seed companies offer a few of the old-fashioned varieties, and there are specialist firms with fabulous ranges.

If you have room, grow plenty of flowers for cutting. Even a small garden can offer a good supply of house flowers, especially if you add greenery (prunings are fine for this)—much nicer, and better for the environment, than those plastic-wrapped bundles of flowers from the supermarket.

Trees

The loss of forests, both temperate and tropical, is one of this century's greatest disasters. Trees have a special place in human consciousness—in Jungian psychology they stand for wholeness. Most of us can remember a tree or two, perhaps from childhood, that played a special part in our lives. For me, there is the apple tree at my grandpa's where I could hide with a book and eat fruit all afternoon.

In nature, trees grow where soil, light, wind, and moisture suit them, but in towns they have to struggle to grow where they are planted.

In *A Pattern Language*, Alexander et al. suggest that urban trees need people as much as people need trees. They should be planted where they provide not just attractive greenery but shade during hot spells, a pleasant spot for a seat or a good place for children to play, because this means that the people who enjoy them will also care for them.

The Organic Lawn

Lawns are something of a dilemma for an organic gardener. Actually, women don't seem to be worried about dandelions in the lawn. It's men who turn into fiendish chemists at the sight of a cheerful little creeping buttercup.

Some environmentalists concerned about famine say that we should devote the land given over to purely ornamental lawns to growing food. There are lots of attractive ways to incorporate food growing even into a front garden. What about a thickly planted bed of potatoes, with their lush foliage and pretty flowers?

LAWN CHECKLIST

❏ Choose an appropriate seed blend. A hard-wearing mixture will be easier to maintain and the weeds won't be quite so obvious.
❏ Spike the lawn with a fork or with special spiked boots.
❏ Feed it with a high-nitrogen natural fertilizer two or three times a year. Seaweed meal is also very good and so is sifted compost.
❏ Arm yourself with an old kitchen knife to dig out dandelions and dock. Or you can leave the dandelions, eat the early sprouts in salad and make the flowers into wine!
❏ Set your mower blades high and keep them sharp: 2 to 3 inches is right for many types of grass, encouraging longer roots.
❏ Leave lawn clippings where they fall to replenish the soil, unless there are too many, in which case they will stick to your feet and get tracked into the house. They make a fine mulch around other plants, and can be added to a compost pile.

Paving

If you decide to increase your paved area, please don't concrete it. Approximately one-third of the land in an average city is already under concrete or asphalt, mostly for roads and parking lots, and this has undesirable ecological consequences.

Solid paving increases water runoff because natural drainage is blocked; it affects the microclimate—think how parking lots hold heat in summer; and does nothing useful with the solar energy that falls on it. Damage can only be repaired by replacing the whole slab instead of just a couple of bricks, and solid paving essentially kills the soil below.

Make a surface with old bricks or paving stones instead, set in dirt so that mosses and plants can grow in the gaps. This sort of surface responds well to weathering—it will look better in 10 years than it does now. The delicate ecology of earthworms, plants, and insect life will be preserved, while you still have a firm, dry surface on which to put a table or for children to push a tricycle. Paths can be laid in the same way, or you can use stepping stones set in grass or low-growing plants.

Outdoor Living

The backyard is your nearest outdoor environment and an important part of home ecology is making it a pleasant and practical living area. Provide as much natural seating as you can. The lawn is fine on warm, dry summer days, but you'll use the garden a lot more if there are sheltered, sunny seats for cool weather. A bench is lovely, if your garden is big enough. Thick sawn logs are good too.

Watch out, however, if you are buying a wooden bench, for endangered tropical hardwoods. Choose a temperate wood instead. Avoid plastics as much as possible—an accessible storage place is vital if you have wood and canvas folding chairs, and for toys.

Think about shelter from the sun, and about whether you want seats to face activity or to be more secluded. Shelter from wind is important much of the year, and a big umbrella will help during hot weather.

A freestanding greenhouse is one way of using solar energy but even better is a greenhouse connected to the house. A greenhouse usefully brings the outside and inside together, is a great solar heat collector, and gives you extra room as well as a place to grow seedlings and houseplants which you can tend in the winter without going outdoors.

If you are going to use your garden in the evening, it is a good idea to grow plenty of white flowers, which show up beautifully at dusk. Some form of lighting will make the garden more enticing.

Privacy can affect how much we use our yards. It is not rude to want privacy from even the friendliest of neighbors, but some diplomacy is a good idea. Climbing plants are very useful, on a trellis or on wires. Whatever you plant, think about how it will affect your neighbors—don't cut off their light. On the other hand, you may want to organize a shared backyard, an open area between six or eight houses with a play area for the kids.

Gardening books always warn you that you'll have to choose between your flowers and your children. But why not design the garden to cope with children and encourage them to care for it? Establish a part where no trespassing is allowed for your tenderer plants, put a simple fence around the vegetable patch, and watch out for prickly plants and dangerous ones if you have babies around. (I don't see why one couldn't use prickly plants as a deterrent to rough 10-year-olds.)

Plant a tough lawn, and install whatever equipment seems appropriate: a low table, perhaps—a wooden cable drum will do, and they're great to roll around; hang a tire swing, or just a rope to climb.

Children love to dig and plant. You can hardly get them started too early. Give them plenty of help and encouragement and their own collection of pots or a designated area for their own garden.

The easiest way to protect precious flower beds is to raise them, although it will require some initial hard work and extra soil. Use railroad ties or bricks to make the walls. Tending raised beds is much easier than stooping to the ground, the flowers are close so you can smell them easily, and children can look at them without scrabbling through your nicest lilies.

Wildlife

Domestic gardens can provide extra habitat for beleaguered creatures whose natural habitats are being chewed up by development. And because a certain amount of casualness is necessary to make the right environment for wildlife, this type of garden should appeal to occasional gardeners. That bed of stinging nettle is there for the butterflies, of course, not because you haven't got around to digging it up.

WILDLIFE GARDENING CHECKLIST

There are many books on gardening to attract wildlife and you'll need to find out about suitable plants for your area, but here are a few ideas:

❑   Set up a bird table or hang a feeder. You can get these at most pet stores. Put it where you can see it from the house, but out of cats' reach.

❑   Plant native trees and shrubs, which support a wide range of insect life. This in turn attracts birds, raccoons, frogs, and toads. An ecological cycle in the making! Thick shrubbery provides a home for many creatures, and you can prune trees that would be too big if left alone into a thick hedge instead. Try to place these as a windbreak, which will perhaps cut your heating bills and make sheltered spots in the garden.

❑   Plant native wildflowers—these include snowdrops, violets, and primroses, as well as poppies, goldenrod, cornflowers, and oxeye daisies.

❑   While you probably want some lawn for sunbathing and the children's football games, why not allow a corner to go wild? Consult a book on the subject—it's no good just letting the weeds grow. A wildflower lawn grows best on poor soil.

❑   Plant to attract bees and butterflies and birds. They like old-fashioned, sweet-scented flowers. Birds like berries and— part of your organic gardening program— insects.

❑   Piles of rocks, bricks or logs will make a home for many small creatures like beetles and centipedes. Think what a wonderful garden you'll have for scientifically-minded children.

❑ Leave the weeds. This is so tempting that it could easily get out of hand, but try setting aside one area for nettles, wild parsley, and buttercups (or whatever grows where you are). My garden is too small to allow much of this, but I can't resist my patch of creeping buttercup. I know they're invasive, but they look so beautiful in a dark corner that I only sporadically try to uproot them.

❑ Build a pond. The easiest way to line it is with a rubber liner. You can put in a variety of water plants and either wait for the insects to come, or get a bucketful of water and mud from a friend's pond to inoculate yours with water beetles and snails. Frogs will find their own way, but if you are in a hurry you can import some from your friend (not from the wild). Frogs and toads include slugs in their diet, another ecological boon. Their habitat is declining in the country-side, so friendly gardens are important for their survival.

Cultivating a Green Thumb

GRADUAL GARDENING CHECKLIST

❏ Garden with someone else if you possibly can. It doesn't matter if they know as little as you do to start with. The important thing is to have someone to admire the emergent sweet peas, to commiserate with you over aphid damage, and to share the initial spadework.

❏ Take it easy. Don't put your back out with improvident digging. Make sure tool handles are long enough, bend your knees and not your back, turn to throw the spadeful of soil after you have straightened up—and don't try to do the whole patch in one afternoon. Wearing gloves helps to prevent blisters. Sticking your fingertips into hand lotion or butter will make cleaning much easier (make sure it goes under your fingernails), and a hat and/or sunscreen will protect your neck and nose.

❏ Buy or borrow decent tools and learn to care for them. Good rubber boots aren't exactly tools but they come first, unless you have sturdy country shoes that can take a battering and that you won't worry about. A good fork won't get bent first time out, and an expensive pair of clippers will last forever. Start with a fairly narrow spade, or a fork if your soil is really heavy (you'll want to have both eventually), a small trowel, a hoe, a pair of clippers, and a mower if you have a lawn. Power mowers are unnecessary for modest domestic lawns.

❏ Get advice. Subscribe to *Organic Gardening*, and join Ecology Action and the National Gardening Association (see Sources).

❏ Read, especially during the winter. Organic gardening is a popular topic, and books in print range from profusely illustrated coffee table showpieces to small manuals on specific techniques. Many mainstream gardening writers tend towards an organic approach, and some newspaper gardening columns are excellent, besides being usefully seasonal.

❏ Look at other people's gardens. If, like me, you cannot get a nice lawn to grow in your front yard, observe what other people do in theirs. Every neighborhood has a few keen gardeners. They are often delighted to know that you admire the fruits of their labors and ready to give tips on dealing with your area's quirks of sun or soil.

❏ When you see a plant you like, find out its name and make a note; this is a great help when the time comes to order plants or seeds. (My list often stays pinned to the bulletin board until I have forgotten what *Campanula poscharskyana* looked like and why I wrote "summer garden" next to it.)

❏ Grow your own plants from seed. This saves money, and it gives you a wider choice and stronger, organically grown plants. There are a number of large seed companies with extensive ranges, but it is preferable to order from the smaller family firms.

❏ Learn to propagate from cuttings and to layer plants. You can increase your stocks dramatically at no cost.

❏ Tackle a small area at a time, and use easy techniques. Gardening writer Ruth Stout was a keen exponent of the No-Dig Method, which is an especially good idea in flower beds where you probably have lots of bulbs planted, as well as in the vegetable garden.

❏ Keep watering to a minimum by choosing suitable plants, mulching, and watering early in the morning.

❏ Grow plants you love. Don't be afraid to mix flowers and vegetables and herbs and fruit.

❏ Remember to plant plenty of bulbs—deeper than you think, and with a handful of bonemeal in the bottom of each hole. They get each new season off to a good start.

❏ Take time to look around you. Enjoy the sights, sounds, and smell of the special place you have helped to create.

Sources

Books

Carrots Love Tomatoes: The Secrets of Companion Planting with Vegetables, Louise Riotte (New York, Garden Way Publishing, 1976). Distributed by Harper & Row.

The Chemical Free Lawn, Warren Shultz (Emmaus, PA, Rodale Press, 1989).

Greywater Use in the Landscape, Robert Kourik (Metamorphic Press, 1988). Available for $6 postpaid (plus $.36 tax for California residents) from Edible Publications, P.O. Box 1841, Santa Rosa, CA 95402.

Grow More Vegetables (than you ever thought possible on less land than you can imagine), John Jeavons (Berkeley, Ten Speed Press, 1982). If you want to grow vegetables, you've got to have this book.

The Hidden Art of Homemaking, Edith Schaeffer (Wheaton, IL, Tyndale House Publishers, 1985).

Herb Gardening, Claire Loewenfeld (Winchester, MA, Faber & Faber, 1964). My favorite basic text on herbs is still in print, but there are dozens to choose from.

Landscape for Wildlife, Carrol Henderson (Minnesota Department of Natural Resources, 1987). Available from the Minnesota Documents Division, 117 University Avenue, St. Paul, MN 55155. $8.45 ppd.

Make Compost in 14 Days, Editors of *Organic Gardening* magazine (Emmaus, PA, Rodale Press, 1988).

Secrets of the Soil, Peter Tompkins and Christopher Bird (New York, Harper & Row, 1989). A fascinating look at different ways of growing.

Worms Eat My Garbage, Mary Applehoff (Kalamazoo, MI, Flower Press, 1982).

Catalogs

Ecology Action/Bountiful Gardens, 5798 Ridgewood Road, Willits, CA 95490. Their catalog has a full range of seed, books, and supplies for the organic gardener.

Nichols Garden Nursery, 1190 North Pacific Highway, Albany, OR 97321. (503) 928-9280. I've loved this company since I was 14.

Smith & Hawken, 25 Corte Madera, Mill Valley, CA 94941. (415) 383-2000. Good-quality garden tools.

Magazines

National Gardening, 180 Flynn Avenue, Burlington, VT 05401. This goes to members of the National Gardening Association, which is well worth joining.

Organic Gardening, Box 3, Emmaus, PA 18099. Invaluable for information and sources of seeds, tools, and equipment.

Organic Gardening is published by Rodale Press, a promoter of sustainable agriculture for many years.

Organizations

American Community Gardening Association, c/o University of California Cooperative Extension Service, 2615 South Grand Avenue #400, Los Angeles, CA 90007. (213)744-4345. Supports a network of community garden organizers.

National Gardening Association, 180 Flynn Avenue, Burlington, VT 05401. (802) 863-1308. Their goal is to help gardeners at home, in community groups, and in institutions because gardening, "adds joy and health to living while improving the environment."

Native Seeds/SEARCH, 3950 West New York Drive, Tucson, AZ 85745. Send SASE for information.

Seed, Bulb, and Nursery Supplies, an annual list of suppliers available from Rodale's *Organic Gardening* Reader Service/Seed List, 33 East Minor Street, Emmaus, PA 18049.

Seed Savers Exchange, P.O. Box 70, Decorah, IA 52101. Send SASE for information about *The Garden Seed Inventory* and the *Seed Savers Exchange Yearbook*.

Ecology Action—see Catalogs for address.

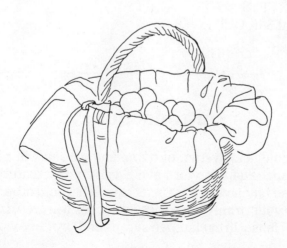

14
PETS

Behavioral changes in our society, with falling birth rate and fewer people in stable marriages with children, probably mean that there are increasing pressures for pet-keeping substitutes. This adds urgency to the need for healthier ecological interaction between [human beings] and [their] pet animals.

—Professor Barrie R. Jones,
Moorfields Eye Hospital, London

Introduction

The ecological system of home and garden will be richer and more successful if you have a variety of creatures in it. Towhees and bluejays will eat insects which would otherwise be nibbling on your primroses. Frogs and toads will grow fat eating your slugs. Hens will eat kitchen scraps and produce wonderful manure for the garden.

Having other living creatures around—birds, rabbits, deer,

hedgehogs, foxes, goats, beetles, butterflies, and earwigs—is just as important to creating a green townscape as providing lawns for sport, trees to doze under, and flowers to smell. Wildlife groups have done a tremendous job of increasing public awareness of endangered animals throughout the world, but we should remember that native, local wildlife needs our help, too.

Many of us are more accustomed to the antics of a black Lab than the night call of owls. Keeping pets is almost *de rigueur* in houses where there are children, and studies show that people live longer when they have a pet.

What role should animals play in our towns and cities? Most children are thrilled by almost any kind of animal, and Alexander et al. suggest that there is some evidence that animals may play a vital role in a child's emotional development (*A Pattern Language*). More than half the households in the United States have at least one cat or dog, and the more children in a family, the more pets they are likely to have.

I might as well tell you. Most pets are not good for the environment. This is not to say that you should get rid of any pets you have. It does mean that we need to think more carefully about the role of animals in our lives, our homes, and our cities.

Ecological Costs

The first dilemma is that our pets consume vast amounts of food—over 9 billion pounds in the United States in 1988. To see a pair of fat Siamese cats eating fresh crab from a Limoges porcelain plate (as I have), contrasted with images of dying children in the Sudan, is monstrous. In 1988, pet food sales were valued at over $5 billion, with millions spent on advertising. This is a phenomenon seen only in North America and Britain; throughout the rest of the world, cats and dogs live on scraps and leftovers, or are treated as wild animals and expected to fend for themselves.

Cats and dogs are carnivorous, and other animals have to be raised and slaughtered in order to feed them. Since it takes approximately 10 pounds of vegetable or grain protein to produce a pound of animal protein—and the grain used to feed livestock is often imported from Third World countries—keeping a pet should need some serious thought. The giant blue bass has been hunted to near extinction in order to feed American dogs and cats, and other marine life is not exempt. A lot of tuna is used in commercial catfood—because its strong flavor means that pets are likely to become addicted to it—but tuna fishing leads to thousands of dolphin deaths.

Canned food is a relatively recent development. In the past pet owners got deliveries of horse meat for the dog and bought inexpensive lamb's liver for the cat. Since most owners now buy canned pet food, packaging is another environmental cost of keeping them—over 3 billion cans a year.

The second dilemma is what has been called the "old lady argument": what about all the little old ladies whose dog or canary is their only companion? Sue Arnold wrote in the London *Observer*, "There must be something seriously wrong with a society which allows its poor little old ladies to become so lonely, so neglected that their only solace is to talk to a budgerigar." Linda Hunter devotes a chapter to pets in *The Healthy Home*, and seems to see nothing alarming about the fact that people like pets because they offer consistency and social security, provide stability, give us praise, and allow us to be intimate in a way that is "more controllable and less threatening than human relationships." Think about it.

Wildlife

Domestic pets can have a devastating impact on local wildlife. A report in the July 1989 issue of *Natural History* gave the results of a study of domestic cats as predators in towns and suburbs, finding that small mammals are the major prey of cats, with birds in second place, presumably because they are more difficult to catch. Nonetheless, a third to half of all sparrow deaths in the areas surveyed had been caused by house cats. This is an area that hasn't received much attention yet, but which you should keep in mind.

The United States is one of the nations that signed the Convention on International Trade in Endangered Species of Wild Fauna and Flora (CITES) in 1976. In spite of this agreement, many animals popular in the pet trade are becoming rare or even endangered. Exotic pets are popular—ranging from lizards, pythons, and iguanas to tropical parrots and llamas. Environmentalists are worried about mortality rates and loss of wild stock, and want a ban on the general trade in wildlife. One wildlife officer commented, "We do not believe wild animals should be used as consumer durables."

What you can do is avoid these pets entirely. It may seem amusing to keep an iguana in your apartment, but by purchasing such an animal you will be supporting an unacceptable and inhumane trade. And rare animals just don't live as long in a cage in your living room as they would in their natural environment.

Choosing to Keep a Pet

If you already have a cat or dog, your choice is probably made for the remainder of its natural life, and you can skip to the sections on feeding and pet care. I have concentrated on cats and dogs because they are the most common pets, and, in general, the largest. If you have second thoughts about keeping the pets you have now—a cat, for example, which kills large numbers of birds, or a large dog in a city apartment—it is always possible to look for another home for it.

If you are thinking about acquiring a pet, the following questions may be helpful.

PET CHECKLIST

❑ How will you feed your pet? Look through the section on feeding.

❑ If you want a dog, have you considered how you will deal with its excrement? Please don't think that public paths and parks are suitable toilet facilities.

❑ What size dog will you choose? Large dogs are comparable to large cars, both in terms of expense and environmental impact.

❑ Think carefully before acquiring more than one animal. Most cats are solitary creatures, and a dog will be happy with your companionship.

❑ Why do you want a pet? Security and companionship can be achieved by other means. And there are alternatives to keeping a cat or dog—geese are excellent guards.

❑ Is it fair to keep a pet in a city or town, particularly if it will have to spend most of its time indoors?

❑ How do your neighbors feel about pets? Would your pet bother them?

❑ If you want a pet for the children's sake, think realistically about whether they will be able to cope with its care. Regular contact with animals—on a city farm, for example—may provide a sensible, conflict-free alternative.

❏ What will you do to prevent your animal from breeding? Puppies and kittens may be sweet, but the numbers of neglected animals that have to be killed every year should give pause to any pet owner. Spaying is essential for responsible pet-keeping.

❏ Can you ensure that your pet does not adversely affect local wildlife? Dogs should not be allowed to roam freely, and declawing a cat will prevent unnecessary carnage.

Feeding Dogs and Cats

The aim here is healthy eating. The first principle is to avoid commercial pet foods. Those packets and cans are not only expensive and wasteful but bad for your pet. The food inside can be contaminated with lead from the soldering, and may be laced with chemical additives, flavorings, salt, and even sugar, just like processed human food.

Dry commercial food is more sympathetically packaged, in cardboard or paper, and it can sometimes be bought in bulk. It is also lighter, which means lower transport costs and energy consumption. It is, however, a highly processed food, and is probably made from the byproducts of intensive meat rearing.

You may find, as we did with our two cats, that your pets seem to be addicted to their current brand of food. Veterinarians suggest that expensive and unhealthy overeating may be caused by our pets' addiction to appetite stimulators and other chemical additives in processed pet foods.

The wild ancestors of today's cats and dogs ate a very different diet from the one we expect our pets to thrive on. It was fresh and raw, rather than cooked, dried, or preserved with chemicals. A famous study with many generations of cats, made by physician Francis M. Pottenger, Jr., in the 1920s, remains an important source of information about dietary health. Pottenger decided to try feeding one group of cats raw meat and unpasteurized milk instead of the standard commercial food used in his laboratory. The raw food cats thrived, while the cooked food animals continued to suffer from allergies, skeletal abnormalities, and a variety of illnesses. The contrast became more pronounced in succeeding generations.

A useful book is *Keep Your Pet Healthy the Natural Way*, by Pat Lazarus. It emphasizes the importance of fresh, mainly raw, unprocessed foods—environmentally sound as well as healthy. Much of the book concentrates on dealing with ill pets, but the fundamental information on diet is relevant to anyone with a cat or dog. A dog's diet should be only one-third meat, while a cat needs some three-quarters of its diet to consist of meat. The balance can be made up of grains, vegetables, and the occasional egg.

Concentrate on liver, kidney, and heart, and do not aim for lean meat. Cats need a high intake of saturated fat. Variety is important for a balanced diet. This diet will probably be cheaper than your pet's present one, as well as healthier. Lazarus reports that animals on a natural diet eat approximately one-third less, and, incidentally, produce far less feces because the food is more nutritious and better digested.

The most difficult thing for most of us is that fresh and unprocessed food cannot be stored on a shelf indefinitely like a tin, and needs to be cut up (but not too much—animals are quite capable of chewing fairly large chunks of meat). If you are squeamish, perhaps you'll want to consider a vegetarian diet for your pet!

Healthy, Whole Foods

A consumer report on pet food confirmed that cats are far more finicky about their food than dogs, something any cat owner knows from experience. I have no experience in converting a dog from a processed to a wholefood diet, but I have struggled with a pair of cats and can offer a few observations.

Like many cats ours were devoted to a leading brand of canned catfood, which we supplemented with dry food. We started by offering small amounts of raw meat, and gradually increased the portions of fresh offal (mainly heart, but sometimes kidney or liver) as we reduced the amount of processed food. There were some failures, when they refused to touch a particular plateful, but after some months they began to dive into their raw food diet with enthusiasm reminiscent of a catfood television commercial.

Hunger does seem to be the best sauce when trying to get cats to switch to something different. This makes for a difficult time if you are soft-hearted when those imploring looks and plaintive meows start coming thick and fast.

Pat Lazarus's suggestion that a quarter of a cat's diet should be made up of cooked cereals (brown rice, for example) and grated carrot, sounds fine to me, but I haven't figured out how to convince the cats. Many cats, however, enjoy table scraps— everything from tossed salad to boiled potatoes. Mixing the grated vegetable into something they like is a good method, at least with a dog. Cats are remarkably skillful at picking out what they want and leaving the rest.

Meat can come from the supermarket during your weekly shop, but I have a butcher nearby and find it convenient to buy a small amount every couple of days. Bulk purchases can be frozen and a small amount thawed each day; it should be near room temperature when offered to your pet. Some pet stores sell large bags of chopped tripe and others sell fresh meat for dogs. Keep a couple of cans or a box of dried food in the cupboard for emergencies. Wholefood shops sell additive-free, natural products which you might want to try.

Vegetarianism

In Chapter 2 we looked at the reasons we should cut our meat consumption, and pets ought to join us in this dietary change. If you start from birth, it is possible to raise a dog as a vegetarian. Although this is against canine nature, in today's world it seems a reasonable compromise.

A vegetarian diet, however, is not appropriate for cats. A vegetarian diet is deficient in arachidonic acid, an essential fatty acid found in the structural fats of meat and fish. Because of this, the Vegetarian Society "urges vegetarian cat owners to consider whether their beliefs are consistent with risking jeopardizing the health of any animal, or whether they should ask any animal to adapt its natural diet to suit the philosophy of the owner, no matter how noble the cause."

It must be said that many pets enjoy foods other than meat. I once had a cat that liked steamed zucchini, and friends have a cat that eats salad. Dogs are even more adaptable. Some dogs seem to eat absolutely anything, and most table scraps can be offered to Fido before going to the compost bucket. Between the dog, the bird table, and the compost heap, you'll have to start asking friends for their leftovers!

Ground Rules for Dogs

While dogs provide companionship for the lonely and excitement for children, they are also a major social menace. Dog feces are not just unpleasant, but dangerous.

Take a guess at the quantities involved—the millions of gallons of urine and thousands of tons of feces that are left on our streets every *day*. I think owners who allow their pets to foul public paths and parks are more antisocial than young graffiti artists. The most irritating aspect of this problem was summed up when I saw a neighbor walking her dog home one afternoon. She stopped to let the dog defecate on the pavement a few houses away from her own door, looking off into the distance while the deed was done. It was not her family who were going to have to look at it or watch their step when they next went outside.

Certain parasites from feces can be carried in on shoes and stick to wheels and may survive for several days on the floor. You might think about switching to slippers and leaving shoes at the door, a good way to avoid carrying street dirt inside, in any case. Park bikes and baby carriages just inside the door if possible, or even under shelter outside. If you have a crawling child, you'll probably want to take special care.

If you move houses, find out whether dogs have had access to the yard.

GROUND RULES CHECKLIST

Here are points to consider if you keep a dog. If they seem overly severe, consider other people's small children. Similar rules will seem perfectly reasonable when applied to them.

❑ Train your dog to defecate in a box or tray or on a piece of newspaper, inside the house or in the backyard. The best way to dispose of feces is by flushing them down the toilet.

❑ Careful worming is important to eliminate parasites—get

advice from your vet. Some experts say that the feces should be burned for two days after worming (that's enough to put me off having a dog).

❏ Certain parasites can survive in soil for over two years so you should ensure that your pet does not use the lawn as a toilet, especially if you have children. Never eat while playing with a dog.

❏ You will need a pooper-scooper, available from pet stores, on outings.

❏ A dog needs a considerable amount of exercise to stay healthy and happy. If you cannot provide this, give serious thought to finding it another home.

❏ Ensure that your pet does not annoy neighbors with constant barking. If it does, you have a responsibility to solve the problem or get rid of the dog.

❏ Use a leash and remember that Trixie should not be allowed to approach strangers, no matter how small and friendly she is. You should be particularly careful around children. If someone wants to say hello to your pet, they will approach you.

❏ See that your pet wears a collar and tag with your name and address.

Pests

Fleas can be controlled without the dangerous insecticides in commercial flea sprays, powders, and collars. The first step in nontoxic flea treatment is to vacuum thoroughly: carpets, rugs, upholstery, cushions, mattresses, everything. Seal the vacuum bag in an old plastic bag and throw it away or burn it. If the problem is acute, put your bedding, pet's bedding, and rugs through a hot wash. Go through this routine again after three or four days.

Next, add nutritional yeast to Trixie's diet. This will make her taste nasty to fleas, and improve her coat. My cats adore yeast, which I sprinkle on top of their meat scraps. Garlic will work the same trick (one mashed clove a day), and I've read that adding cider vinegar to pets' drinking water is effective too (about a teaspoon per quart of water).

Herbal treatment will deal with fleas in the house and yard. Pennyroyal is a mint that has tiny leaves, spreads rapidly, and happens to be a fleabane. It also smells delicious and you can use it to make tea. Plant it all around the yard—plants can be divided as they spread—and use dried leaves to pack a fabric flea collar. You can also buy pennyroyal oil to dab on a collar or bedding; this has caused rare cases of miscarriage so be careful if you have a pregnant pet. Rubbed on your arms and legs it will act as an insect repellent. You can also give your pet a rinse with strong (cool) pennyroyal tea after a bath.

Pets on a fresh, raw diet generally do not suffer from intestinal parasites. A daily dose of garlic is beneficial and some breeders report using nothing but garlic to prevent round-worm. Since garlic in the diet is an ancient remedy for colds and is said to increase resistance to disease, why not give this a try? An easy way to peel a lot of garlic is to separate the cloves and pour boiling water over them. The skins will slip off easily after a couple of minutes. If you like, press the cloves into a jar and mix them to a paste with an unrefined vegetable oil—stir a spoonful into Fido's dish of table scraps or chicken livers once a day.

Other Pets

Choosing a small pet has many practical and environmental advantages. If you are choosing a bird, reptile, or tropical fish, however, it is essential to ensure that they have been bred in captivity—adopting any wild animal, especially one that has come from another part of the world, is supporting a trade that should be eliminated.

Tropical marine fish are a passion of mine but I know that they belong on the coral reefs and not in my living room. Marine fish are always wild-caught and a huge proportion die during shipment; their life expectancy in an aquarium is only a few months. Cyanide-based drugs are sometimes used to capture them. In our home, several fantail goldfish and a pearly koi make fine substitutes. Freshwater tropical fish like guppies are an acceptable choice because they are bred in captivity.

If you keep rodents, it's important to ensure that they do

not escape into the wild, where they can throw the balance of the local ecosystem.

With all these pets, try to cut down on the amount of commercial, packaged food you use, as well as on litter and bedding. Good pet stores sell fresh food, and you can probably use odds and ends from the kitchen too. There are books about every possible kind of pet that will have suggestions for an unprocessed diet.

Animals in Our Lives

Domestic cats and dogs, as Alexander et al. point out, "are pleasant, but so humanized that they have no wild free life of their own. And they give human beings little opportunity to experience the animalness of animals" (*A Pattern Language*).

If you feel that it is essential to share your life with some small living creature, look for alternatives. Your neighbors probably would not welcome a rooster, but if you have a large yard you might keep hens or rabbits. Goats need more room, but they are hardy, friendly, and productive. You'd better think, though, about what you are going to do with the hens once they stop laying and baby bunnies or goats. Can you sell them? Can you face slaughtering them? How will you tell the children?

Domestic animals—goats, ducks, geese—can be raised on common land within communities. In Britain there are city farms, allowing children and older people living in urban areas to experience something of the life of a farm and to buy locally reared food. The animals are fed with reject fruit and vegetables like yellowed cucumbers and slightly faded parsley from the market, and local children help to care for the animals and gardens.

People need contact with other creatures for emotional well-being, and we need a proper picture of the ecological balances that enable us to survive on the earth. Even in the countryside the sight of a pig rolling in the dirt or a flock of chickens scratching for insects has become a rarity, thanks to intensive animal rearing methods. Increasing habitat for wildlife and keeping domestic animals are good ways to expand our contact with the other creatures with which we share the earth.

Sources

Books

Keep Your Pet Healthy the Natural Way, Pat Lazarus (New Caanan, CT, Keats Publishing, 1986).

A Pattern Language: Towns, Buildings, Construction, Christopher Alexander et al. (New York, Oxford University Press, 1977).

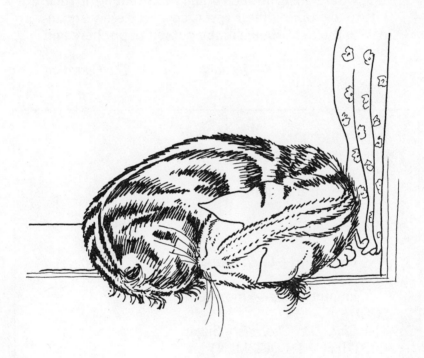

15
CHILDREN

Despite the claim that we are seeking to leave a better world for our children, we know at another level that we are doing no such thing: we are eating up their future, devouring their resources, recklessly squandering their substance in the pursuit of our here and now . . .

—Jeremy Seabrook, *The Guardian*

Introduction

If you have children, you'll be aware of the many choices you make on their behalf, and with their future in mind. But many parents do not realize that we are only beginning to see the consequences of air pollution and global warming from the burning of fossil fuels, radioactive contamination of the seas, and the breakdown of the ozone layer resulting from our use of CFCs. Genetic damage from ionizing radiation and toxic chemicals is certain to affect the physical condition of generations to come. Environmental problems in the news today will have to be faced and dealt with by our children; hazardous waste in today's landfill sites is part of the legacy we leave to our children's grandchildren.

When a Native American tribe had an important decision to make, council members asked themselves how the choice they made today would affect the seventh generation. This attitude is akin to the Christian principle of stewardship. Sadly, the next generation (let alone the seventh one) has been far from our minds. But we can change the way we live—for our own sake, for our children, for the earth, and for the seventh generation.

Pre-conception

Making the decision to bring a child into the world and into your life is one of the most important choices you make. In addition to thinking about whether your present home will accommodate all the shower presents, and about your personal contribution to world population growth, you should give careful consideration to how healthy you and your partner are *before* conception.

It isn't enough to change bad habits after you are pregnant. Animal breeders know that the fitness of both father and mother before conception is of great importance. Sperm cells are just as vulnerable to damage as egg cells. The children of fathers who work at the Sellafield nuclear reprocessing plant in Britain, for example, have greatly increased rates of leukemia. Fathers who smoke are known to have reduced sperm counts and their children are more likely to have birth defects.

Even people who are aware of the importance of how a baby comes into the world, with dim lights and warm baths and a loving welcome, may not realize that parents can help their baby by improving the way they live. Many environmental pollutants affect fetal health, increase the chances of birth defects, and contribute to infant ill health.

Pregnancy

Pregnancy brings many physical changes, but perhaps even more dramatic are the changes in one's plans and priorities. Everyone wants to give advice, and it is difficult to get the unbiased information you want about pregnancy and birth choices. The overwhelming feeling of responsibility for another life leaves a first-time mother vulnerable to pressure, especially from those who are providing prenatal care. I hope that the following information will help you to resolve the issues for yourself.

Chemical Caution

Your doctor or midwife, as well as any good book on pregnancy, will recommend a healthy diet with plenty of fresh fruit and vegetables, and will caution against tobacco, alcohol, and drugs. But you are unlikely to be told that pregnant women should also avoid hazardous household chemicals.

Your nose will tip you off about some of these—many pregnant women find that their sense of smell becomes particularly acute. Pesticides, chemical fertilizers, many cleaning products, paints and paint thinners, contact adhesive, and all aerosols are best removed from your home—Chapter 10 suggests alternatives for many common products.

These changes are also important after your baby is born. Many babies grow up surrounded by dangerous fumes from household disinfectants, used out of misplaced concern about hygiene. Many disinfectants contain cresol, a chemical that can affect the central nervous system and cause organ damage. Hot soapy water will do the trick instead, or you can wipe surfaces down with a mild solution of borax and water.

Even hair dyes have been shown to be carcinogenic and

mutagenic in laboratory tests. Small amounts are absorbed through the scalp, and the fumes are inhaled during application. It is best to avoid all chemical hair treatments—see Debra Lynn Dadd's books (Chapter 10) for gentle, attractive alternative products.

Another thing to consider is your exposure to electromagnetic fields from a computer monitor—you'll find more about this in Chapter 11.

Avoid all medication: many common drugs have been shown to have a deleterious effect on the developing fetus. Make a special effort to stay away from food additives, including artificial sweeteners. Organic fruits and vegetables are not contaminated with pesticide residues so buy them if you can, and eat only lean meat because pesticides, hormones, and antibiotics concentrate in fatty tissue. Better yet, give up supermarket meat or find a source of organically raised meat and dairy products. Tea and coffee, as well as alcohol, should be treated with caution while you're expecting, and while you are planning to conceive.

Instead of thinking of these changes as restrictive, look at pregnancy as an excellent opportunity to make improvements in your life.

Birth

Technology has been creeping up on us in many areas of our lives, but none is more crucial to our health and to the health and wholeness of society than where and how we give birth. This makes birth an important ecological issue.

French obstetrician Michel Odent believes that the period before, during, and immediately after birth affects our immune system, our ability to love and respond to other people, and even the way we age. His first book, which has not been translated into English, is called *Genese de l'Homme Ecologique, L'instinct retrouve*, "The Genesis of Ecological Man." He points out that the technologist sees both women's ability to bear children and the cycles of the natural world as insufficient and inefficient, to be manipulated and improved upon.

According to Dr. Robert Mendelsohn (whose books should

be on the bedside table of every pregnant woman), there are no "decent overall statistics on home-versus-hospital birth in the United States because, I suspect, no one wants to collect them for fear of what they would find." British statistics, however, have shown that home birth is safer than birth in a hospital *in every risk category*. Marjorie Tew, an enterprising statistician at the University of Nottingham Medical School, decided to collate the data from two official perinatal surveys. She found that the presumed connection between hospital birth and reduced infant mortality did not exist. Her results were published in *Place of Birth*.

More recently, Rona Campbell and Alison Macfarlane did another statistical review, again based on official figures, and concluded: "There is some evidence, although not conclusive, that morbidity is higher among women and babies cared for in an institutional setting. For some women, the iatrogenic [doctor-caused] risk associated with institutional delivery may be greater than any benefit conferred, but this has yet to be proven" (*Where to be born? The debate and the evidence*, 1987, National Perinatal Epidemiology Unit, Radcliffe Infirmary, Oxford, England). A woman who has a home birth is continually told how brave she must be, but those of us who have had one often feel that it is going to the hospital that takes courage!

Perhaps the most important factor in a successful labor is that the woman in labor feel comfortable and confident about her own abilities, and at ease in her surroundings. It is embarrassing and inconvenient, but hardly surprising, that women frequently arrive at the hospital only to have their contractions stop. If you were to move a laboring animal, the same thing would happen—this is a natural safety mechanism.

When it comes to avoiding dangerous bacteria, a hospital is the last place a woman about to give birth should be. Babies born at home are, for example, highly unlikely to get staphylococcus, a contagious infection that sometimes runs rife in hospitals. In addition, you are far more likely to end up with what is euphemistically called a "managed labor" in a hospital. A woman who isn't at ease is more likely to need intervention, hospital routine makes a timetable for labor more likely, and the simple fact that equipment, drugs, and staff are available make it more likely that they will be used.

It pays to be skeptical about routine medical procedures during pregnancy and birth. Although the information obtained by testing can be valuable in some cases, there are various risks associated with these procedures, and for most women they are unnecessary.

Melody Weig, a midwife practising in Britain, says that: (1) no form of technological intervention should be used routinely on pregnant women; (2) dependence on information from tests means that practitioners have less incentive to genuinely listen to their patients; and (3) doctors are losing their palpation and observation skills because of excessive reliance on machine data.

Routine fetal monitoring during childbirth is a good example of excessive intervention. In 1985, the World Health Organization stated that "there is no evidence that routine intrapartum electronic fetal monitoring has a positive effect on the outcome of pregnancy." Robert Mendelsohn calls it a "senseless application of medical technology" (*Male Practice*). The use of a fetal monitor makes it more likely that you will need other forms of medical intervention, thanks to the "cascade of management"— an apt expression used to describe the way one act of intervention leads to another. If your waters are manually ruptured to speed up labor, contractions become more painful and you are therefore more likely to need or want painkillers or an epidural. If labor is induced with a drip, you cannot move around freely and will probably have a more difficult and painful time, making the use of further drugs almost certain. And once a woman has anesthetics, she is more likely to need a forceps delivery or Caesarean section.

Many women think that the alternative to a drugged birth is a learned method called natural childbirth, requiring a coach and particular breathing techniques. The idea that we need to learn to give birth makes women feel helpless and incompetent, though of course this is not as negative as the idea of birth-as-an-illness. Learning about the process is a great help, but trusting your body and your instincts, and creating the right environment for giving birth, are the most important things you can do for your baby. See Sources for a number of inspiring books to help you.

Breastfeeding

Scandals about the selling of artificial milk products to women in the Third World, with advertising to persuade them that formula is superior to their breastmilk, has had considerable press coverage.

But what about us? Only a small percentage of American mothers choose to breastfeed their babies at all, and even fewer continue to breastfeed for at least four months, the minimum period recommended by most pediatricians. A recent survey shows that there has been a slight decline in the number of breastfeeding mothers in the 1980s.

Most women in the Third World breastfeed their babies. Surveys in the Third World suggest that no more than one percent of rural women and five percent of urban women are unable to nurse their babies. Yet many well-nourished Americans give up nursing because they "haven't got enough milk." How can this be?

The problems are extremely simple: insufficient support from medical staff and family, and not allowing the baby to nurse enough. Sucking is what stimulates milk production. Rules and schedules which discourage frequent, relaxed feeding are certain to affect your milk supply and your baby's peace of mind. Newborn babies often like to nurse on and off throughout the day (and sometimes at night). Having your baby in bed with you, either at home or in a sympathetic hospital, makes breastfeeding infinitely easier in the early days.

Breastfeeding is physically desirable when a baby is small, but psychological benefits continue with extended breastfeeding. Michel Odent has done an informal survey among children who have been breastfed for at least a year, and finds that these children do not develop an attachment for a transitional object, the psychologist's term for that grubby cot blanket or ragged stuffed bear many small children drag about everywhere.

Young children, and older children and adults too, often feel isolated if they sleep alone, but parents feel a misplaced sense of guilt about the fact that their children like to climb into bed with them. A large family bed is a happy option for some, and a low bed or futon is a great help, especially with a small baby. Odent points out that in many other parts of the world babies always sleep with their mothers. He has also observed that Sudden Infant Death Syndrome (SIDS) is virtually unknown in these countries. Other researchers think that separation from the mother is an important factor in this tragic occurrence.

All new parents need a copy of the *Continuum Concept* by Jean Liedoff. It will transform the way you handle your baby and open your eyes to important ideas about how our very first days affect the rest of our lives.

Social support—from partner, family, and friends—is vital to successful breastfeeding. Women who will happily bare their breasts on a European beach can be desperately shy about feeding a baby, no matter how discreetly. Perhaps this is because they feel that they are the only one doing it! We so rarely see a mother breastfeeding that it doesn't seem normal or ordinary, and any use of our breasts is treated as something sexual. The more common breastfeeding becomes, and the more comfortable all of us—men, women, and children—are with it, the better things will be for mother and baby.

Diapers

When you have a leaky little one, you get obsessed with diapers. Fathers swap notes on the best type, and friends call to tell you about a sale on your favorite brand.

Of course I'm talking about "disposable" plastic-and-paper diapers, not the cloth diapers our mothers or grandmothers used. Some 85 percent of American babies are now put into disposable diapers, and approximately 18 billion are sold every year. Sold, soiled, and discarded.

But unfortunately, not disposed of. The trouble is that disposable diapers simply are not disposable. They are an ecological disaster, contributing to the depletion of limited timber and petroleum reserves—in the United States alone, disposable diapers use 100,000 tons of plastic and 800,000 tons of wood pulp every year. That's some 21 million trees. (This question does not involve babies' diapers only. Many people are concerned about the additional burden of disposable diapers worn by the incontinent aged, in an aging society.)

Anyone who has used disposables will remember how the

garbage cans were suddenly twice as full. A general U.S. estimate is that four percent of solid household waste is made up of soiled diapers, a huge figure for a single item. For every dollar we spend on disposable diapers, taxpayers will spend 10¢ on disposal.

I used disposables on my first child. After all, everyone else seemed to. Tacit medical endorsement, fortified by the free samples given to new mothers, is enough to convince many parents that disposables are the correct thing to use.

Because disposables save time and effort they can seem worth the expense, though it is considerable: about $2,500 for a child potty-trained by two and a half. Washing and drying cloth diapers at home only takes an extra 10 or 15 minutes a day. Think of the lessons even a tiny child will learn from watching you—reusing something instead of throwing it away and making a little extra effort because you care about the planet we share.

There is growing public concern not only over the disposal problem—some states have proposed legislation banning disposable diapers—but also over the health risks they present. Modern sanitation involves the separation of sewage from other waste, but with disposable diapers huge amounts of fecal matter are treated as part of the household trash rather than being processed through the sewage system. When one considers that raw sewage sometimes ends up on our beaches, perhaps this is an idle concern.

Diapers may be a source of groundwater contamination from landfill sites. "Leachate containing viruses from human feces (including live vaccines from routine childhood immunizations) can leak into the earth and pollute underground water supplies. In addition to the potential of groundwater contamination, airborne viruses carried by flies and other insects contribute to an unhealthy and unsanitary situation. ("The Disposable Diaper Myth," *Whole Earth Review*, Fall 1988).

Many children are sensitive to the chemicals, perfumes, and plastic in disposable diapers. The plastic covering efficiently holds in moisture, which causes diaper rash. "Keeps baby drier" means that his blanket or your knee is kept dry—while the moisture is sealed inside the diaper, next to his skin. Because of the high cost of disposables they may not be changed often enough—12 to 15 times a day is recommended for newborns, which would cost nearly $40 a week.

Although the initial expense of using cloth diapers and covers is much greater than that of buying a bag of disposables at the grocery store, in the long run you should cut costs by about half, even taking laundering into account. And subsequent babies add much less to the total.

Another alternative is a diaper service. When my mother had twins in the late 1950s, she got a year's free diaper service as a prize. You hand over your pail of dirty diapers, and in return get a pile of bouncy fresh ones, washed and dried in high-temperature machines. Talk about convenience!

Cloth Tips

As the eldest of five children, I remember the deft way my mother sluiced out diapers, wrung them firmly and tossed them into a covered pail. With modern washing machines and dryers, using cloth diapers should be much easier for us than it was for our mothers. The most important thing is to get a routine established. Here's how:

CLOTH DIAPER CHECKLIST

❑   Make sure you have enough diapers, at least three to four dozen. You will also need a covered pail to hold rinsed diapers until wash time, a supply of borax, and a gentle laundry soap.

❑   Half fill the pail with water and add a tablespoonful of borax, to disinfect the diapers, and reduce odors and staining.

❑   Diapers that are merely wet can go straight into the pail while soiled diapers should first be rinsed in the toilet bowl. Wear rubber gloves at this stage if you like.

❑   When you are ready to wash, drain the excess solution into the toilet, then use a spin cycle to drain dirty water. A toploading washing machine is less economical with water than frontloaders, but is much better when you have diapers to deal with. Hot wash and double rinse.

❑   Dry diapers outside whenever you can: sunlight acts as a natural disinfectant and gentle bleach. Otherwise, use a dryer set on high to help sterilization. Tumbling also makes the diapers softer.

❑   Avoid old-fashioned plastic pants. There are dozens of

different diaper covers available today, made from a variety of materials—felted wool, nylon, and even Goretex!—in a rainbow of colors. Most of these are pinless, with velcro fasteners. Changes are simple—rivalling disposables.

❑ Let your baby go bare whenever you can, inside and out.

❑ Take a plastic bag with you when you go out, to carry home dirty diapers. (Another thing to avoid is those disposable baby wipes. Instead, carry a washcloth in a small plastic bag.) If you use cloth diapers most of the time, don't feel guilty about using a disposable occasionally. Check the Seventh Generation catalogue for the best disposables.

Health

I can think of no better way to introduce this section than to quote from Dr. Robert Mendelsohn's *How to Raise a Healthy Child . . . in Spite of Your Doctor.*

> The best way to raise a healthy child is to keep him away from doctors, except for emergency care in the case of an accident or an obviously serious illness. . . . Most doctors ignore the fact that the human body is a wondrous machine with an astonishing capacity to repair itself. If you take your sick child to a doctor, he probably won't let it do that. Instead, he will interfere with the body's natural defenses by giving your child treatment that he doesn't need and shouldn't get, with side effects that his body is not designed to handle.
>
> If you become convinced that you should accept my advice and avoid your doctor whenever it makes sense to do so, you will learn to avoid the traps that pediatric medicine has laid for your child. The first of these is the "well-baby visit"—a cherished ritual of pediatricians that enhances their income but does nothing constructive for your child. The hazard of these examinations is the proclivity of doctors—a heritage of medical school—to discover illness where none exists. The diagnosis leads to treatment, of course, with consequences that may make your child sick.

Now you're dying to get the book and read more of what Dr. Mendelsohn has to say! Although he does not claim to be presenting an ecological approach to health care, that is exactly what he does.

Immunization

Most health care professionals (Dr. Mendelsohn is a forceful and articulate exception) insist that universal immunization is both safe and necessary. They tell parents, for example, that there's a clear choice between having measles and having a vaccine. It may therefore surprise you to learn that a 1978 survey found that more than half the children who contracted measles had been vaccinated against it.

A common justification for universal vaccination is that it is responsible for this century's reduction in infant mortality. The common childhood diseases were, however, in decline long before many modern vaccines came on the scene. Better hygiene, clean water, and an improved diet were crucial factors. Vaccines may be a valuable source of income to drug companies and pediatricians, but their effectiveness and safety are very much in doubt.

Your pediatrician will press you to have the baby's first set of shots at an early age, especially if you have been making well-baby visits, even though some vaccines are officially acknowledged as ineffective in babies less than a year old. If you have a young baby, take the time to look into this question before you make up your mind.

One might think that a sickly infant would need immunization more than a robust child, but children who are already unwell are most vulnerable to ill effects from vaccination. One study shows a connection between the DPT vaccine and cot death—the most likely explanation being that in these cases the vaccine was the last straw for a child whose system was already under stress.

An Australian doctor has used Vitamin C and zinc supplements to boost immune function before giving vaccines to vulnerable Aboriginal children, and infant mortality in the group virtually disappeared. If you decide to go ahead with vaccination, you might want to give your baby extra Vitamin C and some multimineral drops containing zinc. Read Walen James's excellent book, *Immunization,* and make up your own mind.

Fluoride

Until the 1930s, fluoride was considered a poison. The expanding steel and aluminum industries at the time had serious problems disposing of the soluble fluoride waste that was being generated. A chemist employed by the sugar industry, which wanted to find a way of reducing tooth decay without lowering sugar consumption, noticed that small amounts of fluoride seemed to produce this effect; in larger doses it caused mottling, brittle teeth, and abnormal bone formation.

Instead of being fined for contaminating water supplies with toxic fluoride, the aluminum and steel industries were eventually able to sell the waste fluoride to water authorities. Since most water is used for washing and sewage, an enormous amount of toxic waste could be disposed of. The public was told that this was a health benefit of the modern age.

The chemical is promoted by the medical and dental professions, in spite of the fact that it is implicated in a wide variety of health problems, from allergic reactions to cancer, and even to Sudden Infant Death Syndrome (SIDS). A child who makes a habit of eating fluoridated toothpaste may be getting as much as three times the amount of fluoride officially considered safe.

One potent argument against fluoridated water is that it is involuntary mass medication. This has frightening implications, and can only be explained by the fact that metal production and some consumer products would become more expensive if the true cost of fluoride disposal were borne by industry. It is not surprising that fluoride is called "the protected pollutant."

A diet low in sugar and high in minerals, along with proper brushing habits, will keep your children's teeth in good condition without fluoride. If after further reading you still want your children to have fluoride, why not use fluoride drops in a prescribed dose rather than rely on random intake from toothpaste or water?

You can also order a reprint of an article about fluoride which appeared in *Mothering*, Winter 1989. The author, John Yiamouyiannis is author of *Fluoride: The Aging Factor* (Delaware, OH, Health Action Press, 1986).

Food

All the dietary principles set out in Chapter 2 apply to children just as much as to adults, but there are a few special aspects of feeding the kids which I want to mention.

Getting children to eat what you want them to eat is not easy. My son, for example, who was practically weaned on organic carrots and used to beg for kelp tablets, was singing ditties about ice cream and French fries by the time he was three. But things are not as discouraging as that sounds. In spite of the allure of fries (which he seldom has), he dives into a meal at a vegetarian restaurant—or a bowl of rice and stir-fried vegetables at home—with gusto, and will try pretty much anything.

Many parents think, thanks to the baby food industry, that kids need and like to eat a limited range of children's food. With all good intentions they give the children an early supper of canned baby food or fish sticks and mashed potatoes, and later eat something far more interesting themselves. Is it such a surprise that children become fussy and refuse to try anything out of the ordinary?

A child's palate is more sensitive than ours, but it is easy to get into the habit of adding strong spices to food after setting aside a portion for the little ones. There is no need to use expensive and overpackaged commercial babyfood. And letting children eat with you (from the age of six months they can begin to join in family meals) is quite an incentive to improve your own eating habits.

CHILD DIET CHECKLIST

There's no doubt that changing your child's diet is even harder than changing your own. Move cautiously and make sure that you are willing to stop eating sugary breakfast cereal too. There are bound to be some good foods your children like. Carrot sticks? Apple sauce? Cheese? Here are some general ideas for eating with children.

❏ Let your child join in family meals from the age of six months, with tiny tastes of suitable soft foods. Mash or puree small portions for an older baby.

❑ Eat a variety of foods, both cooked and raw, but don't force anything on a child.

❑ Aim for a balanced diet over the course of each week, not each day.

❑ Don't panic if your child doesn't eat as much as you think he should; a healthy child will not starve himself.

❑ If vegetables are a problem, look at your own attitude toward them. In countries where vegetables are the mainstay of the diet, children wouldn't dream of not liking them. Try cutting salad ingredients finely and use a creamy dressing, perhaps yogurt-based. Or cut raw vegetables into pieces for nibbling—it's a good idea to keep a plentiful supply of these ready in the fridge. Pureeing cooked vegetables can make all the difference to small children.

❑ Don't let a child who isn't eating meals have low–nutrition snack foods. I've noticed that parents sometimes think "at least she's eating something," even though the snacks will spoil her appetite for the next meal. For some children, healthy snacks might be a good idea.

❑ Undermine the attractions of storebought potato chips or French fries by occasionally making some real ones, at home. Crispy roast potatoes are a happy alternative (coat chunks of potato with cold-pressed corn oil and a little butter, and bake in a hot oven). Children quickly understand the notion of real food.

❑ Let them get involved in meal planning and preparation as early as possible. There are illustrated cookbooks for children aged two plus. Ensure that the one you choose emphasizes healthy foods; some come from the mix-two-cans-of-soup cooking school, or concentrate on desserts.

❑ Children will be fascinated by food and development issues —you can talk about additives and food processing, visit an organic farm, and discuss how what we eat affects people in other countries.

❑ Growing at least a little of your food is a terrific way to get children involved in family meals. Encourage cooking skills, even when this means having to deal with flour on the ceiling afterwards. Enjoyment and imagination are the attitudes you want to encourage. One of the most interesting things you can do together is to make foods that generally come from the store: graham crackers, for example, or pretzels or ketchup. See *Better Than Store-Bought* for ideas.

Sugar

In spite of constant publicity about the hazards of sugar consumption—tooth decay and hyperactivity, for example—I am surprised at how many parents just don't bother to curtail the biscuits, sugared drinks, and sweets their children eat. Even the most genteel playgroups and daycare centers seem to offer sweet snacks.

Parental example will help, but the extraordinary visibility of sweets and chocolates is a hard one to deal with. Racks at every supermarket checkout, with bright wrappers and enticing cartoon characters, beckon. Even health food stores have displays of sweets near the till.

This is a battle I'm fighting at home. Here are a few tips: offer yourself as a good example by cutting out sugar from your diet; eliminate refined sweets from the house (have healthy alternatives on hand); serve fresh fruit and cheese as a dessert; and never offer sweet things as a reward. *American Wholefood Cuisine* has useful snack suggestions which are as relevant for children as for adults.

The sugar industry is immensely powerful, as Professor John Yudkin graphically details in a new edition of the classic *Pure, White and Deadly*. Immense pressure has been put on him to stop his research and to discredit his findings that sugar is implicated in some cancers, liver disease, gout, and eye and skin problems, as well as in diabetes. Yudkin asserts: "If only a small fraction of what is known about sugar were revealed in connection with any other material used as a food additive, that material would be banned."

Another point to consider is that sugar is a substantial cash crop in the Third World, thus contributing indirectly to starvation and malnutrition in those countries.

Clothes and Equipment

It is so easy to get carried away, dressing a small child. The miniature trappings are appealing, and with a first baby you're likely to be given lots of frilly little garments. Chapter 3 offers general ideas about buying, and the suggestions about buying secondhand become even more relevant with kids. Tiny garments cost a small fortune, yet have to be replaced every couple of months as a baby grows.

Apart from the environmental reasons for buying less (discussed in Chapter 3), take a moment to assess your feelings about acquiring things for your children. We sometimes feel that we must buy in order to be good parents. But children actually need very little, and they'll be happier and better off with fewer things but lots of love and attention.

You may have friends and relatives who will hand over a nearly new baby wardrobe; it's well worth letting people know that you are not averse to borrowing clothes and baby gear. Otherwise, goodwill stores and garage sales throw up terrific bargains. Tiny clothes get very little wear so they are often in excellent condition. You'll find that you can afford far better quality—and originally more expensive—clothes by careful shopping. There are resale shops in some towns, and while the prices cannot rival those at garage sales they are still considerably cheaper than buying new.

Choose well-made, sturdy garments, in natural fibers whenever possible. If you worry about your child looking uncoordinated because you've acquired clothes here and there, decide on a basic color scheme and stick to it. This may seem fussy—and plenty of parents and children couldn't care less—but if you do care it makes dressing a recalcitrant and opinionated toddler, and hunting through piles of clothes at a rummage sale, a lot simpler.

You'll be staggered at the amount of money you can save by buying secondhand (you might want to send a proportion of the savings to a children's relief organization). A friend of mine who has a well-to-do husband sneaks off to the Salvation Army store when he is away on business!

Baby equipment, too, can be acquired secondhand. Check your local newspaper or place your own advertisement asking for the things you need and specifying the approximate price you are willing to pay. American furniture manufacturers once went through a phase of trying to persuade parents that it was unhygienic to use hand-me-down articles. What nonsense! Be prepared to give your purchases a good scrub (some sellers clean and polish items first, others do not), and as with clothes, check first for the small parts that may be missing or broken, and practically impossible to replace.

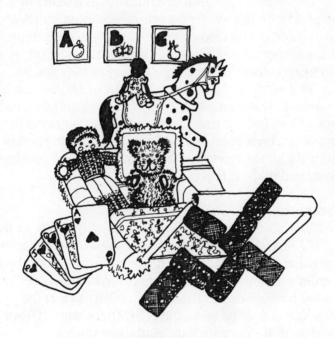

Play

Babies today have cupboards full of battery-driven velour dogs and helicopters with revolving blades. Although children need things to play with, many complex modern toys (even the virtuous, educational sort) are designed for what one box describes as "imaginative play"—that is, play the way the designer imagines it. A far cry from a rag doll and an old box for a playhouse.

What effect does this have on children? Some will annoy their parents by ignoring the miniature kitchen after it has been dismantled, and pulling out all the saucepans for a jam session in the corner. Others will grow up wanting an endless supply of new toys.

Parents are apt to lose their temper when an expensive toy is taken apart by a child who wants to find out how it works. But if you give a small child a toy with complicated internal mechanisms, her native curiosity (the imagination we want to encourage) inspires her to set to work with a screwdriver.

Older children compare notes with friends at school, and the child with the wrong bicycle or computer software feels left out and out of step. How a child copes with this depends on her own independence and self-confidence, and on whether her parents too feel the need to have every new gadget.

The environmental and social consequences of this are profound. The sheer quantity of raw materials used to make toys, most of which don't last long, is one aspect of the problem. Even more important are the lessons children learn before they can walk about ceaseless consumption, readymade entertainment, and disposability.

Companions

The ability to develop close relationships in later life is closely linked to childhood friendships. Some studies suggest that other children are even more important than the mother in a child's emotional development. When people lived in extended families rather than the modern nuclear family, children grew up not only with their brothers and sisters but with cousins, grandparents, and aunts and uncles.

Children need to spend informal time together, not only school time or organized visits. This can be difficult, depending on where you live and whether there are other children of roughly the same age nearby. Solving this is a complicated issue but I'm mentioning it because I suspect an overdependence on toys has a lot to do with not having enough companionship, and you may want to think about this aspect of provision for your children.

Playthings

Considering the price of even the flimsiest toy, you might as well spend a little more and get something that will last. Durable toys made of good, solid materials are expensive, but even if you have only one or two children, toys can be passed to friends, sold through small ads, or saved for the grandchildren. Well made stuffed animals and wooden toys will last nearly forever. You may be lucky enough to find old toys or children's furniture in grandma's attic, or even at a secondhand store—I'm always hoping.

TOYS CHECKLIST

❑ Let children play with real things: put together a childsized collection of pots and pans and dishes, instead of a tiny plastic kitchen (there is a lovely description of a child's kitchen in Louisa May Alcott's *Little Men*).

❑ Look for toys made of natural materials: cloth, paper, leather, natural fleece, and wood. There are many specialist mail order sources; one is HearthSong, P.O. Box B, Sebastopol, CA 95473. (800) 325-2502.

❑ Make playthings. Penelope Leach's *Your Baby and Child: From Birth to Age Five* has good ideas in a special section at the back of the book, many made from recycled household items, and other books about children have similar sections.

❑ Secondhand or hand-me-down toys can be cleaned and mended, or you can make your own—let your child help.

❑ Invest in beautiful, adaptable toys. One example is the wooden train sets made by the Swedish firm Brio.

❑ Swapping toys with friends is a good idea, giving your child more variety and saving you money, which can go towards buying more expensive, lasting toys.

❑ Have a special box or drawer for any sort of miniature item that comes your way: tiny boxes, jam jars, desk supplies. These can be invaluable on a rainy day.

❑ Make a dollhouse, perhaps in an old dining room cupboard with its doors removed. Use scraps of gift wrapping paper for the walls and leftover bits of carpet for the floors. Toothpaste caps make lampshades, or drinking glasses for larger dolls, and all sorts of odds and ends can be put to good use.

❑ A dress-up box is essential. Children love gaudy, glittery, magical clothes, which you can often pick up for next to nothing at goodwill stores. They also adore funny shoes and hats—perhaps you can rustle these up from a great aunt or younger sister.

❑ In general, stick with pencils, chalk, and crayons, instead of plastic pens. And watch out for marking pens that contain chemical solvents—these can be dangerous.

❑ Some children adore filling in coloring books (I did) but they don't encourage a child's imagination like plain paper. Let children use the back of printed sheets of paper to draw on; you can save these from junk mail. Or buy drawing pads made of recycled paper. Blackboards and writing slates are fun too, and good for messages.

❑ All those postpaid return envelopes that come with bills can be used to play office, along with spare order forms and other bits of paper you would otherwise throw away.

❑ Magazines and color catalogs can be cut up and pasted in various ways. Establish a specific place for used magazines, or you'll find your latest *Computer World* being hacked to bits.

❑ A button box, handy for sewing and mending, can be a treasure trove. So can a collection of seashells, coins, or whatever your particular passion is.

❑ Build a playhouse, either indoors or out. This is an excellent way to use scrap wood, moldings, carpet and wallpaper left from a bigger project.

❑ Toys shouldn't be substitutes for hands-on assistance from parents. Often a child just needs a little adult aid to turn a cardboard box into a spaceship or a sturdy fruit crate into a stove.

❑ Let children join in your tasks whenever you can. They may not be able to make the same economic contribution to the family that children did a century ago, but it's good for them to feel that they can help. They can also acquire useful skills early in life—sewing on buttons may seem great fun to an eight-year-old.

❑ Here is a list of criteria to use when you buy toys and play equipment. Look for items that are (1) as free of detail as possible, (2) versatile, (3) large and easily manipulated, (4) durable, (5) roomy, (6) made from materials that are warm and pleasant to touch, and that (7) encourage cooperative play.

❑ Jeffrey Hollander's *How to Make the World a Better Place* has a section on "Nonviolence—Toys, Television, Children, and Adults", which made me take a hard look at my son's toys. This excellent book is one that all parents should have, and you may want to join the National Coalition on Television Violence, P.O. Box 2157, Champaign, IL 61820.

Television

If you spend every evening slumped in front of the box, you can hardly complain about its effect on your children or tell them they should be outside playing instead of watching cartoons on Saturday morning.

Do the effects of violence on television have to be proved before we act on our instinctive knowledge that casual violence is certain to affect our children? I recently read a suggestion that television violence has created a climate of social disease, a feeling that the world outside is a dangerous place; as a result we become more likely to accept authoritarian government in the hope that this will protect us.

Joyce Nelson, in *The Perfect Machine: TV in the Nuclear Age,* writes: "The most powerful impact of TV's hidden curriculum is simply that of keeping people switched off from life outside the living room." This has serious implications for everyone concerned about the environment.

She cites a number of observed characteristics of addicted TV viewers: short attention span, lack of reflectiveness (the ability to think), poor logical ability, and atrophy of the imagination. Children raised on television often do not know how to play—they simply imitate characters and situations they've seen on the tube. And there is persuasive evidence that television is a significant factor in failure at school.

A child is not going to be as amenable to homemade toys after watching fifteen advertisements for the Death Ray from Pluto Wargame. Many parents are concerned about the products advertised on children's TV and the increasing violence of children's programming.

Reading aloud together is a satisfying alternative, and there are a number of books available to help you choose reading material for different ages. Apart from other considerations, reading gives you a chance to answer a three-year-old's incessant questions without missing anything.

Our Future in Theirs

Access to good education is fundamental to any democratic society, and the information and attitudes that today's children acquire at school will affect the future of each of us, whether or not we have children of our own.

Home schooling is an option that appeals to some parents, enabling children to be actively involved in decisions about learning and, often, to make a real contribution to the family economy. On the other hand, local schools have traditionally served an important social function in communities, for parents as well as children, and can be an important factor in neighborhood or village life.

The values that our children need to face and resolve the complex problems of the next century are not going to be acquired in school, but school lessons can help to provide the knowledge and skills they will need to find their places in an uncertain world. Above all, we need to foster a sense of responsibility toward the planet we live on, and of obligation not only to the people with whom we share it now but to future generations.

Sources

Books

Babies, Breastfeeding, and Bonding, Ina May Gaskin (Granby, MA, Bergin & Garvey, 1987). A warm, encouraging guide to caring for your new baby.

Babies Love Books, Dorothy Butler (Bradley Head, 1980; Penguin, 1988). Along with *Five to Eight*, this book will help you to enjoy your children and encourage their imaginations.

Better Than Store-Bought, Helen Witty and Elizabeth Schneider Colchie (New York, Harper & Row, 1979).

The Continuum Concept, Jean Liedoff (Boston, Addison-Wesley, 1986). If I were to recommend one book to parents-to-be, this would probably be it.

The Family Bed, Tine Thevenin (Wayne, NJ, Avery Publishing, 1987).

Five to Eight, Dorothy Butler (Bodley Head, 1986).

Fluoride: The Aging Factor, John Yiamouyiannis (Delaware, OH, Health Action Press, 1986).

Genese de l'Homme Ecologique, L'instinct retrouve (The Genesis of Ecological Man), Michel Odent (Epi, 76 bis rue des Sts-Peres, F-75007, Paris, 1979).

How to Make the World a Better Place, Jeffrey Hollander (New York, Quill, 1990).

How to Raise a Healthy Child . . . in Spite of Your Doctor, Robert Mendelsohn (New York, Ballantine, 1987).

Immaculate Deception: A New Look at Women and Childbirth in America, Suzanne Arms (Boston, Houghton Mifflin, 1975). Things have improved since this book was published, but there is still a long way to go.

Immunization: The Reality Behind the Myth, Walene James (Granby, MA, Bergin & Garvey, 1988). This detailed book will answer your questions about immunization, and gives practical tips about improving your child's health and dealing with school authorities if you decide not to immunize.

Keepers of the Earth: Native American Stories, and Nature Activities for Children, Michael Caduto (Golden, CO, Fulcrum Publishing, 1988).

Let's Have Healthy Children, Adelle Davis (New York, New American Library, 1988). A classic. Davis believed in feeding children healthy food from healthy soil.

Male Practice: How Doctors Manipulate Women, Robert Mendelsohn (Chicago, Contemporary Books, 1982). The information Dr. Mendolsohn offers will horrify you, but this book will give you information, courage, and conviction to take charge of your pregnancy and labor.

The Perfect Machine: TV in the Nuclear Age, Joyce Nelson (Toronto, Between The Lines Press, 1988).

Place of Birth, Sheila Kitzinger and John A. Davis (New York, Oxford University Press, 1978).

The Politics of Breastfeeding, Gabrielle Palmer (London, Pandora Press, 1989). Distributed by Unwin Hyman, 15-17 Broadwick Street, London W1V 1FP. Support the work of the International Baby Food Action Network, c/o ACTION, 3255 Hennepin Avenue South, Suite 225, Minneapolis, MN 55409. (612) 823-1571.

Pure, White and Deadly (2nd Edition) John Yudkin. Out-of-Print.

The Read-Aloud Handbook, Jim Trelease (Magnolia, MA, Peter Smith, 1984). Includes an interesting chapter about television.

Sharing Nature with Children, Joseph B. Cornell (Nevada City, CA, Crystal Clarity, 1979).

The Sneaky Organic Cook, Jean Kinderlehree (Emmaus, PA, Rodale Press, 1971).

What Every Pregnant Woman Should Know: The Truth About Diets and Pregnancy, Gail and Tom Brewer (New York, Random House, 1977).

What to Do After You Turn Off the TV, Frances Moore Lappé (New York, Ballantine, 1985).

Your Baby and Child: From Birth to Age Five, Penelope Leach (New York, Knopf, 1989).

Magazines

The Complete Mother, Box 399, Midmay, Ontario NOG 2JO. (519) 367-2394. A Canadian magazine about pregnancy, birth, and breastfeeding.

Mothering Magazine, P.O. Box 1690, Santa Fe, NM 87504. (505) 984-8166. The best place to start if you want information about alternatives in childbirth, or about virtually any aspect of baby or child care.

P3, The Earth-based Magazine for Kids, P.O. Box 52, Montgomery, VT 05470. Send for a subscription to this "earth-positive project," aimed at children 7–10 years old; 10 issues for $14, and free to elementary school libraries. *P3* stands for Planet 3—earth, the 3rd planet from the sun.

Organizations

Concerned Citizens for Cloth Diapers, P.O. Box 2211, Boulder, CO 80306. (303) 444-4598. A voluntary group that is promoting the use of cloth diapers in hospitals and at daycare centers. You could start a similar group in your area.

La Leche League, P.O. Box 1209, Frankline Park, IL 60131. (312) 455-7730. All new mothers should have a copy of their book, *The Art of Breastfeeding;* LLL has local support and social groups around the country.

Montessori Society, 150 Fifth Ave., New York, NY 10011. (212)

924-3209. Many of Maria Montessori's ideas about education, particularly about children's connection with the natural world, are relevant to home ecology.

National Association of Diaper Services, 2017 Walnut Street, Philadelphia, PA 19103. (215) 569-3650.

The National Committee Against Fluoridation has been absorbed by the National Health Federation, P.O. Box 688, Monrovia, CA 91016. (818) 357-2181.

Join the NRDC's Mothers and Others for Pesticide Limits, and order their book, *For Our Kids' Sake: How to Protect Your Child Against Pesticides in Food.* Write Mothers and Others, P.O. Box 96641, Washington, DC 20090.

POSTSCRIPT

Where do we go from here? How do we change the world around us, influence our friends, politicians, and the companies that make the products we use every day? *Home Ecology* is about changing what we do at home, but I hope you will feel inspired to get involved with some of the larger issues. The next two decades will be decisive. Americans have led the world in creating waste, and now we need to show that an industrialized, consumer society can change direction for the good of future generations. If not us, who? If not now, when?

Becoming better informed is an essential first step. This gets easier every day—environmental issues are given prominent coverage in newspapers and on television, environmental publishing is booming, and campaigning groups can send you information about everything from wood treatment chemicals to aluminum in drinking water. Subscribe to a few of the listed magazines to keep up to date on the environmental, health, and social issues that concern you. My favorites are the *Utne Reader*, *E Magazine*, and *World Watch*, but there are many to choose from.

The layperson is easily bewildered by conflicting information. Dervla Murphy's point about statistics (quoted on page 223) is worth keeping in mind: assess the motives of the person of organization presenting you with "scientific facts." Remember that experts in any particular environmental field—whether nutrition or radiation or toxic chemicals—tend to see their particular area as being of supreme importance. It may be easier for us non-experts to maintain a clear perspective, seeing the links between different subjects.

Some people seem to enjoy preaching doom and gloom, so you need to be alert to the tone of what you read or hear. You don't have to be an environmental activist in order to make a real contribution. The questions we need to keep in mind are simple. What do we value? What do we care about? The Worldwatch Institute puts it this way:

In the end, individual values are what drive social change. Progress toward sustainability thus hinges on a collective deepening of our sense of responsibility to the earth and to future generations. Without a reevaluation of our personal aspirations and motivations, we will never achieve an environmentally sound global community.

Collect some basic books. What you choose depends on your particular interests, but I wouldn't be without these:

❏ Christopher Alexander's *A Pattern Language*. Stewart Brand, founder of the *Whole Earth Catalog*, says that this book "should be in the hands of every citizen, city dweller, home builder, office worker." It is an expensive hardback, so you might get it from the library. Once you're hooked, you'll have to get a copy of your own.

❏ The Worldwatch Institute's annual *State of the World* report is fascinating. It has become an essential reference guide for those concerned about the state of our world. You don't have to read it from cover to cover; an occasional dip will turn up gems of information and insight. The clear, jargon-free English is a pleasure to read.

❏ Frances Moore Lappé's *Diet for a Small Planet* contains some good vegetarian recipes, but I value it most for the author's personal story and for the section "Lessons for the Long Haul." I always put this book down feeling ready for the next task.

❏ My favorite reference guides are Jeffrey Hollander's *How to Make the World a Better Place* (Quill, 1990), which is terrific in its treatment of organizations and social issues, and Debra Lynn Dadd's *The Earthwise Consumer* (Jeremy Tarcher, 1990). Dadd's book is the most comprehensive guide to green products available.

❏ No doubt you already have a copy of *50 Simple Things You Can Do to Save the Earth*. If not, don't miss this publishing phenomenon. It's a stylish, handy little guide.

❏ Get hold of some good cookbooks (suggestions on pages 40–41; I especially like Jane Grigson's) and *Richard's New Bicycle Book*. Why not add a set of tree, flower, and bird guides to help you get to know the world around you?

❏ *The Essential Whole Earth Catalog* (Doubleday, 1986) and the *Whole Earth Ecolog: An Environmental Tool Kit* (Harmony, 1990). These are among my favorite browse books.

❏ Finally, there is Wendell Berry. He is an essayist, novelist, and poet, and a Kentucky farmer. His most recent book is *What Are People For?* Others you might want to start with are *The Unsettling of America* and *The Gift of Good Land.*

Writing letters—to your representatives, manufacturers, and retailers—is a good habit to acquire. Here are a few tips:

❏ Give your letter a subject heading and keep it short and specific.

❏ If you have more than one complaint or subject, write separate letters so they can be directed to the right departments.

❏ Consider writing letters with several friends—you'll save time and postage.

❏ Type it if possible, or at least ensure that it is legibly handwritten. Use a good quality recycled paper.

❏ A word processor makes it easy to produce letters, but try to personalize each one, and address the envelopes by hand.

❏ Make it clear that you are a voter/taxpayer/customer, so the person you have written to will want to keep you on his or her side.

❏ Conclude your letter with a question so the addressee will be obliged to reply.

❏ Keep a copy of everything you write.

Even better than writing letters is joining with other people in a cause you care about. You may be a member of one or more of the national pressure groups, such as the Sierra Club or Greenpeace, but don't forget that local groups need your support, both financial and practical.

Go to a few meetings; you may not find soulmates at every one, but you will almost certainly hit upon a group and a campaign that fits your personal interests and concerns. Developing the confidence to explain, gracefully and politely, how you feel about particular issues becomes easier when you are part of a supportive community or group.

You may want to get involved in protests. Kids find this thrilling, and they'll have plenty to talk about in social studies the next day. Protests range from dressing up like rain forest animals to lying down in front of bulldozers—there's something for everybody.

If the idea of activism makes you nervous, don't underestimate the power of your personal example. Seeing you use cotton diapers, save tea leaves for your compost heap, or ride a bike to the company picnic will inevitably influence the people around you. This isn't a matter of making them feel guilty, but of showing others what is possible by putting ecological principles into action.

Equally important is the example you set for your children and their friends. Take time to explain to them why you carry a string bag to the grocery store, and how turning off lights and putting a blanket around the hot water tank will help to keep the earth from warming up. The other day my son asked why there were so many people in cars and where were they all going. The Department of Transportation should be asking the same questions, and it's something all of us will have to think about over the next decade.

Summarizing the "most important things to do" isn't easy, but here is a modest list of principles. They will not save the earth, but they will help you to live more lightly on it!

❑   Buy less, and recycle whenever and whatever you can.
❑   Get a bicycle, and cut down on the amount of driving you do.
❑   Don't buy tropical hardwoods.
❑   Use as little plastic as possible.
❑   Choose organically grown products, buy humanely reared meat if you eat meat, and cut back on processed food.
❑   Switch to nontoxic household products.

There are difficult times ahead, and each one of us has a part to play. I like to remember this quotation from the Bible: "I have set before you life and death, blessing and cursing: therefore choose life that both thou and thy seed may live" (Deuteronomy 30:19). Don't believe that "people's ordinary

spending is the most powerful agent of change they possess."
Buying is a passive activity. You are far more powerful than that
and have far more to offer. What the world needs now is your
vision, your energy, your imagination, and your courage. We're
in this one together.

BIBLIOGRAPHY

Note: Unfortunately, books go out of print. I've marked those titles in the following bibliography as "OP." I hope you can find the books at your library or through a search service.

Alexander, Christopher et al. *A Pattern Language: Towns, Buildings, Construction.* New York: Oxford University Press, 1977.

Applehoff, Mary. *Worms Eat My Garbage.* Kalamazoo, MI: Flower Press, 1982.

Appleyard, Donald, and Lintell, Mark. *The Environmental Quality of City Streets: The Resident's Viewpoint.* Berkeley: University of California, 1971.

Ardsell, Donald B. *High Level Wellness.* Berkeley: Ten Speed Press, 1986.

Arms, Suzanne. *Immaculate Deception: A New Look at Women and Childbirth in America.* Boston: Houghton Mifflin, 1975.

Artley, Alexandra. *Putting Back the Style.* London: Evans Brothers, 1982.

Aslett, Don. *Is There Life After Housework?* Cincinnati, OH: Writer's Digest Books, 1985.

Ballantine, Richard. *Richard's New Bicycle Book.* New York: Ballantine, 1987.

Barnhart, Ed. *Physician's Desk Reference.* Oradell, NJ: Medical Economics Books, 1989.

Berry, Wendell. *Home Economics.* Berkeley: North Point Press, 1987.

Bertell, Rosalie. *In No Immediate Danger.* Summertown, TN: Book Publishing Co., 1986.

Berthold-Bon, Annie. *Clean and Green: The Complete Guide to Nontoxic and Environmentally Safe Household Cleaning.* New York: Ceres Press, 1990.

Birnes, Nancy. *Cheaper & Better: Homemade Alternatives to Storebought Goods.* New York: Harper & Row, 1988.

Bracken, Peg. *I Hate to Housekeep Book.* London: Arlington Books, 1963.

Brewer, Gail, and Brewer, Tom. *What Every Pregnant Woman*

Should Know: The Truth About Diets and Pregnancy. New York: Random House, 1977.

Brodeur, Paul. *Currents of Death.* New York: Simon & Schuster, 1989.

———. *The Zapping of America.* New York: W.W. Norton, 1977. OP

Brown, Lester R. *State of the World 1988, A Worldwatch Institute Report on the Progesss Toward a Sustainable Society.* New York: W.W. Norton, 1988.

Brown, Michael. *The Toxic Cloud.* New York: Harper & Row, 1987.

Caduto, Michael, and Bruchac, Joseph. *Keepers of the Earth: Native American Stories and Nature Activities for Children.* Golden, CO: Fulcrum Publishing, 1988.

Capra, Fritjof. *The Turning Point: Science, Society & the Rising Culture.* New York: Simon & Schuster, 1982.

Cornell, Joseph B. *Sharing Nature with Children.* Nevada City: Crystal Clarity, 1979.

Council for Economic Priorities. *Shopping for a Better World.* New York: Council for Economic Priorities, 1989.

Dadd, Debra Lynn. *Non-Toxic Home: Protecting Yourself & Your Family from Everyday Toxics & Health Hazards.* Los Angeles: Jeremy P. Tarcher, 1986.

———. *Non-Toxic, Natural and Earthwise.* Los Angeles: Jeremy P. Tarcher, 1990.

Davis, Adelle. *Let's Have Healthy Children.* New York: New American Library, 1988.

EarthWorks Group. *50 Simple Things You Can Do to Save the Earth.* Berkeley: EarthWorks Press, 1989.

Editors of *Organic Gardening* magazine. *Make Compost in 14 Days.* Emmaus, PA: Rodale Press, 1988.

Elkington, John. *The Green Consumer.* New York: Penguin Books, 1990.

Ewald, Ellen. *Recipes for a Small Planet.* New York: Ballantine, 1988.

Gaskin, Ina May. *Babies, Breastfeeding and Bonding.* Granby, MA: Bergin & Garvey, 1987.

Goldbeck, David. *The Smart Kitchen.* Woodstock, NY: Ceres Press, 1989.

Goldbeck, Nicki, and Goldbeck, David. *Nicki & David Goldbeck's*

American Wholefood Cuisine. New York: New American Library, 1983.

Goldemberg, Jose. *Energy for a Sustainable World.* New York: Wiley, 1988.

Grigson, Jane. *The Vegetable Book.* London: Michael Joseph Ltd., 1978.

——. *Jane Grigson's Fruit Book.* New York: Atheneum Publishers, 1982

Grotz, George. *The Furniture Doctor.* New York: Doubleday, 1983.

Halpern, Steven, and Louis, Savary. *Sound Health: Music and Sounds That Make Us Whole.* New York: Harper & Row, 1985.

Hardyment, Christina. *From Mangle to Microwave.* Cambridge, MA: Basil Blackwell, 1987.

Hecht, Susanna, and Cockburn, Alexander. *The Fate of the Forest.* London: Verso, 1989.

Henderson, Carrol. *Landscape for Wildlife.* St. Paul, MN: Minnesota Department of Natural Resources, 1987.

Herbert, Ralph. *Cut Your Electric Bills in Half.* Emmaus, PA: Rodale Press, 1986.

Hollander, Jeffrey. *How to Make the World a Better Place.* New York: Quill, 1990.

Hunter, Linda. *The Healthy Home.* Emmaus, PA: Rodale Press, 1989.

Illich, Ivan. *Limits to Medicine.* London: Marion Boyars Publishers Ltd., 1976.

Innes, Jocasta. *The Pauper's Homemaking Book.* London: Penguin, 1976.

James, Walene. *Immunization: The Reality Behind the Myth.* Granby, MA: Bergin & Garvey, 1988.

Jeavons, John. *Grow More Vegetables (than you ever thought possible on less land than you can imagine).* Berkeley: Ten Speed Press, 1982.

Katzen, Molly. *The Enchanted Broccoli Forest.* Berkeley: Ten Speed Press, 1982.

——. *The Moosewood Cookbook.* Berkeley: Ten Speed Press, 1982.

Kenton, Leslie. *Ageless Aging: The Natural Way to Stay Young.* New York: Grove, 1985

——. *The Ten Day Pure Body Plan.* New York: Pocket Books, 1987.

Kinderlehree, Jean. *The Sneaky Organic Cook.* Emmaus, PA: Rodale Press, 1971.

Kitzinger, Sheila, and Davis, John A. *Place of Birth.* New York: Oxford University Press, 1978.

Kourik, Robert. *Greywater Use in the Landscape.* Santa Rosa, CA: Edible Publications, 1988.

Kuhn, Thomas. *Structure of the Scientific Revolution.* Chicago: University of Chicago Press, 1970.

Lappé, Frances Moore. *Diet for a Small Planet* (10th Anniversary Edition). New York: Ballantine, 1982.

————, and Collins, Joseph. *Food First.* New York: Ballantine, 1979.

————. *What to do After You Turn off the TV.* New York: Ballantine, 1985.

Lazarus, Pat. *Keep Your Pet Healthy the Natural Way.* New Caanan, CT: Keats Publishing, 1986.

Leach, Penelope. *Your Baby & Child: From Birth to Age Five.* New York: Knopf, 1989.

Leckie, Jim. *More Other Homes and Gardens.* San Francisco: Sierra Club Books, 1981.

Liedoff, Jean. *The Continuum Concept.* Boston: Addison-Wesley, 1986.

Loewenfeld, Claire. *Herb Gardening.* Winchester, MA: Faber & Faber, 1964.

Longacre, Doris. *Living More with Less.* Scottdale, PA: Herald Press, 1980.

Mansfield, Peter, and Monro, Jean. *Chemical Children: How to Protect Your Family from Harmful Pollutants.* New York: David & Charles, 1988.

Mazria, Edward. *The Passive Solar Energy Book.* Emmaus, PA: Rodale Press, 1979.

Mendelsohn, Robert. *Confessions of a Medical Heretic.* Chicago: Contemporary Books, 1979.

————. *How to Have a Healthy Baby...In Spite of Your Doctor.* New York: Ballantine, 1987.

————. *Male Practice: How Doctors Manipulate Women.* Chicago: Contemporary Books, 1982.

Moore, Thomas J. *Heart Failure.* New York: Random House, 1990.

Mott, Lawrie, and Snyder, Karen. *Pesticide Alert: A Guide to Pesticides in Fruits and Vegetables.* San Francisco: Sierra Club Books, 1988.

Murphy, Dervla. *A Place Apart.* Greenwich, CT: Devin-Adair Publishers, 1980.

———. *In Ethiopia with a Mule.* London: John Murray, 1968.

———. *Muddling Through in Madagascar.* New York: Overlook Press, 1989.

———. *Race to the Finish? The Nuclear Stakes.* London: John Murray, 1981.

Nelson, Joyce. *The Perfect Machine: TV in the Nuclear Age.* Toronto: Between the Lines Press, 1988.

North, Richard. *The Real Cost.* London: Chatto & Windus Ltd., 1986.

O'Brien, Margaret, and Shepherd, Ursula. *Nature Notes.* Golden, CO: Fulcrum Publishing, 1990.

Odent, Michel. *Entering the World: The De-medicalization of Childbirth.* New York: New American Library, 1984.

———. *Genese de l'Homme Ecologique L'instinct Retrouve (The Genesis of Ecological Man).* Paris: Epi, 1979.

———. *Primal Health.* London: Century Hutchinson Publishing, 1986.

Orwell, George. *The Road to Wigan Pier.* San Diego, CA: Harcourt Brace Jovanovich, 1972.

Ott, John. *Light, Radiation and You.* New York: Devin-Adair, 1990.

Palmer, Gabrielle. *The Politics of Breastfeeding.* London: Pandora Press, 1989.

Pearse, Innes H., and Crocker, Lucy H. *Peckham Experiment.* Wolfeboro, NH: Longwood Publishing Group, 1985.

Pearson, David. *The Natural House.* New York: Simon & Schuster, 1989.

Perlin, John. *A Forest Journey.* New York: W.W. Norton, 1990.

Pirsig, Robert. *Zen and the Art of Motorcycle Maintenance: An Inquiry into Values.* New York: Morrow, 1974.

Renner, Michael. *Rethinking the Role of the Automobile.* Washington, DC: Worldwatch Institute, 1988.

Richman, Beth, and Hassol, Susan. *Everyday Chemicals.* Snowmass, CO: Windstar Foundation, 1989.

Rifkin, Jeremy. *Time Wars: The Primary Conflict in Human History.* New York: Henry Holt and Company, 1987.

Riotte, Louise. *Carrots Love Tomatoes: The Secrets of Companion Planting with Vegetables.* New York: Garden Way Publishing, 1976.

Robbins, John. *Diet for a New America.* Walpole, NH: Stillpoint Publishing, 1987.

Robertson, Laurel et al. *The New Laurel's Kitchen.* Berkeley: Ten Speed Press, 1986.

Rombauer, Irma S., and Becker, Marion Rombauer. *Joy of Cooking.* New York: Macmillan, 1986.

Rousseau, David. *Your Home, Your Health and Well Being.* Berkeley: Ten Speed Press, 1988.

Samuels, Mike, and Bennett, Hal Zina. *Well Body, Well Earth.* San Francisco: Sierra Club Books, 1983.

Samuels, Mike, and Nancy. *The Well Adult Book.* New York: Summit Books, 1988.

——. *The Well Baby Book.* New York: Summit Books, 1979.

Schaeffer, Edith. *The Hidden Art of Homemaking.* Wheaton, IL: Tyndale House Publishers, 1985.

——. *What Is a Family?* Old Tappan, NJ: Fleming F. Revel Co., 1982.

Schumacher, E. F. *Small Is Beautiful: Economics As If People Mattered.* New York: Harper & Row, 1975.

Seymour, John, and Giradet, Herbert. *Blueprint for a Green Planet.* New York: Prentice Hall Press, 1987.

Shulman, Martha. *Fast Vegetarian Feasts.* New York: Doubleday, 1986.

——. *The Vegetarian Feast.* New York: Harper & Row, 1986.

Shultz, Warren. *The Chemical Free Lawn.* Emmaus, PA: Rodale Press, 1989.

Shurcliff, William. *Thermal Shutters and Shades: Over 100 Schemes for Reducing Heat Loss Through Windows.* Andover, MA: Brick House Publishing, 1980.

Stellman, Jeanne, and Henifin, Mary Sue. *Office Work Can Be Dangerous to Your Health.* New York, Pantheon, 1983.

Tepper-Marlin, John, and Bertelli, Domenick. *The Catalog of Healthy Food.* New York: Bantam, 1990.

Thevenin, Tine. *The Family Bed.* Wayne, NJ: Avery Publishing, 1987.

Thomas, Anna. *The Vegetarian Epicure.* New York: Random House, 1972.

Tokar, Brian. *The Green Alternative: Creating an Ecological Future.* San Pedro, CA: R&E Miles Publishers, 1987.

Tompkins, Peter, and Bird, Christopher. *Secrets of the Soil.* New York: Harper & Row, 1989.

Trelease, Jim. *The Read-Aloud Handbook.* Magnolia, MA: Peter Smith, 1984.

Venolia, Carol. *Healing Environments: Your Guide to Indoor Well-Being.* Berkeley: Celestial Arts, 1988.

Webb, Tony, and Lang, Tim. *Food Irradiation: The Facts.* New York: Inner Traditions, 1987.

Weiner, Michael. *Maximum Immunity.* New York: Pocket Books, 1987.

Winston, Stephanie. *Getting Organized: The Easy Way to Put Your Life in Order.* New York: Warner Books Inc., 1978.

Witty, Helen, and Colchie, Elizabeth Schneider. *Better Than Store-Bought.* New York: Harper & Row, 1979.

Yates, Steve. *Adopt-a-Stream.* Seattle, WA: University of Washington Press, 1988.

Yiamouyiannis, John. *Fluoride: The Aging Factor.* Delaware, OH: Health Action Press, 1986.

Yudkin, John. *Pure, White and Deadly.* OP.

INDEX